BASEBALL'S
NO-HIT
WONDERS

BASEBALL'S NO-HIT WONDERS

MORE THAN A CENTURY OF
PITCHING'S GREATEST FEATS

DIRK LAMMERS

FOREWORD BY FAY VINCENT

UNBRIDLED BOOKS

Unbridled Books

Library of Congress Cataloging-in-Publication Data

Names: Lammers, Dirk.
Title: Baseball's no-hit wonders : more than a century of pitching's greatest
feats / by Dirk Lammers ; foreword by Fay Vincent.
Description: Lakewood, Colorado : Unbridled Books, [2016] |
Includes bibliographical references and index.
Identifiers: LCCN 2015031944| ISBN 9781609531256 (paperback edition) | ISBN
9781609531263 (ebook edition)
Subjects: LCSH: No-hitters (Baseball)--United States--History. | Pitchers
(Baseball)--United States--History.
Classification: LCC GV871 .L36 2016 | DDC 796.357/22--dc23
LC record available at http://lccn.loc.gov/2015031944

1   3   5   7   9   10   8   6   4   2

DESIGNED BY MEIGHAN CAVANAUGH

CONTENTS

FOREWORD

My pal Bart Giamatti, who preceded me as Major League Baseball commissioner, often claimed that baseball was a game of stories. A former Yale president, Bart was both a literate man and a devoted baseball fan. He would have taken this book to his bed and devoured it in an evening. This is a book of good stories.

Another literate man, Dirk Lammers, proves in this book that Bart was correct. Baseball people seem to have a special feeling for games in which no one gets a hit. These are the fabled "no-hitters," and this remarkable book is the history—and much more—of what the book title calls "Baseball's No-Hit Wonders." You, dear readers, who have gotten this far are about to have a full meal of delicious baseball stories.

There have been 294 no-hitters in the long history of the major leagues. We fans of the game love the no-hitter because it is relatively rare to experience one and also because we know how difficult it is to keep the other team from getting even one scratch hit. Of course the very rare nature of the no-hit game means many games that head into late innings with the growing tension of turning into a no-hitter end in the failure of someone getting a hit. The groans are loud. Those failures make the no-hitter one of the singular appeals of a well-pitched game. We never know when a no-hitter is going to happen.

This volume is the complete—and I mean fully complete—story of the no-hit games in the long history of Major League Baseball, and it will serve as the place to look if one wonders why baseball makes such a big deal of no-hit games. With prodigious research, Lammers has produced not just the bare bones of each no-hit game but adds to each game story the little and telling details that are so alluring.

I offer one example of many included in the pages that follow. The record for no-hitters pitched by one man is seven, held by Nolan Ryan, who completed his skein on May 1, 1991, when at age 44 he shut out the Toronto Blue Jays 3-0 in a complete-game victory for his Texas Rangers. He struck out 16. As Lammers tells that story, he adds a telling quote from Texas shortstop Jeff Huson, who commented after the game that the Blue Jays "just got in the way of a train." One inestimable value of this book is that it uses such comments to bring the baseball events to life. Happily, Lammers keeps the reader in mind and tells us the human side. Bart would have loved those details. You will as well.

In Chapter 28, Lammers describes an important meeting in New York of baseball's official committee for statistical accuracy. I headed that committee and played a role when our committee established the first official definition of a no-hitter. We decided, not without some debate, that a no-hitter had to be a game "in which a pitcher or pitchers complete a game of nine innings or more without allowing a hit."

The game that led to the definition being clarified was a 4-0 win by the Chicago White Sox over pitcher Andy Hawkins and the Yankees when the White Sox got no hits and yet won the game as a result of various mishaps. The game was in Chicago, so Hawkins did not pitch in the ninth, as his team was ahead and so there was no point in the Yankees batting in the last of the ninth. My committee ruled that Hawkins could not be credited with a no-hitter because he did not pitch the full nine innings. I defended the rule and still do, though there are serious baseball people who disagree. I prefer no-hitters by winning pitchers.

If you like to read good baseball stories and like to be amused and entertained, this book will delight you as it did me. I learned a lot, but the fun is to read the sidebar comments that Lammers lards into this history. There is wit, unusual stuff, and just plain fun in these stories. After all, baseball is at its best when it is seen as a great game. This book is about the game of baseball. There are no dollar signs in this book. Lammers says he had fun writing this book. I see why, and so will you.

—Fay Vincent Jr.

BASEBALL'S NO-HIT WONDERS

The Pirates' Bob Moose briefly interrupted the Miracle Mets'
pennant chase by throwing a September 1969 no-hitter.

(Photo by Dirk Lammers)

INTRODUCTION

The drama and tension keep increasing from the seventh inning on, and every pitch and every subtle movement by every player becomes so critically important.

—Sportscaster Dick Enberg

Like most lifelong baseball fans, I've never had the privilege of witnessing a no-hitter in person.

I am more than a tad jealous that my two oldest sisters knocked that task off their bucket list when they were kids. On September 20, 1969, my dad took Claudia and Jen to Shea Stadium to experience the New York Mets' amazin' late-season run. But the Pirates' Bob Moose had other plans, and he hit the pause button on the Mets' championship quest by throwing a 4-0 no-hitter. Claudia, who couldn't care less about sports then or now, described the experience as "boring" and said her best memory of the actionless game was "when we got ice cream."

I was 11 months old at the time, too young—I guess—to be dragged into the city from Jersey, and perhaps that began my obsession with no-hitters. I eventually got to see Tom Seaver, Jerry Koosman, and "Doc" Gooden pitch some terrific games at Shea, but none of them ended with a zero in the "H" column. As the Mets failed to find a way to throw the franchise's first no-hitter for more than 50 years of existence, my obsession led to a website (NoNoHitters.com) and eventually this book.

Here's why I love the no-hitter.

. . .

COMPLETING A NINE-INNING GAME without yielding a hit is part skill and part luck, with the recipe's ratio always in flux. For a Major League Baseball team chasing a pennant, the no-hitter is a brief celebratory stop along a 162-game marathon. But for the pitcher leaping into his catcher's arms after inducing that tension-filled fly-out, groundout, or strikeout to end the drama, the accomplishment marks the pinnacle of individual success. A no-hitter secures a pitcher's spot on an elite yet diverse list that embraces Hall of Famers, struggling journeymen, and wide-eyed rookies. Guys with nicknames of "Cannonball," "Nixey," and "Hooks" appear alongside such legends as Cy Young, Bob Feller, Nolan Ryan, and Sandy Koufax.

"No-nos," as they are often called (the slang is derived from the more formal "no-hit, no-run game" but has come to be used for all no-hitters) have eluded such greats as Grover Cleveland Alexander, Lefty Grove, Whitey Ford, Steve Carlton, Don Sutton, Roger Clemens, Pedro Martínez, and Greg Maddux while somehow seeking out such short-timers as Bumpus Jones, Iron Davis, Bobo Holloman, Mike Warren, and José Jiménez.

Red Sox pitcher Clay Buchholz, who helped Boston capture World Series titles in 2007 and 2013, said his 2007 no-hitter in just his second major-league start was one of the highest points of his career.

Clay Buchholz of the Boston Red Sox threw a no-hitter in his second major-league start. *(Photo by Dirk Lammers)*

"It's a team sport, so obviously the world championships outweigh anything you can do in baseball," Buchholz said. "But on an individual level, that's one of the greatest feats that you can accomplish as a starting pitcher. It's something that I'll never forget."[1]

Jim Bunning, a Hall of Famer who won 224 games over a 17-year career, was the first major leaguer to throw no-hitters in both the American and National leagues. Bunning said his 1958 Tigers gem is the highlight of his AL career, and his perfect game for the 1964 Phillies versus the Mets is the highlight of his NL career.

"I had the misfortune of not playing in a World Series and not having the opportunity to pitch in one," he said. "You pick regular-season games, and those are the two that stood out."[2]

KIDS BEGIN DAYDREAMING about throwing major-league no-hitters early in their sandlot days.

"This is something I've been dreaming about since I was five years old," the Pirates' John Candelaria said after his 1976 no-no against the Dodgers.[3]

Dick Enberg, a veteran network sportscaster who calls games for the San Diego Padres, said there's no more dramatic sports event for a play-by-play man. "It all builds and builds with each pitch to the ultimate climax," he wrote in his 2004 autobiography, *Dick Enberg: Oh My!* "The payoff is so enormous and so unlikely that the final out is major league ecstasy."[4]

The no-hitter is even impressive from the losing side of the diamond, said former catcher and longtime Brewers broadcaster Bob Uecker.

On June 17, 1967, "Mr. Baseball" struck out and flied to left for the Atlanta Braves before being lifted for an eighth-inning pinch hitter during Houston pitcher Don Wilson's no-hitter at the Astrodome. "I did my part," he joked.[5]

Uecker said many fans just want to see action, but there's something majestic about a dominant pitching performance. "I appreciate good pitching, especially if there's nothing hit good and there are no sensational plays to preserve a no-hitter," Uecker said. "It's just him against you, and he's blowing you away."[6]

Major-league baseball since its 1876 birth has offered fans slightly more than an average of two no-hitters during a typical season, although the sport's history has experienced its share of peaks and valleys. The 1990, 1991, 2012 and 2015 seasons each featured a record seven no-nos, yet more than two dozen seasons have finished without a single one. Over the last decade, the average number of no-hitters has crept up to about 2.7 per season. And from 2010 through 2014, baseball fans got to watch nearly five no-hitters per season.

It took the New York Mets a half-century to get their first no-hitter; the Montreal Expos completed that task by the franchise's ninth game.

As of this writing, the San Diego Padres are still waiting.

The no-hitter display at the National Baseball Hall of Fame features a ball, photo, and caption from each major-league no-no. *(Photo by Dirk Lammers)*

A note about perfect games versus no-hitters: Obviously, a game with all 27 batters failing to reach first base on a walk, hit, or error is also a no-hitter and counts as such. The perfect game is the upper echelon of no-hitters, with about 8 percent of no-hitters carrying the perfect-game mantle as well.

Interesting fact: Although nearly three dozen major leaguers have thrown multiple no-hitters, not a single one has thrown two perfect games.

Most no-hitters are perfect games for a while, only to be lost on a base on balls, a booted grounder, or a misjudged fly. Such blemishes, oft forgotten when they occur in the earlier innings, are magnified amid late-inning murmurs of a pending perfect game. Only three pitchers— the 2015 Washington Nationals' Max Scherzer, the 1972 Chicago Cubs' Milt Pappas, and the 1908 New York Giants' "Hooks" Wiltse— lost their perfect games on the 27th batter yet recovered to preserve their no-hitters.

THIS BOOK IS ABOUT both perfection and *near* perfection, giving us a more mortal, intriguing cast of characters to examine. After all, even a "perfect game" encompasses a pitcher missing the strike zone with a ball from time to time, so what exactly does perfection entail?

Most of us know about Don Larsen's perfect World Series game in 1956. I want to tell the bigger, broader, often very funny and sometimes oh-so-close stories about the 294 official MLB no-hitters, the 30 or so Negro League no-hitters, and the numerous late-inning near misses that have left so many pitchers standing on the mound with heads bowed.

In the '90s, a bunch of no-hitters were taken *off* the record books; I'll recap those as well, notably the 12-inning no-hitter that wasn't. And there will be plenty more stories to add, with young minor leaguers awaiting their chance to get their opportunity to join the club.

. . .

BESIDES THE DOMINATING solo performances, there have been flukes, one-shot wonders, multiple-pitcher no-hitters, a no-hitter on acid—I'm not talking citric—and a partial no-hitter credited to the game's greatest slugger.

A pitcher's quest for a no-hitter is as heroic and complicated as it gets and, like baseball itself, can change a game, career, and life with every pitch.

Read on for the strange but true history of the no-hitter in America's greatest game.

Boston Red Sox teammates Babe Ruth, left, and Ernie Shore are credited with baseball's first combined no-hitter. *(Photo from Bain News Service Collection, Prints & Photographs Division, Library of Congress, LC-USZ62-23241)*

CHAPTER 1

FOUR BALLS AND A
BOP ON THE BEEZER

That's what baseball's made of, moments like that.

—BABE RUTH'S GRANDDAUGHTER LINDA RUTH TOSETTI

When baseball fans reminisce about the legend of Babe Ruth, what comes to mind first are his 60 home runs in 1927 or his gesture toward the Wrigley Field bleachers in Game 3 of the '32 World Series before crushing a ball over the center-field fence. Not to mention his legendary drinking and noteworthy girth. But before the Babe hit his eighth homer ever in his long march toward 714, he secured himself a spot in no-hitter lore by taking a swing of a different sort—with his fist.

GEORGE HERMAN RUTH JR. began his professional career in 1914 as a Boston Red Sox pitcher, and he hadn't yet thought about becoming a slugger despite his love of the batter's box. "There isn't a man in the world who isn't happiest when he's up there at the plate with a stick in his hand, but it was pitching which took my time in Boston," Ruth said in *Babe Ruth's Own Book of Baseball*.[7]

The Babe had amassed an impressive 12-4 record for the Red Sox by June 23, 1917, when the lefty took the Fenway Park mound for the opening game of a Saturday doubleheader against the Washington Senators. Leadoff batter Ray Morgan stepped to the plate, and Ruth tossed his first pitch.

"Ball," yelled umpire Brick Owens, earning a glare from Ruth.

Three more pitches drew the same call, the Babe's temper rising with each. Morgan took his free pass to first base as Ruth continued jawing with Owens, according to *Boston Globe* sportswriter Edward F. Martin.

"Get in there and pitch," the umpire ordered.

"Open your eyes and keep them open," Ruth yelled.

"Get in and pitch or I will run you out of there," Owens warned.[8]

The Bambino threatened to punch Owens in the nose, and Owens had heard enough. The ump gave Ruth the heave-ho.

Ruth's exact words while charging the plate were likely "I'm gonna bop you on the beezer," said his granddaughter Linda Ruth Tosetti.[9]

Ruth's right hook actually missed Owens's beezer, glancing off the ump's mask and landing behind the left ear.

Recalling the game in a newspaper column nearly 25 years later, the umpire had a far tamer memory of the day's events. "Babe got hot under the collar and complained so vigorously that he was ordered off the field," Owens wrote in the *Milwaukee Journal*.[10] The scrum prompted several police officers, players from both benches, and Red Sox player-manager Jack Barry to drag Ruth off the field. Catcher Pinch Thomas, who tried to block Ruth from getting to Owens, also got ejected.

"Baltimore Babe with his temper beyond control went to the dugout under a cloud. His suspension will cripple the Red Sox badly as they need the big portsider very much," the *Globe*'s Martin wrote, dreading Ruth's inevitable punishment to come.[11]

The Sox manager, needing someone to take the mound in a hurry, turned to Ernest Grady "Ernie" Shore, a dependable right-hander who had posted a 19-8 record with a 1.64 ERA two years previously. Shore had just thrown five innings two days earlier, but he grabbed the ball in attempt to bring some calm to Fenway.

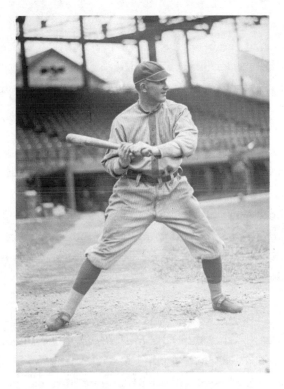

Ray Morgan, the only Washington Senators player to reach first base,
walked on four pitches before being thrown out attempting to steal.
*(Photo from Harris & Ewing Collection, Prints & Photographs Division,
Library of Congress, LC-DIG-hec-02540.)*

Third baseman Eddie Foster stepped into the box, and Morgan took
off to steal second on Shore's first pitch. Replacement catcher Sam
Agnew fired down to the bag to notch the game's first putout.

Shore retired Foster and proceeded to send Senator after Senator back
to the dugout as he filibustered his way down the Washington lineup.
"Shore fanned only two and it did not seem as if he was working hard,"
according to the *Globe*. "He made a number of nifty plays himself."[12]

The only hard chance, according to the *Washington Post*, came in the
ninth inning on a ball hit by Washington catcher John Henry, but Boston left fielder Duffy Lewis saved the no-no.

"Henry drove out what looked to be a sure hit, but Lewis came racing in and smothered the ball," the newspaper said. "Several great infield plays aided Shore in keeping a clean slate."[13]

Shore closed the game by snagging a swinging bunt off the bat of pinch hitter Mike Menosky, and the crowd of more than 16,000 fans rose to give Shore an ovation.

"Relieving Ruth after 'Babe's' scrap with Umpire Owens in the first inning of this afternoon's double-header, Ernie Shore hurled a perfect game," declared one wire report. "Not a Senator reached first."[14] Owens called the contest one of the most exciting games he officiated. "Look through your records and you won't find another instance of a hurler credited with a perfect performance, although facing only 26 men," Owens said.[15]

THE DAY AFTER THE GAME, the *Brooklyn Daily Eagle* wondered how American League President Ban Johnson would react to the young Ruth's assault on Owens, who was considered an esteemed, competent arbitrator of the game. "Ban will probably announce, as he does in all cases, an indefinite suspension, but how long will Ban make it stick?" the newspaper asked.[16]

Johnson suspended Ruth for one week and fined him $100.[17]

As for Shore's accomplishment, the official scorers of the day had a hard time classifying exactly what had occurred on June 23, 1917, according to Owens. "As I said many arguments arose at the end of the contest over this unusual situation," the umpire said, "and finally it was decided that Ernie deserved the highest goal that any pitcher can attain—the perfect game."[18]

FINALLY, THAT IS, until Major League Baseball's committee for statistical accuracy stepped into the fray in 1991. The committee chaired by Commissioner Fay Vincent established an official definition of a no-hitter, saying, "A no-hitter is a game in which a pitcher or pitchers complete a game of nine innings or more without allowing a hit." A perfect game adds the extra requirements of no walks and no errors over nine innings or more.

The committee's rule-tightening effort not only wiped 50 rain-shortened, darkness-shortened, and eight-inning no-hitters off the record books, it also rebranded Shore's accomplishment—the game could not be perfect, as Ray Morgan had reached first base.

So a game that had for 74 years been considered Shore's perfect game was suddenly classified as professional baseball's first combined no-hitter, credited to Ruth (0 innings) and Shore (9 innings). The Babe, whose contribution to *that* game was only four pitched balls and a bop in the beezer, secured his spot on the no-hitters list for perpetuity.

Perhaps fortunately, Ernie Shore, who left baseball in 1920 to return to North Carolina and serve as Forsyth County's longtime sheriff, never knew his perfect game was renamed. He died 11 years before the committee's decision.

NO-HITTERS BY COMMITTEE

A Bazooka Joe cartoon from a Topps baseball card pick celebrates the Astros' six-pitcher no-hitter against the Yankees. *(Bazooka Joe cartoon used courtesy of The Topps Company, Inc., www.topps.com)*

In addition to the Babe Ruth/Ernie Shore combo no-hitter, here are all the others shared by two or more pitchers.

Steve Barber (8 2/3 inn.), **Stu Miller** (1/3 inn.)
Baltimore Orioles @ Memorial Stadium (Baltimore)
Sunday, April 30, 1967 (first game of doubleheader) / Orioles 1, Tigers 2
Barber and Miller combine for a no-hit loss.

Vida Blue (5 inn.), **Glenn Abbott** (1 inn.), **Paul Lindblad** (1 inn.), **Rollie Fingers** (2 inn.)
Oakland Athletics @ Oakland–Alameda County Coliseum

Sunday, September 28, 1975 / A's 5, Angels 0
Final game of season; Blue participates in this multiple-pitcher no-hitter
    after throwing his own in 1970.

John "Blue Moon" Odom (5 inn.), **Francisco Barrios** (4 inn.)
Chicago White Sox @ Oakland–Alameda County Coliseum
Wednesday, July 28, 1976 / White Sox 2, A's 1

Mark Langston (7 inn.), **Mike Witt** (2 inn.)
California Angels @ Anaheim Stadium
Wednesday, April 11, 1990 / Angels 1, Mariners 0
Witt finishes up this multiple pitcher no-hitter after throwing his own in
    1984.

Bob Milacki (6 inn.), **Mike Flanagan** (1 inn.), **Mark Williamson**
    (1 inn.), **Gregg Olson** (1 inn.)
Baltimore Orioles @ Oakland–Alameda County Coliseum
Saturday, July 13, 1991 / Orioles 2, A's 0

Kent Mercker (6 inn.), **Mark Wohlers** (2 inn.), **Alejandro Peña**
    (1 inn.)
Atlanta Braves @ Atlanta–Fulton County Stadium
Wednesday, September 11, 1991 / Braves 1, Padres 0

Francisco Cordova (9 inn.), **Ricardo Rincon** (1 inn.)
Pittsburgh Pirates @ Three Rivers Stadium
Saturday, July 12, 1997 / Pirates 3, Astros 0 (10 inn.)

Roy Oswalt (1 inn.), **Peter Munro** (2 2/3 inn.), **Kirk Saarloos**
    (1 1/3 inn.), **Brad Lidge** (2 inn.), **Octavio Dotel** (1 inn.),
    Billy Wagner (1 inn.)
Houston Astros @ Yankee Stadium in interleague play

Wednesday, June 11, 2003 / Astros 8, Yankees 0
Most pitchers used in a no-hitter at six; first interleague no-hitter
  excluding Don Larsen's 1956 World Series perfect game.

Kevin Millwood (6 inn.), **Charlie Furbush** (2/3 inn.), **Stephen**
  Pryor (1/3 inn.), **Lucas Luetge** (1/3 inn.), **Brandon League** (2/3
  inn.), **Tom Wilhelmsen** (1 inn.)
Seattle Mariners @ Safeco Field in interleague play
Friday, June 8, 2012 / Mariners 1, Dodgers 0
Ties for most pitchers used in a no-hitter.

Cole Hamels (6 inn.), **Jake Diekman** (1 inn.), **Ken Giles** (1 inn.),
  Jonathan Papelbon (1 inn.)
Philadelphia Phillies @ Turner Field
Monday, September 1, 2014 / Phillies 7, Braves 0

"Toothpick" Sam Jones in 1955 became the first
African American to throw a major-league no-hitter
(Photo from National Baseball Hall of Fame and Museum)

CHAPTER 2

I DO NOT LIKE HITS,
SAM I AM

I never had much luck hitting against Sam. But I wasn't by myself.

—ROY CAMPANELLA ON SAM JONES

The Cleveland Buckeyes' Sam Jones was developing a formidable fastball under the tutelage of player-manager Quincy Trouppe in 1947 when Jackie Robinson unlocked Major League Baseball's doors to African Americans.

Jones, a 21-year-old rookie whose light complexion and reddish-brown hair earned him the nickname "Red," helped the Buckeyes capture the 1947 Negro American League pennant. Jones would take on two additional nicknames over his 21-year career, and the quirky yet affable hurler would twice carve his name into baseball's annals before succumbing to cancer at the young age of 45.

As integration began to deplete the once powerful Negro League rosters, Jones played one more season for the Buckeyes in 1948. He spent the next couple of years bouncing around minor, semipro, and winter Caribbean leagues but took advantage of the time to develop a sweeping curveball that landed him a major-league contract with the Cleveland Indians.

Jones had since become known as "Sad" Sam Jones, usurping the nickname from the seldom-smiling journeyman who had pitched 40 years before him. Sportswriters decided that the new Jones's forlorn facial expressions mimicked the original "Sad" Sam, and the nickname stuck.

Jones made his first major-league relief appearance in 1951, and a 39-year-old Trouppe rejoined him in Cleveland a year later to make history. On May 3, 1952, Jones took the mound in the seventh inning to throw two-thirds of an inning against the Washington Senators with his old Negro League player-manager squatting behind the plate. The pairing created the first all–African American battery to play in an American League game.

BUT THE 6-FOOT-4, 200-POUND right-hander struggled to earn a starting slot in an Indians rotation stacked with such stars as Bob Feller, Bob Lemon, and Early Wynn. Cleveland demoted Jones to AAA Indianapolis before trading him to the Chicago Cubs at the close of the 1954 season.

Jones, who always pitched with a toothpick hanging out of the side of his mouth, finally earned a starting job with the Cubs in 1955 under his newly minted moniker of "Toothpick" Sam Jones. "I'm strictly a flat-toothpick man," Jones explained to *Time* magazine. "Those round ones get stuck between the bicuspids and molars. And I don't go much for those perfumed quill kind either—too dangerous."[19]

Jones was intimidatingly wild, but his sweeping curve had matured into the majors' best, noted Brooklyn Dodgers catcher Roy Campanella. The pitch was particularly troublesome for players who batted from the right side, as a ball that appears aimed for a hitter's head can break in to nip the inside corner.

"His curve ball, easily the most spectacular in the league, breaks about three feet," Campanella wrote in *Jet* magazine. "His fastball runs into you and if you don't meet it right, it'll almost knock the bat out of your hands."[20]

Jones on May 12, 1955, was holding the Pittsburgh Pirates hitless through eight innings despite walking four batters. The Cubs provided a

4-0 lead heading into the ninth inning, and Jones needed to retire just three batters to give the 2,200 fans scattered throughout Wrigley Field the ballpark's first no-hitter since the famed Fred Toney–Hippo Vaughn battle of 1917. But Jones kicked off the frame by issuing back-to-back-to-back walks, inviting a terse mound visit from his frustrated manager.

"Get that ball over," growled Stan Hack. "That's all."[21]

Jones hunkered down and struck out Dick Groat and Roberto Clemente before facing slugger Frank Thomas. Jones was oblivious that he was on the verge of history. "I didn't know I had a chance at a no-hitter until Thomas came up there," he told a reporter. "Then the crowd yelled so loud when I threw the first pitch to him, I knew there must be something."[22]

Jones's 1-2 curveball caught Thomas looking, and the 29-year-old Toothpick accomplished what Negro League legends Dick "Cannonball" Redding, Satchel Paige, "Bullet" Joe Rogan, and Ray Brown could only dream of—he was the first African American to throw a major-league no-hitter.

Jones graciously deflected kudos to the Cubs' veteran catcher, Clyde McCullough. "I was just out there throwing fast balls and curves," Jones said. "Clyde deserves all the credit. I just kept throwing what he told me."[23]

WGN-TV announcer Harry Creighton, who had kidded Jones during batting practice that he would buy him a gold toothpick if he threw a no-hitter, made good on his promise. Creighton tracked one down for $11 and presented the peculiar luxury item to the pitcher.[24]

JONES'S DISPARATE STATISTICS that season illuminate his struggles to parlay his dominance into better career numbers. He led the AL in 1955 with 198 strikeouts, but he also issued the most walks (185) and hit a league-leading 14 batsmen. During his best career season as a member of the 1959 San Francisco Giants, Jones posted a 21-15 record with a 2.83

ERA. He topped 200 strikeouts for the second straight season, but he again walked more than 100 batters.

Jones nearly had two additional no-hitters that year. On June 30, 1959, he was no-hitting the Los Angeles Dodgers through seven and two-thirds innings when shortstop Andre Rodgers fumbled an infield chopper hit by Junior Gilliam. The official scorer ungraciously ruled it a single instead of an error, and Jones had to settle for a complete game one-hitter. "Can you imagine anyone calling that a hit?" Jones asked a reporter after the game. "They don't want no-hitters thrown around here."[25] Jones also threw a seven-inning rain-shortened no-hitter on September 26, 1959, but such partial accomplishments were stricken from the major-league record books in 1991. Jones placed second in voting for the 1959 Cy Young Award honoring the majors' best pitcher, ceding the honor to former teammate Early Wynn.

Jones's 270 innings of work during 35 starts and 15 relief appearances that year took their toll on his oft-sore arm. Said one trainer to *Time* magazine, "You name it, that arm has it—bone chips, arthritis, a pathological condition, anything that can go wrong."[26]

The 1961 expansion draft allowed the New York Mets and Houston Colt .45s to fill their inaugural rosters with players from existing NL teams. Each of the eight clubs had to make 15 players available from their 40-man rosters, and the Colt .45s selected Jones. Less than two months later, Houston traded him to the Detroit Tigers. Jones had been complaining about stiffness when doctors found two enlarged lymph nodes on the back of his neck in 1962. Surgeons removed the growths and initially thought they were benign, but they later discovered a "low grade malignancy," wrote Bob Green.[27] Radiation treatments hampered Jones's performance that year, and he was released at the end of the season. He threw some additional games for the 1963 Cardinals and the 1964 Orioles before finishing his career in the minors in 1967.

A recurrence of Jones's neck cancer led to his death on November 5, 1971.

. . .

JUST HOW GOOD was "Toothpick" Sam Jones's curveball? Roy Campanella used Dodgers shortstop Pee Wee Reese, facing Jones in 1955 with a 3-2 count, to illustrate the point. "Jones went into that herky-jerky motion of his and let the ball go," Campanella wrote. "Reese hit the deck, thinking it was headed toward him. But it turned out to be a strike and Reese was out." An exasperated Reese returned to the Dodgers dugout, grumbling, "In all my years playing baseball, I've never struck out sitting down."[28]

St. Louis-born Max Scherzer threw two no-hitters in 2015, giving the Missouri metropolis the top spot in the list of cities producing no-no throwers. *(Photo by KeithAllisonPhoto.com)*

In the world of no-hitters, the city of St. Louis is the most prolific hometown having given birth to four no-hitter throwers. Philadelphia and Oakland had been tied for the top spot until St. Louis-native Max Scherzer threw two no-nos in 2015. Six other cities have each produced three no-no pitchers.

5 **St. Louis, Missouri**
   Ted Breitenstein, Jerry Reuss, Ken Holtzman, Pud Galvin, Max Scherzer (2)

4 **Philadelphia, Pennsylvania**
   Bill Dietrich, Bill McCahan, Matt Kilroy, Sam Kimber

4 **Oakland, California**
   Dave Stewart, Monte Pearson, Dennis Eckersley, Jim Tobin

3 **Brooklyn, New York** *
Larry Corcoran, Ed Morris, Sandy Koufax

3 **Fresno, California**
Jim Maloney, Ewell Blackwell, Tom Seaver

3 **Kansas City, Missouri**
David Cone, Vern Kennedy, "Smokey" Joe Wood

3 **New York, New York**
Jim Palmer, John Candelaria, Bo Belinsky

3 **Rochester, New York**
George Mogridge, Bob Keegan, Charles "Old Hoss" Radbourn

3 **Sacramento, California**
Bob Forsch, Ken Forsch, Jim Jay Hughes

* If we were to rank the cities in terms of total no-nos, the honor would go to . . .
drumroll . . . Brooklyn with 8: Koufax (4), Corcoran (3), and Morris (1). Second
place? Brooklyn's 8 just edges out Refugio, Texas, with 7, all by Nolan Ryan.

Baseball, as depicted in this 1866 portrait, was a much different game before the turn of the century. *(Photo by G. F. Davis, New York Public Library, A. G. Spalding Baseball Collection, b13537024)*

CHAPTER 3

THE FATHER OF NO-NOS

The Hartfords were for the third time this week whitewashed by the St. Louis Club to-day. The batting of the Hartfords was execrable, not a single safe hit being made off Bradley.

—1876 WIRE REPORT OF GEORGE BRADLEY'S NO-HITTER

When St. Louis Brown Stockings pitcher George Washington Bradley tossed what Major League Baseball considers its first no-hitter on July 15, 1876, the setting and rules varied greatly from the current state of the national pastime. Instead of taking to a mound of dirt and clay at the Grand Avenue Ball Grounds in St. Louis, the 24-year-old Bradley found his spot inside a flat 6-foot-square pitching box with a front line just 40 feet from home plate. (It's hard to imagine this now; feels more like cricket!)

The 5-foot-10½-inch, lanky right-hander picked up a ball far different from the tightly wound spheres of today. An 1876 "Dead Ball Era" baseball was essentially a ball of yarn wound around a rubber center and covered by two stitched-together strips of white horsehide or cowhide. A brand-new ball was already soft, and it grew softer during the rigors of a game until it began to unravel.

None of the Brown Stockings fielders wore gloves, and Bradley's catcher, "Honest John" Clapp, was no exception. He took his spot far behind home plate, nearly against the backstop, as he waited to field Bradley's first pitch on a bounce.

Umpire Charles Daniels took his spot off to the side. National League rules at the time awarded a walk after nine balls, and getting plunked by a pitch was simply another ball. A third strike in 1876 yielded not a trip back to the dugout but a mere warning from Daniels: Swing at good pitches or you'll be out on the next (fourth) strike.

When Hartford Dark Blues leadoff hitter Jack Remsen stepped up to bat, he was given the option of calling for a high ball, a low ball, or a "fair ball" (an area similar to today's strike zone). Once Remsen decided, he had to stick to that strike zone for the duration of his at-bat.

Bradley was allowed to begin his windup with a running start within the pitching box as long as he released the ball before stepping across the front line. An overhand pitch was illegal, so "Grin" and fellow hurlers of his day threw underhand or in a submarine style with their arm never reaching above the waist.

George Washington Bradley, top row center, had a phenomenal 1876 season, posting a 45-19 record with a 1.23 ERA and baseball's first official no-hitter.
(Photo from Wikimedia Commons)

On this day in 1876, Bradley began the game by retiring Remsen and worked his way down the lineup during the 1-hour-50-minute contest (wouldn't we like that game length back?), striking out three batters while walking one. The Brown Stockings' defense was of little help, committing eight errors while somehow preserving Bradley's 2-0 no-hit shutout victory.[29]

Bradley's blanking of Hartford was one of his astonishing 16 shutouts during a stellar 1876 season, by far the best of his nine-year career. Equally impressive was his 45-19 record with a league-leading 1.23 ERA. Bradley was not merely a member of the Brown Stockings' pitching staff; he *was* the pitching staff. He started every game.

Despite his success, due to new leagues being formed, teams moving cities, and trades, Bradley bounced around the NL before pitching his final game as a member of the Cincinnati Outlaw Reds of the Union Association in 1884. He returned to Philadelphia to become a police officer, retiring only when he was forced out at the age of 75 after 40 years of service.

"I had four years on the patrol wagon," he said. "That was when my hair and mustache began to whiten, and I could hear the boys behind my back call me 'the old man.' But I never would think of getting old. Now they are retiring me. They brought me face to face with age. I don't like it."[30]

WHAT HE WOULD LIKE, however, is the safe aging of his 1876 pitching gem. It remains the oldest no-no recognized by MLB despite the unearthing of one and possibly two earlier no-hitters tossed by a man named Joe Borden. On July 28, 1875, a year before Bradley's no-no, Joe Borden threw a 4-0 no-hit, no-run game for the Philadelphia Athletics against the Chicago White Stockings.[31] Researchers took so long to uncover this because Joe Borden played under the alias "Joseph E. Josephs," as he didn't want his parents to know he was playing ball! (Baseball was not seen as a "gentleman's game" then.)

The 1875 game was great, says Major League Baseball, but the MLB timeline begins in 1876 with the birth of the National League, and 1871–1875 National Association games aren't part of MLB history. But in 1950, baseball historian Lee Allen discovered what might be an 1876 National League no-hitter thrown by Borden for the Boston Red Caps on May 23—nearly two months before Bradley's no-no. The box score from that day shows two hits charged to Borden in the 8-0 win over the Cincinnati Red Stockings, but Allen surmised that those hits were actually bases on balls, not singles.[32] Early baseball rules and standards in that day were quite fluid, and some official scorers still considered reaching base on a walk a base hit. Official scorer Opie Caylor commonly called walks base hits, but it's not known how Caylor scored that particular game.[33]

Joe Borden's time in baseball was short-lived. The 22-year-old developed arm soreness by July 1876 and was cut after a 15-0 loss to the Chicago White Stockings. Still under contract with the Red Caps, Borden had to finish the season selling tickets and serving as groundskeeper.[34]

THE NEW RESEARCH hasn't fazed Major League Baseball, which has declined to revisit old box scores and continues to recognize George Washington Bradley as the father of the no-hitter. That was good news for Bradley, who never wanted to give up his police badge and likely felt the same about his inaugural no-no status. "That badge, a baseball or two and a ragged glove are among my prized possession," he said.[35]

WHERE WERE THE NO-NOS THROWN, AND ON WHAT DAY?

If a pitcher is going to try to throw a no-hitter on a given day or night, he might want to wait until he arrives in the Windy City. And/or hope to pitch on a Saturday. Chicago has hosted more no-nos than any other major-league city with 30, accounting for more than 10 percent of the total since 1876. That's amazing, considering that the Cubs avoided becoming a victim of a no-hitter from September 1965 through July 2015. Here's the breakdown of no-hitters by city.

The Top 5

Chicago	30
New York	25
Boston	23
Philadelphia	21
Cincinnati	17

In double digits

Brooklyn	15
Cleveland	15
St. Louis	14
Los Angeles	12
Detroit	11

The rest

Pittsburgh 9, Baltimore 9, San Francisco 9, Oakland 9, Houston 8, Milwaukee 7, Anaheim 7, Atlanta 6, Seattle 6, Washington, D.C. 5, Kansas City 4, San Diego 4, Miami 4, Minneapolis 3, Montreal 3, Arlington 3, Providence 2, Louisville 2, Buffalo 2, Toronto 2, St. Petersburg 2, Worcester 1, Rochester 1, Denver 1, Phoenix 1

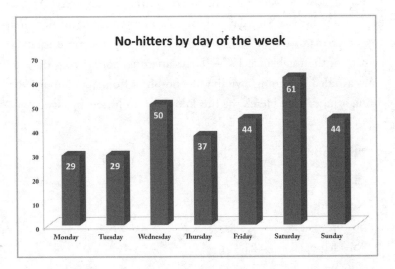

No-hitters by day of the week

(Graphic by NoNoHitters.com)

BREITENSTEIN, NEW ORLEANS

Ted Breitenstein, shown in an old American Tobacco Company card, threw a no-hitter for the St. Louis Browns on the last day of the 1891 American Association season in his first major-league start. *(Baseball card photo from the Benjamin K. Edwards Collection, Prints & Photographs Division, Library of Congress, LC-DIG-bbc-1086f)*

CHAPTER 4

BOFFO DEBUTS FOR BUMPUS, BREITENSTEIN, AND BOBO

Everything Bobo threw was belted and everywhere the ball went, there was a Brownie to catch it.

—St. Louis Browns owner Bill Veeck

The 1890s and 1950s couldn't be further apart in every way, save for three baseball milestones—all by fellows with names or nicknames starting in B. (Nicknames *were* better back then.)

Our first two B's—Bumpus Jones and Ted Breitenstein—threw their no-hitters from a flat pitcher's box, not a mound, but at least it had been moved back from 40 to 50 feet from home plate by the time they came along.

Our third, Alva "Bobo" Holloman, threw his stuff from a raised mound at the proper 60-foot-6-inch distance from home plate.

CHARLES LEANDER "BUMPUS" JONES was crisscrossing the heartland as a minor leaguer in the fall of 1892 when he was given the opportunity of a lifetime. The 22-year-old right-hander received an invitation to play in an exhibition game against the big-league Cincinnati Reds in Wilmington, Ohio.

Jones was summoned from the outfield to pitch one inning, and his stifling of the Cincinnati offense impressed player-manager Charles Comiskey. The Reds' skipper upped the ante by offering Jones an even greater opportunity—the chance to start the Reds' October 15 finale against the Pittsburgh Pirates.[36]

"That the youngster had enough faith in his own ability is shown in the fact that he came here yesterday to pitch without a cent of pay," the *Cincinnati Enquirer* wrote. "All he asked was his expenses."[37]

Jones had visited Cincinnati two years earlier while pitching for a semipro team. But the Ohio-native was now standing in the Bank Street Grounds pitchers box facing such Bucs' greats as Connie Mack. A nervous Jones walked the first two batters but worked his way out of the jam by inducing a ground-ball double play. He walked another Pirates batter in the second but again was saved by a double play.[38] "He is small in stature but is very quick and muscular," the local paper wrote of Jones. "He wastes little motion in delivering the ball and has great speed and splendid curves."[39]

Jones issued his fourth base on balls to Patsy Donovan in the third inning (the hometown paper proclaimed it should have been called a strikeout), and Donovan advanced by stealing second. Donovan scored the Pirates' lone run when Jones fielded Duke Farrell's bunt and threw the ball past first base into right field.[40]

Still, of course, the no-hitter was intact.

Jones settled down and began to retire batter after batter to the cheers of 800 faithful who "made enough noise for ten times that many people."[41]

"Not once did the interest lag," according to the *Enquirer*. "Everybody stayed to the finish."[42]

The game ended with a 7-1 score and bubkes in the "H" column. Bumpus Jones made history as the only pitcher ever to throw a no-hitter in his first major-league appearance, though Boston Red Sox left-hander

Bill Rohr came within one strike of the feat in 1967. Two other pitchers have thrown no-hitters in their first big-league starts, *but* Ted Breitenstein and Alva "Bobo" Holloman had each made earlier relief appearances.

TED BREITENSTEIN THREW an 8-0 no-hitter for the St. Louis Browns on the last day of the 1891 American Association season. The 23-year-old southpaw had five calls from the Browns' bullpen before earning a start against the Louisville Colonels during the opener of an October 4, 1891 doubleheader. Breitenstein's only blemish in front of a crowd of 5,000 Sportsman's Park spectators was a lone walk.

"Not a hit was secured off him, and only twenty-seven men came to bat," said a report in the *Chicago Tribune*. "The Browns fielded perfectly, which materially aided him."[43]

Alva "Bobo" Holloman threw a no-hitter in 1953 during his first major-league start *(Photo from National Baseball Hall of Fame and Museum)*

Fast-forward to the 1950s.

Alva Holloman, a 6-foot-2, 207-pound hurler who liked to refer to himself in the third person as "Bobo," had been relegated to the American League Browns' bullpen early in 1953 and was struggling with a 9.00 ERA in five and one-third innings over four appearances.

"I'm a starting pitcher," the 27-year-old sinkerballer told manager Marty Marion.[44]

When Marion finally gave Bobo his May 6 start, he made the most of it. He held the Philadelphia Athletics without a hit while issuing five walks and committing one error. Browns owner Bill Veeck, who gave Holloman a $100 suit for the feat, was not otherwise impressed, he wrote in his 1962 autobiography *Veeck—as in Wreck*: "Just when it appeared Bobo was tiring and running out of gas, a shower would sweep across the field and delay the game long enough for Bobo to rest and be refreshed."[45]

A POSTSCRIPT on our three gents who did so well their first times out:

Bumpus Jones's debut performance so impressed Charles Comiskey that the Reds' player-manager guaranteed the pitcher a job to start the 1893 season. But a rule change pushed the pitching box 10 feet 6 inches farther from home plate than Bumpus was used to, and the extra distance proved troublesome. The Reds relegated Jones to the bench, forcing him to sign midseason with New York Giants. Facing Cy Young in his last major-league appearance, Jones walked 10 and gave up six runs. He finished his career in minor and semipro leagues in the 1890s and into 1901.[46]

Bobo Holloman, too, proved to be a one-shot wonder. He pitched 22 more games in 1953 before Veeck released him. A few minor-league seasons and time as a scout followed.

Back to the 1890s, and we find that Ted Breitenstein established a longer, more successful career. In fact, nearly seven years after tossing that no-hitter in his first start in 1891, he would throw his second on April 22, 1898, as a member of the Cincinnati Reds. And not only that, on the same day, Jim Hughes threw one for the Baltimore Orioles. It marked the first time two no-hitters were thrown on the same day—doubling Breitenstein's reason to pop open the bubbly.

FIRST NO-HITTERS AFTER MAJOR RULE CHANGES

Ledell "Cannonball" Titcomb pitched the first no-hitter after baseball established a walk as four balls. *(Photo from New York Public Library, A. G. Spalding Baseball Collection, b13537024)*

Rule changes over the history of baseball have often been drastic, from the DH to mound height. Spanning 1883–1973, here are the first no-hitters thrown after some of the game's major rule changes.

First no-hitter under 1883 rule allowing pitchers to deliver the ball from above the waist:
Charles "Old Hoss" Radbourn
Providence Grays (NL) @ Kennard Street Park (Cleveland)
Wednesday, July 25, 1883 / Providence Grays 8, Cleveland Blues 0

First no-hitter after batters are no longer allowed to ask for a high, low, or "fair ball" pitch in 1887:
Adonis Terry
Brooklyn Bridegrooms (AA) @ Ridgewood Park (Brooklyn)
Sunday, May 27, 1888 / Brooklyn Bridegrooms 4, Louisville Colonels 0

First no-hitter after baseball establishes a walk as four balls, settling
    on that number in 1889 after earlier rules awarded runners first
    base after nine, eight, six, and five balls:
Ledell "Cannonball" Titcomb
Rochester Broncos (AA) @ Culver Field (Rochester)
Monday, September 15, 1890 / Rochester Broncos 7, Syracuse
    Stars 0

First no-hitter after 1893 rule changes establishing the now
    standard 60-foot-6-inch pitching distance and replacing the
    pitching box with a rubber slab:
Bill Hawke
Baltimore Orioles (NL) @ Boundary Field (Washington)
Wednesday, August 16, 1893 / Baltimore Orioles 5, Washington
    Senators 0

First no-hitter after baseball limits the height of the pitcher's
    mound to 15 inches in 1904:
Cy Young
Boston Americans (AL) @ Huntington Avenue Grounds (Boston)
Thursday, May 5, 1904 / Boston Americans 3, Philadelphia
    Athletics 0 (perfect game)

First no-hitter since the 1968 rewriting of the anti-spitball rule:
Tom Phoebus
Baltimore Orioles (AL) @ Memorial Stadium (Baltimore)
Saturday, April 27, 1968 / Baltimore Orioles 6, Boston Red Sox 0

First no-hitter after the pitcher's-mound height is reduced from 15
    inches to 10 inches in 1969 and the strike zone is reduced to an
    area from the armpits to the top of the batter's knees:
Bill Stoneman

Montreal Expos (NL) @ Connie Mack Stadium (Philadelphia)
Thursday, April 17, 1969 / Montreal Expos 7, Philadelphia
    Phillies 0

First American League no-hitter with the designated hitter in use:
Steve Busby
Kansas City Royals (AL) @ Tiger Stadium (Detroit)
Friday, April 27, 1973 / Kansas City Royals 3, Detroit Tigers 0

First no-hitter under 2015 rules to speed up games:
Chris Heston
San Francisco Giants (NL) @ Citi Field (New York)
Tuesday, June 9, 2015 / San Francisco Giants 5, New York Mets 0

New York Yankees catcher Yogi Berra jumps into Don Larsen's arms
after Larsen threw a perfect game in the 1956 World Series.
(Library of Congress, Prints & Photographs Division, LC-DIG-ppmsca-18786)

CHAPTER 5

POSTSEASON PERFECTION

Three days before, I was a dejected young pitcher who had let himself and his teammates down in Game 2. I had just hoped to hell that Casey would give me another chance in the Series to redeem myself.

—DON LARSEN IN *The Perfect Yankee*

Lists chronicling the most memorable moments in World Series history often focus on walk-off victories erupting in home-plate mayhem. Los Angeles Dodgers fans relish replays of Kirk Gibson pumping his arm while hobbling through the ninth-inning home-run trot that ended Game 1 of the 1988 fall classic. Championship-starved New York Mets fans can't go a season without watching Ray Knight cross the plate on Mookie Wilson's 10th-inning dribbler past Bill Buckner for the Game 6 victory over the Boston Red Sox in the 1986 World Series. Hall of Famer Bill Mazeroski is forever remembered in Pittsburgh for his Game 7, ninth-inning home run that crowned the Pirates 1960 world champions.

But one pitcher's 1956 accomplishment trumps them all, as the New York Yankees' Don Larsen had to notch 27 consecutive memorable moments to cement his spot in baseball history. Larsen, on October 6, 1956, threw the first—and only—perfect game in World Series history.

Larsen said in a 2014 interview that he still thinks about his victory over the Brooklyn Dodgers several times a day. "It was the best thing that ever happened to me," he said.[47]

The 6-foot-4, 215-pound right-hander began his career with the St. Louis Browns/Baltimore Orioles organization, but the Orioles traded him to the Yankees in 1954 as part of an 18-player swap. The 27-year-old Indiana native was splitting his time between starter and reliever in 1956 when manager Casey Stengel gave him the start for Game 2 of the World Series at Ebbets Field.

"I did a lousy job," Larsen recalled.[48]

The Yankees' offense built a 6-0 lead, but four walks, an error and a hit prompted Stengel to yank Larsen and turn to the bullpen after just 10 Brooklyn batters. The Dodgers evened the score by the end of the second inning and won 13-8 to establish a 2-0 series lead.

New York evened the series by taking back two in the Bronx on strong performances by Yankees pitchers Whitey Ford and Tom Sturdivant. No one knew who would start Game 5; Larsen figured that Stengel would opt for Bob Turley or Johnny Kucks. But when he arrived at his Yankee Stadium locker on October 6, he found that coach Frank Crosetti had left the game ball in Larsen's shoe, signaling that he was the chosen one.

"He picked me," Larsen said, ecstatic with Stengel's vote of confidence. "I don't know the reason because nobody told me. I was happy, happy to get a second chance."[49]

A perfect game wasn't on anyone's mind when Larsen nearly walked Pee Wee Reese in the opening frame. He established a 1-2 count before throwing two consecutive balls but recovered to catch Reese looking at a slider for the strikeout. Yankees catcher Yogi Berra said it was the only time during the entire game that a count against a Dodgers batter reached three balls, as Larsen threw 97 pitches—70 for strikes.

"I never had such good control in my life," Larsen said. "Every time Yogi put the sign down, I threw it pretty close, except for a couple of mistakes. The defense made a couple of nice plays for me."[50]

The Dodgers threatened Larsen's no-no in the second inning when

Jackie Robinson lined a ball down the third-base line. The ball ricocheted off third baseman Andy Carey's glove and landed in front of shortstop Gil McDougald, who scooped it up and threw a perfect strike to first to beat Robinson by a half-step.

THE GAME REMAINED scoreless until Mickey Mantle hit a solo homer in the fourth. Larsen continued mowing through the Dodgers' lineup but survived a couple of scares in the top of the fifth.

Gil Hodges entered the batter's box with one out and drove a long fly ball into the left-center field gap. Mantle gave chase from center field and made a stellar backhand grab "that saved my bacon," Larsen recalled.[51]

Mantle's grab marked the game's 14th out, meaning Larsen was now more than halfway through a game he hadn't yet realized remained perfect. Next up was Sandy Amoros, and the Cuban-born lefty pounced on a high fastball and launched it toward the right-field stands. Umpire Ed Runge, who was stationed in the outfield on the right-field line, watched the ball drift right of the foul pole before throwing out his arms, prompting a stadium-full of relieved sighs.

"Back before you had those wire screens, those balls were sometimes hard to call," Runge said in the book *Umpires: Classic Baseball Stories from the Men Who Made the Calls*.[52]

"He hit the ball pretty good," Larsen said. "It wasn't foul by much."[53]

Amoros then grounded out to second to end the inning.

Larsen helped provide some insurance in the bottom of the sixth inning. Carey led off the inning with a single, and Larsen was called upon to lay down a sacrifice bunt despite his reputation as being a good-hitting pitcher. Larsen let the count drop to 0-2 and figured he'd be asked to swing away, but Stengel ordered another bunt attempt—a risky move. Larsen tapped the ball in front of the plate, and Carey reached second as the throw went to first.[54]

Hank Bauer followed with an RBI single, and the Yankees had a 2-0 lead. Mantle could have broken open the game with two runners on, but he hit the ball right at Hodges for what developed into a double play.

An autographed baseball and scorecard from Don Larsen's perfect game in the 1956 World Series *(Photo by Dirk Lammers)*

Larsen said the close score continued to keep him and his teammates on their toes, and he's not sure how fate might have treated him if Mantle had homered and extended the Yankees' lead to 5-0. He retired the side in the seventh and eighth innings, and the decibels emanating from the 64,519 fans packed into Yankee Stadium grew to the roar of a subway train with each Dodgers at-bat. So did Larsen's nerves.

In the latter innings he began reaching for the rosin bag after nearly every pitch, and "that wasn't my style." Larsen didn't realize the uncharacteristically frequent grabs until 2007, when he got together with Berra and some other former teammates to watch the television broadcast for the first time.

"I guess you get in a groove or something, and if it works nice, you keep on doing it," he said. "Maybe it's unnatural, but you're probably not aware you're doing certain things."[55]

In the ninth, Larsen enticed outs from Carl Furillo and Roy Campanella before Dodgers manager Walter Alston called back pitcher Sal Maglie and sent pinch hitter Dale Mitchell to the plate. The batting change gave Larsen a short break from the tension. "I turned to center field and I said a little prayer," he said. "That helped, I guess."[56]

Berra thought his "eardrums were gonna burst from the crowd noise," he wrote in the foreword of Larsen's autobiography. With a 2-2 count, Berra called for a fastball. Mitchell tried to check his swing, but it didn't matter as home-plate umpire Babe Pinelli bellowed "Strr ... iii ... ke three."

Berra said he felt like a kid on Christmas morning.[57] "I came out of my squat and ran toward Don," Berra wrote. "Then I leaped on him and hugged him like a brother."[58]

That moment, captured in stills and film reels from many angles, remains one of the most iconic images in World Series history. The image was all the more striking due to Larsen's 6-foot-4 versus Yogi's 5-foot-7. Larsen said he expected Berra to do something to celebrate, but the leap surprised him a bit. At the time, Larsen knew only that he had thrown a no-hitter to help the Yankees win their seventh championship in 10 years. "I didn't know it was a perfect game until someone told me in the clubhouse after the game," Larsen said.[59]

IT WAS ANOTHER New York Yankees pitcher, Bill Bevens, who nearly beat Larsen to the postseason no-no punch by nine years. In Game 4 of the 1947 World Series, Bevens held the Dodgers hitless through eight and two-thirds innings despite walking 10 batters. In the bottom of the ninth inning with two runners aboard, pinch hitter Cookie Lavagetto lined a double off the right-field wall to drive home two runs, kill the no-no, *and* give Brooklyn a 3-2 victory.

A banner honors the
Philadelphia Phillies'
Roy "Doc" Halladay
for throwing the second
postseason no-hitter
in baseball history.
(Photo by Dirk Lammers)

Larsen's perfecto and Bevens's near miss were thrown in an era when postseason baseball and the World Series were synonymous. The addition of the wild card, divisional, and league championship series over the years has added additional opportunity for postseason no-hitters, and Larsen finally drew some company in his one-man club after 54 years of exclusivity. The Philadelphia Phillies' Roy Halladay, in his first postseason start, no-hit the Cincinnati Reds for a 4-0 victory in Game 1 of the National League Divisional Series on October 6, 2010.

"It's just one of those special things that I'll always remember," Halladay told the *Philadelphia Inquirer.*[60]

The Phillies went on to sweep that series from the Reds but dropped the National League Championship Series to the San Francisco Giants in six games.

While Larsen's achievement was surprising considering his overall MLB record of 81-91, Halladay had already thrown a perfect game earlier that season against the Marlins on May 29.

WELCOMING A NEW MEMBER into the postseason no-no club didn't faze Larsen. "It didn't bother me a bit," he said. "It was the playoffs. That wasn't a World Series game, anyway." And although Larsen continues to

cherish that day at Yankee Stadium, he gave up a piece of prized memorabilia from the accomplishment in 2012. Larsen put his jersey and
pants from that game up for auction, raising $756,000 to help pay for
his grandchildren's college education.[61]

SEE APPENDIX B for a list of all of MLB's perfect games to date.

DID YOU KNOW?

MILWAUKEE SEEKS
HOME-BREWED NO-NO

Milwaukee's Miller Park hosted a neutral-site no-hitter by the
Chicago Cubs' Carlos Zambrano, but Brewers fans have yet
to witness a home-brewed no-hitter. *(Photo by Dirk Lammers)*

Baseball fans in the city of Milwaukee got to celebrate their first
home-field no-hitter way back in 1884 in the original Brewers franchise's second game as a Union Association replacement team. On
September 28, 1884, pitcher Ed Cushman no-hit the Washington
Nationals for a 5-0 win at Milwaukee's Wright Street Grounds.

After the Boston Braves relocated to Wisconsin in 1953, fans
packing Milwaukee County Stadium got to watch plenty of home-
team no-nos in the 1950s and '60s.

Jim Wilson threw a no-hitter against the Philadelphia Phillies in 1954, and Lew Burdette no-hit the same team in 1960. Warren Spahn no-hit the Phillies in 1960, then followed up with a second no-hitter against the San Francisco Giants in 1961.

THE BRAVES left for Atlanta in 1966, and despite the arrival of the American League Brewers in 1970, Milwaukee fans continue to root, root, root for the home team to throw a no-no.

The Kansas City Royals' Steve Busby threw his second no-hitter at County Stadium in 1974, but his was at the expense of the Brewers. And when the Brewers' Juan Nieves finally notched the team's first (and only) no-no in 1987, the site was Baltimore's Memorial Stadium.

Brewers television analyst Bill Schroeder, who caught Nieves's no-no, said CC Sabathia should have been credited with the team's second no-hitter in Pittsburgh on August 31, 2008. The Pirates' only hit during the Brewers' one-hit victory that day came when Sabathia fumbled Andy LaRoche's fifth-inning swinging bunt, allowing La-Roche to reach first.

"I've got to believe you call that an error," Schroeder said. "A play like that can't be the only hit in the game. That's a sore spot."[62]

BUT MILWAUKEE holds the distinction of hosting the majors' only neutral-site no-no. The Houston Astros in 2008 were forced to move their September 14 home game against the Chicago Cubs to Milwaukee's Miller Park because of damage from Hurricane Ike. The Cubs' Carlos Zambrano apparently liked the setting, as he no-hit the Astros for a 5-0 victory.

The Cincinnati Reds' Fred Toney, pictured, and the Chicago Cubs'
Hippo Vaughn combined for baseball's only double no-no in 1917.
*(Photo from Bain News Service Collection, Prints & Photographs
Division, Library of Congress, LC-DIG-ggbain-24924)*

CHAPTER 6

HEAD-TO-HEAD
NO-HITTER DUELS

When nine rounds had been played neither one of the stalwart hurlers had allowed a base hit, but in the tenth the break came and it went against Vaughn.

—JAMES CRUSINBERRY, *Chicago Daily Tribune*

What is the best pitchers' duel of all time?

One nominee is a July 2, 1933, contest between the New York Giants and the St. Louis Cardinals. Some 50,000 Polo Grounds fans watched as the Giants' Carl Hubbell outlasted St. Louis starter Tex Carleton to stifle the Cardinals' lineup for an 18-inning 1-0, six-hit victory.

Another finalist is the 16-inning battle between the Milwaukee Braves' Warren Spahn and the San Francisco Giants' Juan Marichal on July 2, 1963 in front of nearly 16,000 enthusiasts at Candlestick Park. The scoreless gridlock ended in the bottom of the 16th inning when Willie Mays tagged Spahn for a walk-off homer.

A World Series Game 7 is baseball's ultimate pressure cooker, and the October 27, 1991, finale in that year's fall classic was all about pitching. The Minnesota Twins' Jack Morris outdueled the Atlanta Braves' John Smoltz to eke out a 1-0 victory in front of more than 55,000 fans who packed the Metrodome.

. . .

BUT THE 3,500 CUBS FAITHFUL who braved a bone-chilling wind at the friendly confines of Weeghman Park on May 2, 1917, wouldn't have accepted nominees. They'd already given the award to their own James "Hippo" Vaughn and the Cincinnati Reds' Fred Toney. Why? The two pitchers battled through the only *double* nine-inning no-hitter in baseball history.

The duo upheld a rivalry dating back to their minor-league days, when Toney pitched for the Louisville Colonels of the American Association and Vaughn played for the Kansas City Blues. "Vaughn and I were always after each other," Toney told a reporter many years later.[63] Their feud carried over into the majors, and it would reach unprecedented heights that day in Chicago as Toney and Vaughn continually sent batters back to their dugouts.

"Inning after inning the players were set down in order and the fans enjoyed a marvelous pitching duel between two crafty, resourceful and cunning pitchers," according to one game-day wire report.[64]

Chicago Daily Tribune sportswriter James Crusinberry deduced that Vaughn outpitched Toney, striking out 10 while walking just two. A third Reds batter reached first when Cubs shortstop Rollie Zeider fumbled an easy grounder.[65]

"Vaughn really was the more brilliant of the two pitchers for nine innings," Crusinberry wrote. "Only twenty-seven men faced him in that time, because each time he walked a man double plays occurred, clearing the bases, and the one fellow who reached first on Zeider's fumble was tagged out trying to steal."[66]

Toney issued two bases on balls and struck out just one batter through nine, but his defense was perfect.

"The duel was so desperate that when the ninth inning was over and the honors were even the crowd cheered both men," Crusinberry wrote.[67]

The dual no-hitters went to extra innings.

The Cincinnati Reds' Fred Toney and the Chicago Cubs' Hippo Vaughn,
pictured, combined for baseball's only double no-no in 1917.
*(Photo from Bain News Service Collection, Prints & Photographs
Division, Library of Congress, LC-DIG-ggbain-16744.)*

Vaughn said he knew he was tired when he took the mound for the
top of the 10th inning, but he felt he still had his stuff. But after an easy
first out, Larry Kopf, the Cincinnati shortstop, smacked a liner into
right field. "Fred Merkle made a desperate lunge to his right with one
hand stretched out, and perhaps came within a foot of the ball, but it
was out of reach, and the terrible suspense was broken," the *Chicago
Daily Tribune* report said.[68]

A second out ensued, but then Hal Chase hit a liner at the center
fielder, who appeared to misjudge the ball before trying to catch it at his
ankles. The ball dropped, and runners now stood on first and third.

Famed Native American athlete Jim Thorpe then stepped up to the plate. After Chase stole second, Thorpe poked a swinging bunt that Vaughan came off the mound to field, but he knew instantly that trying to throw out the 1912 Olympics pentathlon and decathlon gold medalist would be fruitless. He threw to home plate, but catcher Wilson "just went paralyzed."

"The ball hit him square on the chest protector—I'll never forget it—it seemed to roll around there for a moment—and then dropped to the ground," Vaughn recalled.[69] Kopf scored from third before Wilson recovered to pick up the ball and tag out Chase for the third out, and the damage was done. The score was 1-0 in favor of the Reds.

A rejuvenated Toney took the mound for the bottom of the 10th, and "the big Tennessee man called on all the reserve power in his right arm to make sure of the honor of a no hit game."[70] Toney struck out Larry Doyle for the first out. Merkle hit a deep fly ball to the left-field wall, but outfielder Manuel Cueto snagged it for out number two. Cy Williams stepped in as the Cubs' last hope. Toney had intentionally walked the power hitter in the second and fifth innings, but he had to face him in the 10th. Williams fouled an early pitch against the grandstand. "For some reason, the umpire didn't throw the ball out of the game," Toney said. "When I got it back, it had a big scuffed place on it—and I knew I had Williams."[71] Toney completed the strikeout for the 10-inning no-hitter.

"Toney pitched a better game," Vaughn told his teammates after the game. "He didn't give any hits."[72]

Baseball fans have enjoyed plenty of great pitchers' duels in the century since Toney and Vaughn's 1917 matchup, but no other major-league game has gone nine full innings without a hit from either side.

THE CLOSEST ATTEMPT was on September 9, 1965, when Dodgers legend Sandy Koufax and the Cubs' Bob Hendley dueled. It was the greatest southpaw battle of all time. Koufax rightfully grabbed the spotlight by throwing a perfect game for his fourth career no-hitter, but Hendley was no slouch. He yielded just a single hit—a seventh-inning double—and the game set the record for fewest hits yielded in a game (one) and fewest base runners allowed in a nine-inning game (two).

Well, there was a 0-0 10-inning affair once. More on that soon.

Ben Sanders might have been credited with a no-hitter he didn't deserve, according to a Louisville sports writer. *(Photo from New York Public Library, A. G. Spalding Baseball Collection, b13537024)*

Questionable calls on whether a booted ball should be ruled a hit or an error take on extra-special meaning when a pitcher has a no-no on the line.

In 1991, the Kansas City Royals' Bret Saberhagen thought he'd lost his no-hitter when Chicago's Dan Pasqua hit a liner toward left-center field and the ball grazed off the glove of Kirk Gibson. It was immediately ruled a hit, but the official scorer reversed the ruling, making it an error.

IN TODAY'S 24-hour-news-cycle world, fans across the globe know pretty quickly what the official ruling is, but that wasn't always the case.

Here are a handful of early no-hitters with a play or two still in doubt.

Ben Sanders: Louisville Colonels (NL) / Monday, August 22, 1892 / Louisville Colonels 6, Baltimore Orioles 2 / Eclipse Park (Louisville)

The local paper's headline for this game reads "Only One Hit" based on George Van Haltren's sharp grounder toward third in the fourth inning. The shot was just missed by third baseman Hughie Jennings. Shortstop Charley Bassett snagged the ball about 20 feet behind third base, but his desperate throw was about 3 feet wide, and Van Haltren was safe at first. "At the time of the play, there was no question about it being a hit," noted the story in Louisville's *Courier-Journal*. "However, when the game was over and that proved to be the only hit made, a few inflammable cranks set up the claim that Jennings and Bassett had made bad errors. They wanted to improve Sanders' already splendid record, though it could only be done by robbing Van Haltren."[73]

The *Courier-Journal* box score recorded it as a hit, but Sanders is in baseball's record books as having thrown a no-hitter.

Cy Young: Cleveland Spiders (NL) / Saturday, September 18, 1897 (first game of doubleheader) / Cleveland Spiders 6, Cincinnati Reds 0 / League Park (Cleveland) / *His first of three no-hitters*

Four Reds reached first in this game on a walk and three errors, with two of the errors coming on balls hit by Bug Holliday to third baseman Bobby Wallace. On the first of those, Wallace considered the play too easy, and it got through him, noted a special dispatch in the *Cincinnati Enquirer*. "Again Holliday hit a hard one at Wallace," the newspaper said about the second nonhit. "It fell at his feet, and he had plenty of time to throw the runner out, but his throw took O'Connor off the bag."[74] Young's Hall of Fame page notes that that ball was originally ruled a hit, but Wallace sent a note to the press box after the eighth inning indicating that he had actually made an error. The ruling on the field was changed.

"Young considered the game to be a one-hitter, despite a valiant effort from his teammate," the Hall notes.[75]

Vic Willis: Boston Beaneaters (NL) / Monday, August 7, 1899 / Boston Beaneaters 7, Washington Senators 1 / Huntington Avenue Grounds (Boston)

According to David Fleitz's book *Ghosts in the Gallery at Cooperstown: Sixteen Forgotten Members of the Hall of Fame*, six Washington Senators reached base in this game on four walks, a hit batsman, and a slow roller by opposing pitcher Bill Dinneen that third baseman Jimmy Rollins couldn't handle. All four of Boston's newspapers declared it a hit, but the *New York Times* and *Sporting Life* ruled it an error—thus making Willis's performance a no-hitter.

Sporting Life ran a correction ruling it a hit a week later, but the game has been recorded in history as a no-hitter.[76]

Ernie Koob: St. Louis Browns (AL) / Saturday, May 5, 1917 / St. Louis Browns 1, Chicago White Sox 0 / Sportsman's Park (St. Louis)

The banner headline across the top of Part 2 of the *Chicago Sunday Tribune* for May 6, 1917, reads, "KOOB TAMES SOX IN ONE HIT GAME, 1-0." Sports writer I. E. Sanborn noted in his story that Buck Weaver's lone hit came with one out in the first inning. "He chopped a high bounder to the first base side of Koob," according to the *Tribune*. "Ernie Johnson, who was subbing at second, tore in and tried to pull a brilliant stop and throw, but failed."[77] The *New York Times* and *Washington Post* both printed stories noting the game's one hit. A dispatch out of St. Louis that appeared in the *Morning Tulsa Daily World* touched on the controversy, saying that official scorer J. B. Sheridan was not in the press box when Weaver hit the ball.

"However he accepted the decision of a local reporter and marked the play an error," the paper said. "Therefore Koob officially is credited with a no-hit game though according to the other scorers the play was clearly a hit."[78]

Howard Ehmke: Boston Red Sox (AL) / Friday, September 7, 1923 / Boston Red Sox 4, Philadelphia Athletics 0 / Shibe Park (Philadelphia)

This game had two questionable plays. "Ehmke's record was tainted in that Bryan Harris of the Athletics hit into center for a double in the sixth inning but was called out for not touching first base," noted one game-day dispatch.[79]

Then, in the eighth, Frank Welch hit a liner to Mike Menosky, which the left fielder fumbled. "The official scorer gave it a single, but later, on consultation with the players, Menosky was given an error," the report noted.[80]

Ehmke still has his no-no.

The Houston Colt .45s' Ken Johnson is the only single pitcher
to throw a complete nine-inning no-hitter for a loss.
(Photo from National Baseball Hall of Fame and Museum)

CHAPTER 7

HOUSTON, WE HAVE A PROBLEM

So I made history. Heckuva way to get into the record books.

—COLT .45S PITCHER KEN JOHNSON

The Cincinnati Reds' 6-foot-4, 210-pound knuckleballer Joe Nuxhall was nursing a 1-0 lead on April 23, 1964. The 35-year-old veteran had, decades earlier, etched his footnote into modern baseball history by pitching two-thirds of an inning for the 1944 Reds as a 15-year-old, becoming the youngest player to appear in a major-league contest.

But Nuxhall, standing one pitch away from finalizing a complete-game shutout of the Colt .45s, wasn't the real story on this night in Houston.

Houston starter Ken Johnson sat motionless in the Colt .45s' dugout, unable to affect the game's outcome. The Colt Stadium scoreboard showed one run on zero hits and two errors for the Reds, zero runs on five hits and two errors for the Colt .45s. Johnson had finished the top of the ninth having held the Reds hitless, but it didn't matter if Houston couldn't manage to score in the bottom of the ninth.

Bob Lillis, the potential tying run, took his lead off first, and Nuxhall readied to deliver a two-out, 3-2 pitch to Houston's John Weekly. "This is a real weird one tonight," noted Gene Elston, Houston's radio play-by-play broadcaster.[81]

As Nuxhall's pitch crossed the plate, conflicting emotions permeated both sides of the diamond. "Call strike three," bellowed Elston. "The ball game is over and Cincinnati wins it by the score of one to nothing, as Johnson pitched a no-hitter and lost the ball game by a run."[82]

NUXHALL'S PITCH gave him and his Reds the win, but it earned Johnson a place in history. Until that moment, no single pitcher had thrown a complete nine-inning no-hitter for a loss, and it has not happened since.

"I was proud of the no-hitter, but I wasn't happy with the loss," Johnson recalled 50 years later.[83]

How the Reds scored their one run is part of the story, as it involved the taboo of bunting to break up a no-hitter. The contest had been scoreless through eight innings, with Johnson allowing only walks in the first and fifth. Johnson got the top-of-the-ninth leadoff hitter out easily, but things were about to unravel when the 23-year-old Pete Rose stepped to the plate. Bunting to break up a no-hitter was not considered fair play, but Johnson knew "Charlie Hustle" would try anyway.

"It wasn't even a good bunt," Johnson told a reporter months after the game. "He dragged it toward the mound instead of down the line, but I didn't grab the ball right and it sank as I got rid of it."[84]

Johnson's errant throw to first sailed into the outfield, and Rose scampered to second.

Next up was Chico Ruiz, who smashed a comebacker to the mound that caromed off Johnson's shin. Third baseman Bob Aspromonte grabbed the ball and fired to first for the out, but Rose advanced to third.

Vada Pinson stepped to the plate with two out and hit a routine grounder that should have ended the inning, but second baseman Nellie

Fox booted the ball. Rose scored, and the Reds were up 1-0 without a base hit.

The veteran Fox was near tears in the Houston locker room as he approached Johnson after the loss.

"Ken, I'm sorry I had to mess it up," Fox told his pitcher.

"Don't feel bad about it, Nellie," Johnson replied. "I put the guy on myself."[85]

Johnson, displaying a plum-colored leg bruise, said he was done for the night even if the Colt .45s managed to send the game into a 10th inning.

"Even if we had tied it," Johnson said, "I couldn't have gone on."[86]

ALTHOUGH JOHNSON REMAINS the only single pitcher to throw a complete-game no-hitter loss, the loss half of that "accomplishment" was matched by a pair of O's pitchers three years later.

During the first game of an April 30, 1967, doubleheader between the Orioles and Tigers, Baltimore starter Steve Barber threw eight innings of no-hit ball despite struggling with his control. The O's broke the 0-0 deadlock in the bottom of the eighth on a sacrifice fly by Luis Aparicio, handing Barber a 1-0 lead into the top of the ninth.

Not so fast.

Barber kicked off the inning by walking Norm Cash and Ray Oyler, and the runners advanced to second and third on a sac bunt. After Detroit replaced both Cash and Oyler with speedier pinch runners, Barber got the second out by jamming pinch hitter Willie Horton into lofting a foul pop-up behind home plate.

It was appearing as if Barber might be able to work out of the jam as Mickey Stanley stepped to the plate, but Barber threw a wild pitch and Cash's pinch runner, Dick Tracewski, crossed home to make it a 1-1 game. But it was still a no-hitter.

When Barber issued his 10th walk of the night to Stanley, Baltimore manager Hank Bauer stepped out of the dugout and signaled to the bullpen for reliever Stu Miller. "I tried to get it for you," the skipper said as he reached the mound.

"If you can't get the ball over, you don't deserve to win," Barber replied.[87]

Miller got Don Wert to hit a grounder to short, but second baseman Mark Belanger dropped Aparicio's throw and the go-ahead run came around. Miller got Al Kaline to ground out to retire the side, but still the Orioles were down 2-1 with the no-hitter about to go for naught. Even the likes of Frank Robinson, Brooks Robinson, and Mike Epstein couldn't save the day, going out 1-2-3 as the game ended as a combined no-hit loss for Barber and Miller.

Barber, resting his arm in ice after the game, said he would have been pulled long before the ninth inning if he hadn't been pitching a no-hitter. He was more upset about losing the game.

"No-hitters are not worth anything in the books unless you win," Barber said.[88]

HERE'S A SITUATION to consider, one that negated four no-hitters.

If you're pitching on the road, and your team is losing by the middle of the ninth, you, of course, don't get to take the mound again. You've lost the game, despite your no-hitter.

Eight-inning no-no losses have occurred only four times:

- June 21, 1890: Silver King for the Chicago Pirates, a 1-0 no-hit Players League loss to the Brooklyn Ward's Wonders
- July 1, 1990: Andy Hawkins for the New York Yankees, a 4-0 no-hit loss to the Chicago White Sox
- April 12, 1992: Matt Young for the Boston Red Sox, a 2-1 no-hit loss to the Cleveland Indians
- June 28, 2008: Jered Weaver (six innings) and Jose Arredondo

(two innings) for the Los Angeles Angels, a 1-0 no-hit loss to the Los Angeles Dodgers

Eight-inning no-hitters had been considered complete-game no-hitters until 1991, when Major League Baseball's committee for statistical accuracy established an official definition of the no-hitter. A pitcher had to pitch nine innings, not eight.

That knocked King's and Hawkins's pre-'91 games off the official list, and Young and Weaver/Arredondo never got a chance to join the club.

A *Brooklyn Daily Eagle* box score shows Sam Kimber's no-hitter that ended in a 0-0 tie. (*Image taken from* Brooklyn Daily Eagle)

There is one more singular achievement: a no-hitter thrown in 1884 that resulted in *neither* a win *nor* a loss.

Sam Kimber, of the American Association's Brooklyn Atlantics, no-hit the Toledo Blue Stockings for 10 innings on October 4, 1884, in a scoreless game that was called due to darkness. The *Brooklyn Daily Eagle* noted that the 0-0 contest "was a rather uninteresting pitcher's game," lacking the "exciting situations and fine fielding work" of other games at Washington Park that year.[89] But it holds its title as a no-hitter by MLB rules because it had no hits, went at least nine innings, and was a complete game.

A CROWNING ACHIEVEMENT

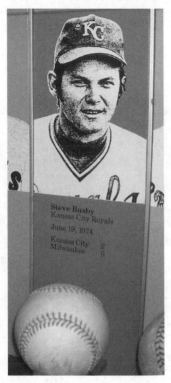

Steve Busby
Kansas City Royals
June 19, 1974
Kansas City 2
Milwaukee 0

Steve Busby threw no-hitters for the Kansas City Royals in 1973 and 1974. *(Photo by Dirk Lammers)*

Steve Busby is gratified to have thrown the first two no-hitters in Kansas City Royals history, but the pitching gems take a backseat to what he considers the defining moment of his eight-year career: the Royals' first division title in their expansion history.

Busby and teammates John Mayberry, George Brett, and Hal McRae spent years beating their heads against the wall trying to catch and beat Oakland, and in 1976, "finally we had gotten to the point where we did."

"To have it all pay off, all the work and all the blood, sweat, and tears, it really was a defining moment for all of us, and the organization, too," he said.[90]

BUSBY WAS still a rookie when he no-hit an aging Detroit Tigers lineup on a cold 1973 night in Detroit, walking six batters and striking out four. The 6-foot-2, 205-pound right-hander said the no-no came out of the blue.

"I never considered myself in those terms of being capable of throwing a no-hitter," he said. "I didn't think I was a power pitcher. I grew up watching Koufax and Drysdale, and I could see where those guys would, but there was no way I thought I was going to be able to throw one."[91]

Busby had sharper control during his second no-hitter against the Milwaukee Brewers in June 1974, walking just one batter as his defense made some stellar plays behind him. The humble pitcher downplayed the accomplishment.

"For a guy like me to throw a no-hitter was about 90 percent luck, getting balls hit at people and having things go exactly right," he said.[92]

BUT BUSBY's '74 no-no put him in some elite company as he became just the 23rd pitcher in major-league history to throw multiple no-hitters, beating Nolan Ryan to the punch by about three months.

"Believe me, I'm very proud of the two of them," Busby said. "It was a great thrill, and I certainly would never give them back."[93]

Years before he entered the majors, Satchel Paige threw no-hitters for the Pittsburgh Crawfords in 1932 and 1934. *(Photo from Robert Lerner, photographer, LOOK Magazine Photograph Collection, Library of Congress, Prints & Photographs Division, LC-L905-52-1778)*

CHAPTER 8

AHEAD OF THEIR TIME: NEGRO LEAGUE NO-HITTERS

Just take the ball and throw it where you want to. Throw strikes. Home plate don't move.

—SATCHEL PAIGE

Three decades before Don Larsen threw his perfect game in the '56 World Series, a 22-year-old Negro League pitcher "down the Shore" beat his big-city counterpart to the postseason punch.

Claude "Red" Grier joined the Atlantic City Bacharach Giants midway through the 1925 season after spending a year and a half with the Washington (and later Wilmington) Potomacs. Grier boasted "a wide assortment of pitches and good control," James Overmyer wrote in *Black Ball and the Boardwalk*, and the southpaw helped lead the 1926 Bacharach Giants to an Eastern Colored League championship.[94]

Atlantic City was set to face the Negro National League champion Chicago American Giants in the third-ever Colored World Series, with three of the games staged at neutral sites. Game 1 ended in a tie, and Grier took the loss in Game 2.

On October 3, 1926, Grier got the start for Game 3 at Maryland Baseball Park in Baltimore and dominated the American Giants lineup for a 10-0 no-hit victory in front of just 2,857 fans.

·   ·   ·

GRIER'S GEM IS one of the dozens of no-nos thrown in the Negro Leagues before the majors integrated in 1947, though incomplete game accounts and the gray lines between professional, semipro, minor league, and barnstorming teams make it tough to come up with an exact number.

There's no doubt that many Negro League pitchers could have etched their spots into the major-league record books if baseball had welcomed them earlier, but their numerous accomplishments received far less media attention.

"CANNONBALL" DICK REDDING, who played for a variety of teams from 1911 through 1928, has been cited as throwing as many as 30 career no-hitters—seven in 1912 alone—but it's difficult to uncover enough box scores to prove or disprove those estimates.

Redding's August 28, 1912, no-no for the Lincoln Giants against the Cuban Stars in Atlantic City is considered the first documented no-hitter between two high-level African American teams.

"Redding's speed was terrific, and the Cubans were helpless before his delivery," noted a *New York Press* game account uncovered by researcher Gary Ashwill. "This was the second hitless game Redding has pitched this season."[95]

The other 1912 no-no, according to the *Press*, was an August 5 perfect game against the Cherokee Indians during that club's East Coast barnstorming tour. If there are others (and there most certainly are), they're difficult to dig up.

ANOTHER NEGRO LEAGUE PITCHER of note is the Kansas City Monarchs' Hilton Smith, who threw the Negro American League's first no-hitter on May 16, 1937. Smith led the Monarchs to a 4-0 win over the Chicago American Giants.

FANS ACROSS THE NATION gushed over Bob Feller in 1940 when the Iowa farm sensation pitched the majors' first Opening Day no-hitter, but detailed game accounts are scarce on Leon Day's 1946 Opening Day no-no for the Newark Eagles of the Negro National League.

Like Feller prior to his second no-no, the quiet, soft spoken Day had just returned from serving his country in World War II, having stormed Utah Beach during the Allied Forces' invasion of France. In James A. Riley's book *Of Monarchs and Black Barons: Essays on Baseball's Negro Leagues*, Day said he had few opportunities to pitch while stationed overseas.

"I was discharged in February at Fort Dix, and went home to Newark until spring training," Day recalled. "We trained in Tampa that year, but my arm wasn't too good."[96]

Day, as usual, was way too modest. The right-hander took the mound at Newark's Ruppert Stadium on May 5, 1946, and used his illusory no-wind-up delivery to no-hit the Philadelphia Stars for a 2-0 win. He allowed just three runners to reach first via a pair of walks and an error, but he struck out just six batters. For Day, any game with a "K" count below 10 was a sign that he "didn't have good stuff."[97]

IN STARK CONTRAST to Leon Day's modesty was the larger-than-life Satchel Paige, who estimated he threw 55 no-hitters over his long, storied career that included stints with numerous teams. When Paige wasn't pitching in league games, he was barnstorming across the country competing against anyone who would take the ball field against his All-Stars.

Just two Paige no-hitters are documented. On July 15, 1932, he threw the first no-no at the newly built Greenlee Field in Pittsburgh's

Hill District, the nation's first black-built and black-owned major-league ballpark. His Pittsburgh Crawfords topped the New York Black Yankees 6-0.

"The elongated speed ball artist from the far South was at his best and literally had the Yanks eating out of his hand," said a *Pittsburgh Courier* account.[98]

Paige's second no-no for the Crawfords came against the Homestead Grays. On July 4, 1934, Paige struck out a Negro National League–record 17 batters.

It would be 14 years before he finally got the opportunity to face big league batters in the regular season. In 1948, at the age of 42, he made his major-league debut with the Cleveland Indians.

The list of Negro League no-hitters, as best as anyone has been able to verify, includes other such greats thrown by Bill Gatewood, "Smokey" Joe Williams, and Jesse "Nip" Winters.

A complete list follows.

Six years after Bob Feller pitched baseball's first Opening Day no-hitter, the Newark Eagles' Leon Day opened the 1946 Negro National League season with a no-no. *(Painting by Dick Perez, www.dickperez.com)*

Negro League games weren't well documented, which makes it impossible to come up with a complete list of no-hitters. The teams' use of classifications such as barnstorming, semipro, and minor league further clouds what to include and what not to include.

This list, put together by the Society for American Baseball Research (SABR) Negro League Committee and Noir Tech Research is perhaps the best when the goal is to look at feats considered on a par with those thrown in the preintegrated majors. The list includes pre–Negro League games between legitimately top-level black teams irrespective of a league affiliation. It also includes a number of interleague games, postseason games, and exhibition games between teams comprising top-level Negro League players. The Negro Leagues Baseball Museum in Kansas City boasts an incredible collection of photos, stories, and memorabilia. But its many brilliant displays don't include an official no-no list.

The following is a list of 34 Negro League no-hitters, but ongoing research may turn up more. Former Negro League pitchers such as "Toothpick" Sam Jones who threw their no-nos in the majors appear on the official Major League Baseball list.

John Goodgame
West Baden Sprudels
Friday, April 21, 1911 / West Baden Sprudels 3, French Lick
    Plutos 0

"Cannonball" Dick Redding
Lincoln Giants
Wednesday, August 28, 1912 / Lincoln Giants 1, Cuban Stars 0

Louis Decatur "Dicta" Johnson
Chicago American Giants
Sunday, June 8, 1913 / Chicago American Giants 9, Paterson Smart
    Set 0

Charles Dougherty
Chicago American Giants
Monday, June 9, 1913 / Chicago American Giants 8, Paterson Smart
    Set 0

Frank Wickware
Chicago American Giants
Wednesday, August 26, 1914 / Chicago American Giants 1,
    Indianapolis ABCs 0

Dizzy Dismukes
Indianapolis ABCs
Sunday, May 9, 1915 / Indianapolis ABCs 5, Chicago Giants 0

Dick Whitworth
Chicago American Giants
Sunday, September 19, 1915 (first game of doubleheader) / Chicago
    American Giants 4, Chicago Giants 0

Bill Gatewood
St. Louis Giants
Saturday, May 13, 1916 / St. Louis Giants 4, Cuban Stars 1
Gatewood's first of two no-hitters on this list.

Bernardo Baró
Cuban Stars
Sunday, July 21, 1918 (first game of doubleheader) / Cuban Stars
    11, Indianapolis ABCs 0

"Smokey" Joe Williams
Lincoln Giants
Sunday, May 4, 1919 (first game of doubleheader) / Lincoln Giants
    1, Brooklyn Royal Giants 0

Tom Johnson
Chicago American Giants
Tuesday, June 17, 1919 / Chicago American Giants 7, Detroit
    Stars 3

Bill Gatewood
Detroit Stars
Monday, June 6, 1921 / Detroit Stars 4, Cincinnati Cubans 0
*First Negro National League no-hitter; Gatewood's second of two no-
    hitters on this list.*

Phil Cockrell
Hilldale (Darby, Pennsylvania)

Monday, September 5, 1921 (second game of doubleheader) /
  Hilldale 3, Detroit Stars 0
Cockrell's first of two no-hitters on this list.

Bill Force
Detroit Stars
Tuesday, June 27, 1922 / Detroit Stars 3, St. Louis Giants 0

Jesse "Nip" Winters
Atlantic City Bacharach Giants
Wednesday, July 26, 1922 / Atlantic City Bacharach Giants 7,
  Indianapolis ABCs 1
Winters's first of two no-hitters on this list.

Phil Cockrell
Hilldale (Darby, Pennsylvania)
Saturday, August 19, 1922/ Hilldale 5, Chicago American Giants 0
Cockrell's second of two no-hitters on this list.

José Méndez (5 inn.), Bullet Rogan (4 inn.)
Kansas City Monarchs
Sunday, August 5, 1923 (second game of doubleheader) / Kansas
  City Monarchs 7, Milwaukee Bears 0
Méndez pitched 5 perfect innings; Rogan allowed one base runner.

Jesse "Nip" Winters
Hilldale (Darby, Pennsylvania)
Wednesday, September 3, 1924 (first game of doubleheader) /
  Hilldale 2, Harrisburg Giants 0
First Eastern Colored League no-hitter; Winters's second of two no-hitters
  on this list.

Andy Cooper
Detroit Stars
Sunday, June 28, 1925 (second game of doubleheader) / Detroit
    Stars 1, Indianapolis ABCs 0

Rube Currie
Chicago American Giants
Tuesday, July 13, 1926 / Chicago American Giants 16, Dayton
    Marcos 0

Claude "Red" Grier
Atlantic City Bacharach Giants
Sunday, October 3, 1926 / Atlantic City Bacharach Giants 10,
    Chicago American Giants 0
Game 3 of 1926 Colored World Series.

Laymon Yokely
Baltimore Black Sox
Sunday, May 15, 1927 (second game of doubleheader) / Baltimore
    Black Sox 8, Cuban Stars 0

Joe Strong
Baltimore Black Sox
Thursday, August 4, 1927 / Baltimore Black Sox 2, Hilldale 1
    (11 inn.)

Willie Powell
Chicago American Giants
Sunday, August 14, 1927 / Chicago American Giants 5, Memphis
    Red Sox 0

"Army" Cooper (7 1/3 inn.), Chet Brewer (1 2/3 inn)
Kansas City Monarchs
Saturday, June 29, 1929 / Kansas City Monarchs 4, Chicago
    American Giants 0
*Cooper was relieved with one out in the eighth after walking bases
    loaded.*

Paul Carter
Hilldale (Darby, Pennsylvania)
Monday, September 7, 1931 (second game of doubleheader) /
    Hilldale 6, Baltimore Black Sox 0

Satchel Paige
Pittsburgh Crawfords
Friday, July 8, 1932 (second game of doubleheader) / Pittsburgh
    Crawfords 6, New York Black Yankees 0
Paige's first of two no-hitters on this list.

Bill Foster
Chicago American Giants
Sunday, September 24, 1933 (first game of doubleheader) / Chicago
    American Giants 6, New Orleans Crescent Stars 0

Satchel Paige
Pittsburgh Crawfords
Wednesday, July 4, 1934 / Pittsburgh Crawfords 4, Homestead
    Grays 0
Paige struck out 17 batters; his second of two no-hitters on this list.

Hilton Smith
Kansas City Monarchs

Sunday, May 16, 1937 (first game of doubleheader)/ Kansas City
    Monarchs 4, Chicago American Giants 0
First Negro American League no-hitter.

"Schoolboy" Johnny Taylor
Negro All-Star Team
Sunday, September 19, 1937 / Negro All-Star Team 2, Paige's
    Dominican All-Stars 0
Benefit All-Star Game played at the Polo Grounds.

Gene Smith
St. Louis Stars
Friday, June 27, 1941 / St. Louis Stars 6, New York Black Yankees 1

Leon Day
Newark Eagles
Sunday, May 5, 1946 / Newark Eagles 2, Philadelphia Stars 0
An Opening Day no-hitter.

Eugene Marvin Collins
Kansas City Monarchs
Sunday, May 22, 1949 / Kansas City Monarchs 14, Houston
    Eagles 0

Sources: SABR Negro League Committee and Noir Tech Research using the *Chicago Defender, Chicago Tribune, Baltimore Afro American, Kansas City Call, Kansas City Star-Times, Pittsburgh Courier,* and *St. Louis Argus.*

Johan Santana, who pitched for the New York Mets from 2008 through 2012, broke the Mets' 50-year curse on June 1, 2012. *(Photo by Dirk Lammers)*

CHAPTER 9

THE 50-YEAR CURSE

At least I had the satisfaction of having him break his bat.

—TOM SEAVER ON LERON LEE, WHO BROKE UP
SEAVER'S 1972 NO-HITTER IN THE NINTH

The New York Mets' David Cone had all of his pitches working on April 28, 1992, and a stifled Houston Astros lineup could do little to evict the big fat zero planted firmly on the Shea Stadium scoreboard. Cone and his clique of Conehead-wearing bleacher bums were starting to wonder if this could finally be the night for the first Mets no-no.

"I started thinking about it early in the game," Cone told a reporter. "I couldn't help it."[99]

Over in the Bronx, 12-year-old Mets fan Robert Ford fixed his eyes to his 4-inch black-and-white portable TV. When Cone reached the sixth inning without yielding a hit, Ford convinced his mom to tune the 30-inch living room console to WWOR so he could witness history in glorious color.

But the baseball gods had other ideas, and the deities imposed their alternate fate with one on and one out in the eighth. Astros pinch hitter Benny Distefano, whose claim to fame is as the majors' last left-handed catcher, nicked a well-placed split-fingered fastball.

"I can still see it—it was a splitter that was down," said Ford, now the

Astros' radio play-by-play man. "Distefano just hits it off the end of the bat, and it just rolls up the third-base line."[100]

Shea Stadium's 16,000 fans watched in incredulity as third baseman Dave Magadan charged the grass and made a late throw to first. The no-hitter was no more.

"It's the Tom Seaver–Nolan Ryan jinx," Cone declared.[101]

As a New Yorker for just six seasons, Cone was acclimating to what lifelong Mets fans had been enduring since the club's 1962 birth: What *could* be the night always ended in disappointment. Cone completed the two-hit shutout, but the Mets' no no-hitters count reached 4,816 games.

"I think if you grew up a Mets fan, it's just one of the things that you kind of accept," Ford said.[102]

THE NOLAN RYAN part of the jinx involves what is widely considered to be one of the most lopsided trades in baseball history. Hindsight helps illuminate the irony packed into sports writer Joseph Durso's lead for the December 10, 1971, edition of the *New York Times*:

> NEW YORK—The Mets finally gave up on Nolan Ryan's wandering fastball today. They traded the 24-year-old pitcher and three prospects to the California Angels for Jim Fregosi, six times the American League's all-star shortstop.[103]

Ryan and his "wandering fastball" went on to win 324 games over a 27-year Hall-of-Fame career, throwing seven no-hitters and 12 one-hitters and striking out 5,714 batters—all major-league records.

Fregosi, "six times the American League's all-star shortstop," batted just .233 for the Mets before he was sold to the Texas Rangers midway through the 1973 season.

. . .

THE NEW YORK Metropolitan Baseball Club—a.k.a. "the Mets"—
began play in 1962. The team, which adopted its name from a 19th-cen-
tury American Association team, was born out of city leaders' efforts to
return National League baseball to New York after westward moves by
the Brooklyn Dodgers and New York Giants. (The team colors of blue
and orange, as well as the Mets' home-jersey script and fancy road-jersey
"New York" font, are a tip of the cap to the Dodgers' and Giants' uni-
forms.)

Sandy Koufax, a Brooklyn native relocated to Los Angeles, intro-
duced the Mets to the dark side of the no-hitter on June 30, 1962, in the
fledgling franchise's 73rd game. The Dodgers' Koufax wowed the Dodger
Stadium crowd by striking out 13 batters, walking five and yielding nary
a hit for his first of what would be four career no-hitters.

Two years later, the Philadelphia Phillies' Jim Bunning disappointed
fathers and sons who flocked to shiny new Shea Stadium to root for the
home team during a June 21 Father's Day doubleheader. Bunning retired each of the 27 Mets batters he faced during the opener for what
would stand as the ballpark's sole perfect game.

A Mets no no-hitters streak could have been averted long ago if
Spring Training contests counted. On March 21, 1965, in St. Petersburg, Florida, Mets pitchers Gary Kroll and Gordie Richardson combined to no-hit the Pittsburgh Pirates over nine innings during a 6-0
shutout. But, although several newspaper headlines branded the game as
the "first Mets no-hitter," official record books decline to support such
bold-font proclamations for Spring Training contests.

Al Jackson nearly threw an authentic no-no against the same team
four months to the day after the exhibition effort by Kroll and Richardson. Jackson held the Pirates hitless through seven and one-third innings
on July 21, 1965, but Willie Stargell tagged the lefty for a one-out
eighth-inning single. Probably no one was counting back then, but
Stargell's hit marked the 580th Mets game without a no-hitter.

Although Tom Seaver is wearing a Mets cap on his Hall of Fame plaque, he got his only no-hitter as a member of the 1978 Cincinnati Reds. *(Photo by Dirk Lammers)*

The Tom Seaver portion of the jinx cited by Cone refers to Seaver's several late-inning failed no-hitter attempts that began in 1968. Seaver, a top prospect who signed with the Mets in 1966, won 198 games for the ball club, earning Rookie of the Year honors in 1967 and picking up Cy Young Awards in 1969, 1973, and 1975. On August 30, 1968, he was no-hitting the St. Louis Cardinals into the eighth inning when Orlando Cepeda led off with a double. It was Seaver's first of four tastes of no-hit frustration, and it marked the Mets' 1,111th game void of the rare feat.

Seaver had thrown eight innings of perfect baseball against the Chicago Cubs on July 9, 1969, when Randy Hundley unsuccessfully tried to spoil Seaver's perfecto with a ninth-inning leadoff bunt. Seaver fielded the ball in front of the mound and threw to first to shrink his to-do list to two outs. Rookie utility player Jim Qualls then stepped to the plate and drove a clean single to left-center field for the Mets' 1,217th non-no-hit game. Seaver placed his hands on his hips as the ball touched the outfield grass, and Shea's 59,000 faithful arose to give "Tom Terrific" a standing ovation in appreciation for making it that far.

As Seaver sealed his one-hit shutout on Don Kessinger's fly-out, the somewhat deflated pitcher returned his hands to his hips and his eyes to the left-center-field spot where Qualls's ball had touched green. Catcher Jerry Grote trotted out and interrupted the somber moment by patting Seaver on the back and shaking his hand. The mound then erupted into a celebration of a key division win in a tightening pennant race that would lead to the club's first world championship.

BUT NO-NO DISAPPOINTMENTS continued as the Mets entered the 1970s.

On May 13, 1970, Gary Gentry took a no-hitter into the eighth inning against the Chicago Cubs before Ernie Banks connected for a two-out single. Gentry completed the one-hit, 4-0 victory as the Mets streak reached 1,330 games.

Tom Seaver again reached the ninth inning with a no-hitter alive during the opening game of a July 4, 1972, doubleheader at Shea. He got the San Diego Padres' Dave Roberts to ground out before Leron Lee lined a ball up the middle to end the no-no bid.

"As soon as he hit it, I knew it was a hit," Seaver told a reporter.[104]

Seaver got Nate Colbert to ground into a 6-4-3 double play to end the game for a 2-0 complete-game shutout—his fourth career one-hitter—as the Met's no no-hitter streak hit 1,692.

ACROSS THE COUNTRY in Anaheim, Nolan Ryan's formerly wandering fastball continued to hit its marks as the Texan developed into the league's most dominant pitcher. The California Angels ace tossed four no-hitters between 1973 and 1975, tying the career mark set by Koufax.

Back at Shea, a 22-year-old Mets rookie named Randy Tate embarked on a valiant attempt to break the curse in his lone major-league season.

On August 4, 1975, Tate took a no-hitter into the eighth inning but was upset by a Montreal Expos pinch hitter. Jim Lyttle drove a one-out single to left for the Mets' 2,208th game with no no-no before the Expos piled on for a 4-3 win.

That year Seaver made his last late-inning attempt at a Mets no-hitter, finally surpassing the mark of one out in the ninth. In a scoreless pitchers' duel with the Cubs' Rick Reuschel, Seaver lost the no-no with two outs in the ninth as Joe Wallis singled to right. It's etched in history as Mets fan disappointment No. 2,259.

But as much as Mets fans wanted that no-hitter, the disappointment paled in comparison with the disenchantment felt after the midnight massacre of June 15, 1977, when the cost-cutting Mets dealt Seaver to the Cincinnati Reds and fellow fan favorite Dave Kingman to the Padres. And as if it were scripted to drive the dagger deeper into Mets' fans hearts, Seaver finally got his only career no-hitter a year later on June 16, 1978—wearing a *Reds* uniform.

"I always felt I'd get one if I got the breaks," Seaver said after the game. "Tonight I did."[105]

PERHAPS "THE BREAKS" equate to a trade to another team, as Ryan continued to throw no-hitters after stripping off his Mets uniform. He tossed his fifth no-no in 1981 as a member of the Houston Astros, and others would soon join Ryan and Seaver in the ex-Mets no-hitters club.

But Pat Zachry, one of the Reds who came to New York in the Seaver swap, nearly redeemed the '77 trade five years later. On a frigid April 10, 1982, within the less-than-friendly confines of Wrigley Field, Zachry completed seven and two-thirds innings of a no-no before pinch hitter Bob Molinaro reached safely on a ball off the glove of Wally Backman that dribbled into right field. The play was ruled a hit, and the Mets count climbed to 3,182 games.

Dwight "Doc" Gooden, a rookie phenom who pitched for the Mets from 1984 to 1994, nearly solved the Mets' conundrum on June 6, 1984. In just his 11th major-league start, the emerging strikeout artist reached the eighth inning with a no-hitter intact before yielding a lead-off single to the Pirates' Doug Frobel. New York won 2-1 in 13 innings, and the streak reached 3,552 games.

AS THE METS' woes continued, former stars who had moved on to other ball clubs left little doubt that the curse attached itself to the team, not the pitcher.

Houston's Mike Scott, a Mets rotation anchor from 1979 to 1982, threw a no-hitter against the San Francisco Giants on September 25, 1986, to clinch the National League West division for the Astros. The 1986 Eastern Division champion Mets would get the last laugh, topping Houston in the National League Championship Series weeks later and then squeaking by Boston in the World Series.

The franchise's tally after 1986: two World Championships, no no-hitters. Which, of course, is amazin', but the no-hitter drought would take more twists than anyone could have expected.

Near misses continued through the late 1980s:

- On June 28, 1987, pitcher Ron Darling—now in the Mets' television booth—no-hit the Phillies through seven innings before giving up a Greg Gross pinch-hit triple to lead off the eighth. The Mets lost 5-4; the streak hit 4,062.
- On June 5, 1988, Gooden again reached the eighth inning and again lost it on the leadoff batter as the Cubs' Damon Berryhill singled. Gooden held on for an 11-3 complete-game victory, but the count climbed to 4,205.
- On June 19, 1988, Cone reached the eighth inning with a no-hitter still a possibility when the Phillies' Steve Jeltz crushed his hopes with a two-out single for no no-no No. 4,217.

. . .

Ryan, meanwhile, continued pitching well into his 40s, breaking his own record with sixth and seventh no-hitters in 1990 and 1991 as a member of the Texas Rangers.

Back in New York, the count continued to climb. On June 14, 1997, in the first year of interleague play, Mark Clark took a no-hitter into the eighth inning against the Boston Red Sox but lost it on pinch hitter Reggie Jefferson's leadoff single. The streak hit 5,604 games.

New York City is primarily Yankees territory, a reality evidenced in every Manhattan tourist store. Walk inside any outlet and count the number of Yankees items compared to the number of Mets items. Reasons? Longevity, history, championships, and parent-child ties for generations.

Mets fans have had to embrace an inferiority complex as a survival mechanism, and two late-'90s games across the East River in the Bronx did little to help. Gooden, who battled back from a yearlong drug suspension in 1995, embarked on a 1996 comeback with the crosstown Yankees. On May 14, 1996, in front of a Yankee Stadium crowd of just under 21,000, "Doctor K" threw his only career no-hitter against the Seattle Mariners.

Then Cone, who pitched for the Kansas City Royals and Toronto Blue Jays before joining the Yankees, earned a part in a Bronx made-for-Hollywood story. July 18, 1999, was deemed "Yogi Berra Day" at Yankee Stadium as the Hall of Fame catcher made his triumphant return to the Bronx after a 14-year absence fueled by a dispute with owner George Steinbrenner. Yankee alumni in attendance that day included Don Larsen, the only pitcher to toss a World Series perfect game, who threw out the game's ceremonial first pitch.

Cone threw out the real first pitch and followed with 87 more—60 for strikes—as he retired 27 straight Montreal Expos. The only interruption of his perfect game came in the form of a half-hour, third-inning rain delay. Suddenly the society of pitchers throwing no-nos after hanging up their Mets pinstripes had grown to four: Ryan, Seaver, Gooden, and Cone.

A NEW MILLENNIUM brought additional disappointments for the Mets.

Tom Glavine, elected to the Hall of Fame in 2014, was a key member of the Mets pitching staff from 2003 through 2007. On May 23, 2004, he took a no-no into the eighth inning when the Colorado Rockies' Kit Pellow pounced on a 1-0 changeup and drove it over Shane Spencer's head to the wall for a double. The Mets' no no-no count reached 6,716 games.

Pedro Martínez, who signed a four-year, $53 million contract with the Mets ahead of the 2005 season, took a no-hitter into the eighth inning on August 14 of that year. The Dodgers' Antonio Pérez led off the inning with a triple, and the Mets count rose to 6,951.

ON SEPTEMBER 29, 2007, the penultimate day of the 2007 season, John Maine was fighting to keep the Mets' postseason hopes alive. He dominated the Florida Marlins through seven and two-thirds innings before Paul Hoover tapped "a little dribbler out in front of the plate in no-man's-land that winds up being the only hit that Maine gave up," recalled Robert Ford, the Mets fan turned Astros radio announcer.[106]

The bullpen secured a 13-0 victory, but few were mourning that the no no-no count reached 7,319. Maine's victory ensured that the next day's game would matter.

Those hopes were crushed quickly as Glavine gave up seven first-inning runs in the must-win Game 162. The Mets, who on September 12 had been set to coast to an Eastern Division title with a seven-game lead, completed the worst late-season collapse in major-league history. The choke ensured a wealth of fired-up callers to local sports radio shows, but that off-season eventually brought some disenfranchised Mets fans some hope.

On February 1, 2008, the Mets signed baseball's best pitcher, Johan Santana, to a $137.5 million, six-year contract, returning fans to their oft-uttered murmurs of "Maybe next year." If any pitcher had a chance to break the now 46-year-old streak, it clearly was Santana.

HOPES WERE HIGH for Mets during the March 31, 2008, season opener against the Florida Marlins in Miami. Santana retired the first nine batters he faced and was one-third of the way toward breaking his new team's streak, but Josh Willingham tagged him for a fourth-inning homer.

Santana pitched seven solid innings for the Opening Day victory, but the Mets dropped to 0-for-7,321 in the no-hitters department.

As construction on the Mets' future home progressed just outside Shea's outfield fences, the 2008 Mets still playing inside the old ballpark fought for a division title. The team's postseason hopes were again crushed by a late-September collapse, and the team vacated its 45-year home without ever giving fans a chance to witness a Mets no-hitter.

The Mets no no-no count continued to climb as the club settled into Citi Field for the 2009, 2010, and 2011 seasons. The team reached the 8,000-game mark on May 11, 2012 with a leadoff triple by ex-Met José Reyes, killing Santana's potential no-hitter before it even started.

FOUR STARTS LATER, in the Mets' 8,020th game, on June 1, 2012, Santana faced the visiting St. Louis Cardinals at Citi Field. The fifth inning had ended, and the Cards still lacked a hit.

Could this be the night?

With St. Louis down 2-0 in the sixth, ex-Met Carlos Beltrán stepped into the batter's box and lined a ball down the third-base line. Third-base umpire Adrian Johnson quickly swung out his arms to signal "foul," but television replays showed the ball had sailed just over the edge of the bag and hit the edge of the outfield chalk.

Such plays were not reviewable in 2012, and as Cardinals third-base coach José Oquendo continued pleading his case to Johnson, Beltrán grounded out to third for the inning's first of three consecutive outs.

Maybe this really could be the night.

Ford, who was preparing to host the Kansas City Royals' postgame radio show at Kauffman Stadium, got word that Santana was working on a no-no. Even though the New York native had moved past fandom into a professional broadcasting career, there was no way he could just check in on such a potentially history-altering moment.

"It wasn't enough for me just to monitor," he said. "I had to watch it, so I pulled it up on my phone and watched the last three innings on my phone."[107]

With the Mets' lead extended to 5-0, Santana got David Freese to lead off the seventh by popping out to first. Yadier Molina then pounced on a one-out breaking ball and drove it to deep left for what looked like a sure double. Mets left fielder Mike Baxter made a beeline for the warning track and snagged the ball just before slamming shoulder-first into the fence. Baxter writhed on the ground in pain, unable to show the ball tucked safely into his glove, but the no-hitter was intact.

Trainers helped Baxter to the dugout, and his next stop was the disabled list, but he had saved Santana's no-no. Matt Adams grounded to first, and the inning was over.

Santana had a Mets' no-hitter through seven, joining a Mets dynamic dozen to have made it that far: Jackson, Seaver, Gentry, Tate, Zachry, Gooden, Darling, Cone, Clark, Glavine, Martínez, and Maine.

This *had* to be the night, right?

The Mets padded the score to 8-0, and Santana took the mound for the eighth. He got Tyler Greene to fly out to left and struck out pinch hitter Shane Robinson before letting Rafael Furcal reach first on a walk. He again had to face Beltrán, but this time Beltrán's liner headed to second without umpire controversy. The inning was over, and Santana was now sailing into waters charted only by Seaver.

As the game entered the bottom of the ninth, the 27,069 fans inside Citi Field were thrown into an anticipatory tension not seen in Flushing Meadows since 1975. The decibels grew as Matt Holliday jumped on the first pitch and hit a blooper to center fielder Andres Torres, who hustled in and snagged it for the first out.

Allen Craig emerged from the on-deck circle and worked the count to 2-2 before reaching for a low breaking ball. He popped a short fly to left, and Kirk Nieuwenhuis—who had shifted from center to left after Baxter's injury—chased it down for the second out.

The crowd's clamor kicked into a deafening roar as Freese stepped in as the last potential impediment to New York Mets history. Santana threw the first ball in the dirt and tossed two more balls before firing a fastball for strike one. Freese fouled off the next pitch just left of third, prompting SportsNet New York television announcer Gary Cohen to flash back to the infield hit that had killed Maine's no-no in 2007.

"That was shades of Paul Hoover right there," Cohen said.[108]

With the count now 3-2, Santana enticed Freese to swing and miss at a low changeup.

"He struck him out!" Cohen roared. "It has happened. In their 51st season, Johan Santana has thrown the first no-hitter in New York Mets history."[109]

The Citi Field stands erupted into pandemonium as teammates mobbed Santana at the mound. A reporter in the postgame news conference asked Santana if he had ever thrown a no-hitter at any level.

"I don't even think I threw a no-hitter in video games," Santana replied to laughter.[110]

The Mets ace had just thrown a career-high 134 pitches, and many a New York sports columnist has wondered if the long outing could have contributed to some of the injuries that have dogged Santana's recent years. But whatever the future holds for Santana, he has forever etched himself into Mets' glory.

"To be able to accomplish this is an honor," Santana said that night. "I know how much this means to New York and to the New York Mets, and it definitely is something that I'm proud of."[111]

NO-HITTER DROUGHTS BY TEAM, DAYS, AND FIELD

Philadelphia Phillies fans such as the Phillie Phanatic had to endure a 55-year drought of no-hitters. *(Photo by Dirk Lammers)*

Although the New York Mets hold the record (for now; watch the Padres) for the longest no-hitter drought since a team's inception, the streak was not the longest overall for a major-league team. Here are some other significant no-hitter droughts.

Longest team drought: Philadelphia Phillies—8,945 games

Between 1906 and 1964, the Phillies went 58 years, 1 month, 18 days without a no-hitter.

The streak began after this no-hitter … **Johnny Lush:** Philadelphia Phillies (NL) @ Washington Park (Brooklyn) / Tuesday, May 1, 1906 / Philadelphia Phillies 6, Brooklyn Superbas 0 … *and ended with this perfect game thrown on Father's Day …* **Jim Bunning:** Philadelphia Phillies (NL) @ Shea Stadium / Sunday, June 21, 1964 (first game of doubleheader) / Philadelphia Phillies 6, New York Mets 0.

Note: The Mets' 50-year streak of 8,019 games fell 926 games short of this all-time record. If the Padres continue without a no-no, the team would reach Philadelphia's mark in 2024.

League drought: A dozen National League no-nos whiz by the American League

From 2012 through 2015, the National League amassed an unprecedented 12 no-hitters without the American League chiming in. *The streak began with this no-hitter …* **Homer Bailey:** Cincinnati Reds (NL) @ PNC Park (Pittsburgh) / Friday, September 28, 2012 / Cincinnati Reds 1, Pittsburgh Pirates 0 … *and ended with this one …* **Hisashi Iwakuma:** Seattle Mariners (AL) @ Safeco Field (Seattle) / August 12, 2015 / Seattle Mariners 3, Baltimore Orioles 0.

A good drought! Longest streak for a team *not* being no-hit: Chicago Cubs—7,920 games

Not all no-no droughts have a negative connotation. The Cubs avoided being on the opposite end of a no-hitter for 7,920 games beginning in 1965. *The streak began with this perfect game …* **Sandy Koufax:** Los Angeles Dodgers (NL) @ Dodger Stadium / Thursday, September 9, 1965 / Los Angeles Dodgers 1, Chicago Cubs 0 … *and ended with this no-hitter …* **Cole Hamels:** Philadelphia Phillies (NL)

@ Wrigley Field / Saturday, July 25, 2015 / Philadelphia Phillies 5, Chicago Cubs 0.

The near 50-year streak was chronicled by our friends at @CubsNoHitStreak, and the Twitter account has reset in a quest to reach the mark again.

As for overall droughts across all of MLB, here are two significant gaps:

Game days between no-hitters by *any* team/pitcher: 535

The longest drought of days with games scheduled between no-hitters lasted three years.

The streak began after this gem ... **Bobby Burke:** Washington Senators (AL) @ Griffith Stadium (Washington, D.C.) / Saturday, August 8, 1931 / Washington Senators 5, Boston Red Sox 0 ... *and ended with this one:* **Paul Dean:** St. Louis Cardinals (NL) @ Ebbets Field / Fri., September 21, 1934 (second game of doubleheader) / St. Louis Cardinals 3, Brooklyn Dodgers 0.

Dean's brother Dizzy pitched a three-hit complete-game shutout in the first game of that doubleheader.

Games between no-hitters by *any* team/pitcher: 6, 364

Although the 1931–1934 streak still reigns for major-league game *days* without a no-no, the mark had no chance of holding up in a postexpansion era as far as total games. Back in the 1930s, a regular season in the 16-team majors consisted of 1,264 games per season. Now, with 30 teams, that number is up to 2,430 games per season. The majors—between early 2004 and late 2006—went 6,364 games without a no-hitter. *The streak began with this perfect game ...* **Randy Johnson:** Arizona Diamondbacks (NL) @ Turner Field (Atlanta) / Tuesday, May 18, 2004 / Arizona Diamondbacks 2, Atlanta Braves 0 *... and ended with this no-hitter ...* **Aníbal Sánchez:** Florida Marlins (NL) @ Pro Player Stadium (Miami) / Wednesday, September 6, 2006 / Florida Marlins 2, Arizona Diamondbacks 0.

As of this writing, the 2005 season continues to be the last full season to feature not a single no-hitter.

Forbes Field, the Pittsburgh Pirates' home from 1909 through 1970, never hosted a no-hitter. *(Photo from Detroit Publishing Company photographic collection. Prints & Photographs Division, Library of Congress, LC-DIG-det-4a23349)*

And then there's the legacy of Forbes Field, home of the no-nos

Pittsburgh's Forbes Field, which served as the Pirates' home ballpark from 1909 through 1970, hosted one of the city's most spectacular sports moments. It was here that Bill Mazeroski blasted his Game 7 homer in the 1960 World Series to give the Pirates a 10-9 win over the New York Yankees and the city's third world championship. But no pitcher, throwing for either the home Pirates or the visitors over 61 years of games, ever pitched a no-hitter within the confines of Forbes Field.

The $1 million ballpark erected in Pittsburgh's Oakland district— that price tag was unprecedented in 1909—was the first built using steel and concrete instead of the traditional wood. It boasted a seating capacity of 25,000, but 30,338 fans showed up to watch the Pirates take on the Chicago Cubs for the field's June 30, 1909, debut. The Pirates lost 3-2. "Every seat in the boxes, grandstand and bleachers was filled, and hundreds crowded onto the field, making necessary ground rules on long hits, which incidentally may have lost the game for the locals," said one report in the *Morning Herald*.[112] Fortunately for the Pirates, the franchise notched its first no-hitter at Exposition Park before moving into Forbes Field or the Pirates could have been looking at a Mets-like no no-no streak.

Nick Maddox

Pittsburgh Pirates (NL) @ Exposition Park (Pittsburgh) / Friday, September 20, 1907 / Pittsburgh Pirates 2, Brooklyn Superbas 1.

The team waited 44 years for its next no-hitter, and the three thrown by Pirates during from the early 1950s to the early 1970s all came on the road:

✓ **Cliff Chambers:** Pittsburgh Pirates (NL) @ Braves Field (Boston) / Sunday, May 6, 1951 (second game of doubleheader) / Pittsburgh Pirates 3, Boston Braves 0
✓ **Bob Moose:** Pittsburgh Pirates (NL) @ Shea Stadium (New York) / Saturday, September 20, 1969 / Pittsburgh Pirates 4, New York Mets 0
✓ **Dock Ellis:** Pittsburgh Pirates (NL) @ San Diego Stadium / Friday, June 12, 1970 (first game of doubleheader) / Pittsburgh Pirates 2, San Diego Padres 0

About one month after Ellis's no-no in San Diego, the Pirates moved to Three Rivers Stadium. The modern stadium's first no-no came six years later, and it was followed by another 21 years after that:

✓ **John Candelaria:** Pittsburgh Pirates (NL) @ Three Rivers Stadium (Pittsburgh) / Monday, August 9, 1976 / Pittsburgh Pirates 2, Los Angeles Dodgers 0

✓ **Francisco Cordova** (9 inn.), **Ricardo Rincon** (1 inn.): Pittsburgh Pirates (NL) @ Three Rivers Stadium (Pittsburgh) / Saturday, July 12, 1997 / Pittsburgh Pirates 3, Houston Astros 0 (10 inn.)

The now demolished Forbes Field may always be known for Mazeroski's shot, but the stadium holds the distinction of being baseball's longest-reigning home of the no no-no.

A brick mural outside the Bob Feller museum in Van Meter, Iowa, honors
the man who threw the majors' only Opening Day no-hitter.
(Photo by Dirk Lammers)

CHAPTER 10

OPENING STATEMENT

Big league baseball's first bite was as luscious as spring's first straw-
berry, and the flavor will linger for days.

—Associated Press, April 17, 1940

B ob Feller was a 15-year-old sensation from the town of Van Meter,
Iowa, in 1936, mowing down teenagers on high school and American Legion fields. Six years later, he completed a task left undone by the
New York Giants' Red Ames and the Chicago Cubs' Lon Warneke—he
threw Major League Baseball's first Opening Day no-hitter.

The attempts by Ames and Warneke came oh so close. On April 15,
1909, Ames no-hit the Brooklyn Superbas through nine innings, but his
teammates couldn't score a run. He wound up losing the no-hitter in the
10th inning and losing the game in the 13th inning.

"Ames did not allow a hit in the first nine innings, only 27 men facing him in this time," noted a report in the *Washington Post*. "In the extra
periods the Brooklyns got to him strongly, making four hits in the last
round."[113]

Warneke got his first taste of Opening Day stardom on April 12,
1933, outdueling fellow Arkansas native Dizzy Dean to lead the Cubs to
a 3-0 win over the St. Louis Cardinals. Warneke's 18 wins and 26 complete games that season earned him the start for Opening Day the next

year, and the "Arkansas Hummingbird" didn't disappoint. Flirting with baseball immortality, the Cubs right-hander held the Cincinnati Reds hitless through eight and one-third innings and needed just two more outs to throw baseball's first Opening Day no-hitter.

Reds left fielder Adam Comorosky thought otherwise, and the former Pennsylvania coal miner popped a single up the middle with one out in the bottom of the ninth. Warneke had to settle for a one-hit, complete-game shutout. "Pitching in mid-season form, Warneke missed a no-hit, no-run game by one throw," wrote AP sportswriter Hugh S. Fullerton Jr., "as he blanked the Redlegs 6-0 and whiffed 13 batsmen."[114]

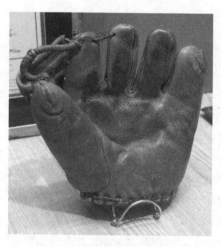

The glove Feller used to throw his Opening Day no-hitter is displayed in the Bob Feller museum in Van Meter, Iowa. *(Photo by Dirk Lammers)*

The honor of throwing the majors' first Opening Day no-hitter would have to wait for Feller and his trademark "Heater from Van Meter" fastball. Feller was making his second Opening Day start on April 16, 1940, at Chicago's Comiskey Park, where 14,000 fans braved chilly temperatures and unrelenting winds to watch the 6-foot, 185-pound right-hander outduel the White Sox' Eddie Smith.

Feller got into trouble early. He struck out Luke Appling to start the second inning, but center fielder Roy Weatherly misjudged Taffy Wright's windblown fly ball, and Wright took second base on the error. Feller struck out Eric McNair for out No. 2 but walked Mike Tresh and Smith to load the bases. He settled down to strike out rookie Bob Kennedy on a fastball to leave the three runners stranded.

Feller let another runner reach scoring position in the third when Joe Kuehl walked and stole second. "But then he abandoned the curve entirely and his fast one was good enough to subdue the next 20 batters in order," wrote *Cleveland Plain Dealer* sportswriter Gordon Cobbledick.[115]

Meanwhile, the Indians scored the team's lone run in the fourth inning. Jeff Heath reached base on a one-out single, and catcher Rollie Helmsley drove him home with a triple. Feller kicked off the ninth inning by retiring Mike Kreevich and Moose Solters to put himself one out from glory.

"I knew I had a chance for a no-hitter in the ninth," he told the *Plain Dealer*, "but I tried to put the thought out of my head by reminding myself you never have a no-hitter until the last man is out."[116]

The next batter was Appling, and "Old Aches and Pains" wouldn't go down quietly as he repeatedly worked the 2-2 count. Appling gave Feller "and the cheering fans several anxious moments," according to the AP report. "Appling drove four foul smashes to right before drawing a walk on the tenth pitch."[117] Feller later said that he was tiring and the repeated fouls prompted him to throw two outside pitches to get rid of the pesky shortstop, but game stories from the day make no mention of Appling's walk being intentional.

Next up was Wright, and the lefty hit a hard grounder to the right side of the infield. Second baseman Ray Mack knocked down the shot, picked up the rolling ball, and threw to first for the final out in the first-ever Opening Day no-no.

"I had some pretty fancy support out there," Feller told the *Plain Dealer*.[118]

Feller's catcher, Helmsley, joked in the clubhouse that everyone was mobbing Feller even though it was Helmsley's triple that had scored the winning run. "He would pick today to pitch a no-hit game," Helmsley remarked. "I was all set to be the hero of that game on account of driving in the only run. Now nobody'll even know I was in the game."[119]

No one had thrown an Opening Day no-hitter before Feller's gem, and no one has since.

Nolan Ryan might have duplicated the feat 50 years after Feller, but the baseball lockout of 1990 wiped out nearly all of spring training. The 43-year-old Ryan had worked just seven preseason innings by April 9, 1990, when he took the ball at the Ballpark at Arlington for the Texas Rangers' season opener. He threw five innings of no-hit ball, but Rangers manager Bobby Valentine sat him after Ryan walked three batters in the fifth inning. The aging veteran, who at the time had five no-hitters under his belt, had reached 90 pitches.

"Hey I'm a fan like anybody else," Valentine said after the game. "But it's the first game of the season and he had hit his pitch limit and he was tired. I'm managing to win the game."[120]

Mike Jeffcoat took the ball in the sixth inning and gave up a two-out Kelly Gruber double to negate the chance of a combined no-no, though Texas secured a 4-2 win for Ryan. The fast-throwing Texan needed just two months to capture his sixth no-hitter with a 5-0 June 11 win over the Oakland Athletics. And he threw his seventh no-hitter a year later but couldn't duplicate Feller's Opening Day feat. Feller threw two more no-hitters in 1946 and 1951, for a career total of three.

Ryan and Feller do share one pitching statistic: Each threw 12 *one*-hitters during his career, tied for the major-league record.

AN OPENING DAY FOOTNOTE: The 1959 Baltimore Orioles turned a rare triple play in that season's inaugural game, but as the AP report from that game noted, the trick failed to trump Feller's Opening Day accomplishment.

ONE-HIT WONDERS

Though these jerseys of Bob Feller and Nolan Ryan read 19 and 30, respectively, the pitchers share the record for most major-league one-hitters with 12 each. *(Photo by Dirk Lammers)*

Bob Feller and Nolan Ryan represented two of the most dominant pitchers of their eras, combining for 590 career wins, 8,295 strikeouts, and 10 no-hitters. Their careers shine even more brightly when you consider that each of them also threw 12 *one*-hitters. Here's the list, with the sole hit that broke up the potential no-no.

BOB FELLER *ONE*-HITTERS, ALL FOR
THE CLEVELAND INDIANS

✓ Wednesday, April 20, 1938 / Indians 9, St. Louis Browns 0 / League Park (Cleveland) / 6th-inning bunt single by Billy Sullivan

✓ Thursday, May 25, 1939 / Indians 11, Boston Red Sox 0 / Fenway Park / 2nd-inning single by Bobby Doerr

✓ Tuesday, June 27, 1939 (first-night game in Cleveland) / Indians 5, Detroit Tigers 0 / Cleveland Stadium / 6th-inning single by Earl Averill

✓ Friday, July 12, 1940 / Indians 1, Philadelphia Athletics 0 / Shibe Park (Philadelphia) / 8th-inning, no-out single by Dick Siebert

✓ Friday, September 26, 1941 (second game of doubleheader) / Indians 3, Browns 2 / Sportsman's Park (St. Louis) / 6th-inning bunt single by Rick Ferrell

✓ Wednesday, September 19, 1945 / Indians 2, Detroit Tigers 0 / League Park / 5th-inning single by Jimmy Outlaw

✓ Wednesday, July 31, 1946 / Indians 4, Red Sox 1 / League Park / 2nd-inning single by Bobby Doerr / *Feller ties Addie Joss (AL) and Charles "Old Hoss" Radbourn (NL) for the major-league mark of 7 one-hitters.*

✓ Thursday, August 8, 1946 (first game of doubleheader) / Indians 5, Chicago White Sox 0 / Comiskey Park (Chicago) / 7th-inning pop-up by Frankie Hayes lands between shortstop and two outfielders / *Feller breaks one-hitter record.*

✓ Tuesday, April 22, 1947 / Indians 5, Browns 0 / Cleveland Stadium / 7th-inning single by Al Zarilla

✓ Friday, May 2, 1947 / Indians 2, Red Sox 0 / Cleveland Stadium / 1st-inning single by Johnny Pesky

✓ Wednesday, April 23, 1952 / Browns 1, Indians 0 (an Indians loss) / Sportsman's Park / Leadoff triple by Bobby Young; Young scores when Marty Marion reaches base on an error by third baseman Al Rosen. Bob Cain also pitched a one-hitter in this game and got the victory.

✓ Sunday, May 1, 1955 (first game of doubleheader) / Indians 2, Red Sox 0 / Cleveland Stadium / 7th-inning single by Sammy White

NOLAN RYAN ONE-HITTERS

For the New York Mets

✓ Saturday, April 18, 1970 / Mets 7, Philadelphia Phillies 0 / Shea Stadium / Leadoff single by Denny Doyle

For the California Angels

✓ Sunday, July 9, 1972 / Angels 3, Red Sox 0/ Anaheim Stadium / 1st-inning single by Carl Yazstremski

✓ Wednesday, August 29, 1973 / Angels 5, New York Yankees 0 / Anaheim Stadium / 1st-inning single by Thurman Munson

✓ Thursday, June 27, 1974 / Angels 5, Texas Rangers 0 / Anaheim Stadium / 1st-inning single by Alex Johnson

✓ Friday, April 15, 1977 / Angels 7, Seattle Mariners 0 / Anaheim Stadium / 5th-inning single by Bob Stinson

✓ Friday, May 5, 1978 / Angels 5, Indians 0 / Anaheim Stadium / 6th-inning single by Duane Kuiper

✓ Friday, July 13, 1979 / Angels 6, Yankees 1 / Anaheim Stadium / 9th-inning, one-out single by Reggie Jackson

For the Houston Astros

✓ Wednesday, August 11, 1982 / Houston Astros 3, San Diego Padres 0 / Jack Murphy Stadium (San Diego) / 5th-inning single by Terry Kennedy

✓ Wednesday, August 3, 1983 / Houston Astros 1, Padres 0 / Jack Murphy Stadium / 3rd-inning single by Tim Flannery

For the Texas Rangers

✓ Sunday, April 23, 1989 / Texas Rangers 4, Toronto Blue Jays 1 / Exhibition Stadium (Toronto) / 9th-inning, one-out triple by Nelson Liriano

✓ Saturday, June 3, 1989 / Texas Rangers 6, Seattle Mariners 1 / Kingdome (Seattle) / Leadoff single by Harold Reynolds

✓ Thursday, April 26, 1990 / Texas Rangers 1, White Sox 0 / Arlington Stadium/ 2nd-inning single by Ron Kittle

Detroit Tigers fans booed the Angels' Erick Aybar for trying to break up Justin Verlander's July 31, 2011, no-hitter with an eighth-inning bunt attempt. *(Photo by KeithAllisonPhoto.com)*

CHAPTER 11

LIE DOWN—OR
LAY IT DOWN?

The Code is a crock.

—*Detroit Free Press* COLUMNIST DREW SHARP

San Diego was trailing Arizona 2-0 on May 27, 2001, when the Padres' Ben Davis stepped to the plate with one out in the eighth inning to face Diamondbacks pitcher Curt Schilling. To anyone reproducing the pictures, descriptions, and accounts of the game, the main plotline at this point clearly was that Schilling was five outs away from completing a perfect game. But the Padres were more concerned with trying to win a ball game.

Davis, looking to bring the potential tying run to the plate, dragged a bunt past the pitcher's mound, breaking one of baseball's unwritten rules demonizing batters for bunting when an opposing pitcher's no-hitter reaches the latter innings. By the time second baseman Jay Bell fielded the ball, Davis had earned first base for the game's first hit.[121]

Schilling said he was a little stunned that Davis would bunt so late in a perfect game in progress. Diamondbacks manager Bob Brenly called the move "chickenshit."[122]

Wouldn't most major leaguers try to reach base any way they could when down 2-0 in the eighth? When did protecting an opposing pitcher's no-hitter become more important than winning a game for *your* team? Or is it just a macho thing—get a *real* hit? And in what inning does a bunt suddenly become taboo?

THE EXACT BIRTH DATE of this unwritten rule is not clear. The great Bob Feller had been holding the St. Louis Browns hitless for five innings in Cleveland on April 24, 1938, when left fielder Mel Mazzera unsuccessfully tried to bunt. The next batter, catcher Billy Sullivan, tried the same thing. The former teammate of Feller's bunted sharply to the left of the mound and beat out Feller's throw by a half-step, according to the AP account. A hometown official scorer easily could have scored the play an error to preserve Feller's no-hitter, but he went with the correct call—a hit.

"I'm awfully sorry I got that hit," Sullivan told Feller after the game. "As long as we had to lose, I wish you'd got your no-hitter."[123]

Feller finished the game with a 9-0 victory, one of his record-setting 12 one-hitters. He had no hard feelings for either Sullivan or the official scorer.

There was also no outrage on May 18, 1953, when the Cincinnati Reds' Gus Bell tapped a bunt toward an unguarded third base to break up Carl Erskine's no-hitter in progress for the Brooklyn Dodgers.[124] Erskine, who already had one no-hitter under his belt and would throw a second in 1956, made no postgame comments of frustration.

The great Warren Spahn was working on his second no-hitter against the San Francisco Giants on April 28, 1961, when pinch hitter Matty Alou came to the plate with one out in the ninth inning. Spahn told *Sports Illustrated* he knew that Giants manager Alvin Dark was sending in the speedy Alou to bunt.

"I know how much Alvin wants to win and I knew he wanted to spoil the no-hitter for his team's sake," Spahn told sportswriter Tex Maule. "The only thing [that] surprised me was Alou bunted on the first pitch."[125]

Spahn grabbed the dead ball, tossed a backhand throw to first to nab Alou, and finished the 1-0, no-hit victory. No bitterness was expressed.

And no one seemed shocked on July 9, 1969, when the Chicago Cubs' Randy Hundley tried to spoil Tom Seaver's perfect game in progress with a ninth-inning bunt attempt. The Mets pitcher fielded the ball in front of the mound and threw to first to pull within two outs of the perfecto. Seaver lost it on the next batter when Jim Qualls signaled to left-center.

BUT BY THE 1980S, players and managers begin citing the apparently newly unwritten rule in postgame interviews. According to an AP report, Kansas City Royals southpaw Danny Jackson was "downright peeved" at Devon White for trying to bunt his way on in the eighth inning to break up his October 1, 1986, no-hitter. White's bunt attempt rolled foul, and Jackson's next pitch brushed White off the plate. Still, Jackson wound up losing his no-no in the ninth on a clean single.

"You try to swing the bat and try to hit the ball," Jackson said after the game. "That was kind of uncalled for."[126] White said he was just trying to get something started. Jackson's teammate Hal McRae took issue with the bunt attempt. "That's certainly not the way they did things in the old days," McRae said.[127]

Tony LaRussa, who managed at the major-league level for 33 years, grumbled when the Kansas City Royals' Greg Gagne broke up Bobby Witt's no-hitter for the Oakland Athletics with a sixth-inning bunt single on June 23, 1994. Replays showed that Witt beat Gagne to the bag, and the A's manager cited the "unwritten code" in postgame comments. "There will be a lot of regrets about that play," LaRussa said. "When you see a bad hop break up a no-hitter, you say that's part of the game."[128]

McRae, who had cited the code to support his Royals teammate Jackson in the 1980s, shifted 180 degrees as the Royals manager defending Gagne. "We're trying to win a ballgame," McRae said. "Gagne bunted on his own and he put it down beautifully."[129]

Justin Verlander completed his July 31, 2011, no-hitter despite Erick Aybar's
eighth-inning bunt attempt. *(Photo by KeithAllisonPhoto.com)*

The Detroit Tigers' Justin Verlander had a no-hitter going with a 3-0
lead when he took the Comerica Park mound in the top of the eighth on
July 31, 2011. Los Angeles Angels leadoff hitter Erick Aybar laid down
a bunt in front of the mound.

Verlander fielded the ball cleanly, but his throw sailed into right field,
giving Aybar second base. Aybar probably would have beaten out a perfect throw, but the hometown official scorer generously ruled it an error
to keep the no-hitter alive. Verlander lost the shutout on a bungled run-
down later in the inning and lost the no-hitter on a Maicer Izturis base
hit to left.

Detroit fans booed Aybar when he took the field in the ninth. But
Angels manager Mike Scioscia defended his player, saying Aybar was
trying to spark a rally. Verlander's manager, Jim Leyland, called it a
"beautiful play." Verlander called it "bush league" from a pitching stand-
point but acknowledged arguments on both sides.[130]

Detroit Free Press columnist Drew Sharp asked readers why a guy should be required to assist someone no-hitting his club: "How is it disrespectful of sainted baseball tradition if a team predicated on speed that leads the American League in infield hits and bunt singles tries to get a leadoff runner on base in a still winnable game through one of its overall strengths?" Sharpe asked.[131] Such silliness, he wrote, reinforces the criticism that baseball is a game too full of itself.

"It's that pretentiousness, that wink-and-a-nod 'inside baseball' that drives people crazy," Sharp wrote. "You don't see this nonsense in football."[132]

THE MUSIC OF BASEBALL

Fans at Fenway Park sing Neil Diamond's "Sweet Caroline" during the eighth inning of a 2015 Red Sox game. *(Photo by Dirk Lammers)*

Nearly every baseball fan can belt out the chorus to "Take Me Out to the Ball Game" when the midseventh arrives, but how many could fumble through even the first line of the 1908 tune's seldom-sung opening verse, "Katie Casey was baseball mad / Had the fever and had it bad"?

Few, no doubt.

But blast Terry Cashman's "Talkin' Baseball," John Fogerty's "Centerfield," or Bruce Springsteen's "Glory Days" through the stadium loudspeakers and you're sure to get a crowd rockin' and rollin'.

MUSIC AND BASEBALL have always paired well, and nowhere has this been more evident than in Boston. After the Boston Marathon bombing in 2013, Neil Diamond flew in to sing "Sweet Caroline" in front of the gathered and grieving at Fenway Park.

The Baseball Project, a band that penned the tune "Harvey Haddix" (see Chapter 15), gave Beantown a doubleheader of due respect on its second album, *Volume 2: High and Inside*.

"Tony (Boston's Chosen Son)" honors Tony Conigliaro, the Red Sox right fielder whose career was cut short by a pitch to the face. "Buckner's Bolero" rightly spreads the blame for the Sox' loss to the Mets in Game 6 of the 1986 World Series. It lists the game's numerous other miscues before asking, "If one play killed the Sox, can you please tell me which?"

In the Red Sox' early days, a group of fanatical followers called the Royal Rooters sang the song "Tessie" to cheer on their team. The fan club disbanded in 1918, and the Red Sox entered their World Series drought, Babe or no Babe. But the Dropkick Murphys modernized the classic Red Sox anthem in 2004, and Boston captured its first World Series title in 86 years.

Hear the crowd roar to your sound
Don't blame us if we ever doubt you
You know we couldn't live without you
Boston, you are the only, only, only

The Murphys' rewrite of "Tessie" mentions Boston no-hitter throwers Bill Dinneen and Cy Young.

And a 2010 song penned by local rock band the Remains pays tribute to another Red Sox hurler who tossed a no-no in 1962: Bill

Monbouquette. Monbouquette at the time was suffering from leuke-
mia, and "Monbo Time" was intended to help raise money for cancer
research.

SOME NOTES about Monbo and Dinneen:

- **Bill Monbouquette:** In 1965, he was the starting pitcher versus
  58-year-old Satchel Paige, then with the Kansas City A's. Of course,
  Paige has two of his own Negro League no-hitters to his credit.
  Monbouquette threw a complete game for his 10th win of the
  season but was a strikeout victim of Paige in the third inning.
- **Bill Dinneen:** In addition to his 1905 no-hitter (not to mention
  his three victories for the Boston Beaneaters over the Pirates in the
  first World Series in 1903), Dinneen went on to be a very well-re-
  garded umpire and called balls and strikes for five no-hitters (a
  sixth was broken up in extra innings). He remains one of only two
  individuals in major-league history both to pitch a no-hitter and to
  call one as plate umpire. (Adonis Terry, who threw two no-nos for
  Brooklyn, umpired Frank "Noodles" Hahn's 1900 no-hitter for the
  Cincinnati Reds. "Noodles"? I'll say it again: They had better nicknames back then.)

Johnny Vander Meer shows off his pitching technique to some kids at the New York World's Fair. *(Photo from Manuscripts and Archives Division, New York Public Library, 1935–1945)*

CHAPTER 12

VANDER MEER BIST
DU SCHÖN

It was the first major-league game my father and mother had ever seen me pitch. Naturally I wanted to win for them as well as my team, but I frankly confess I never dreamed I would pitch another no-hit game.

—JOHNNY VANDER MEER, WRITING IN THE *Saturday Evening Post*

Coasting through three innings with a 6-0 lead is not exactly a pressure situation for most major-league pitchers, but the Cincinnati Reds' Johnny Vander Meer was sailing into uncharted territory on June 19, 1938, as he faced the Boston Bees for the second time in nine days. The 22-year-old lefty was a bundle of nerves in the top of the fourth as he prepared to deliver a one-out, 2-1 pitch to the Bees' Debs Garms. Vander Meer let out a sigh of relief when the third baseman popped the ball into short left-center field for a clean base hit.

"I'm glad that's over," Vander Meer said after the game. "I only wish the first man up could have hit and ended the strain."[133]

Garms's single—the first hit yielded by Vander Meer in 21 and two-thirds consecutive innings—came on the heels of Vander Meer's unprecedented back-to-back no-hitters, and the 33,000 fans at Braves Field were starting to wonder if he could score a hat trick.

Vander Meer's innings streak, a new National League record, fell just shy of the major-league mark of 23 innings set by the great Cy Young, who traveled to Boston to see if someone could dethrone him. But Vander Meer already had set his own mark: A major-league pitcher had never before thrown no-hitters in consecutive starts, and no major leaguer has done it since.

THE 6-FOOT-1, 190-POUND LEFTY began his no-no streak on June 11 back home against those same Boston Bees, with Garms out of the lineup. The contest would have been long forgotten if not for a sensational one-handed catch by Reds rookie center fielder Harry Craft to rob a base hit in the second inning.[134]

Vander Meer knew he was gunning for a no-hitter from the seventh inning on thanks to Bees manager Casey Stengel, who tried to jinx the young pitcher on the way to the bench, according to a UP account.

"So you've got a no-hitter in your hands," Stengel jabbed. "Well you won't get it because we are going to get you in the next inning."[135]

A ticket stub from Vander Meer's second no-hitter bears the shape of a lightbulb, signifying the first night game at Ebbets Field.
(Photo from Robert Edward Auctions)

Vander Meer buckled down and made it through the eighth. Stengel, vowing to keep his promise, sent up three pinch hitters in the ninth, but Vander Meer retired all three for the 3-0 no-hit win.

Vander Meer's next assignment came four days later during the Brooklyn Dodgers' inaugural night game at Ebbets Field. The fastball ace didn't know he was the starter until about an hour and a half before game time. "It doesn't make much difference though," he told a reporter. "I just go out and pitch my own natural ballgame. The fielders behind me really make it possible, anyway."[136] Vander Meer walked five

Dodgers but kept the Brooklyn squad hitless through the first eight frames as the anticipation grew among the 36,000 fans.

Decades later, during a conversation in Cooperstown, New York, with former baseball Commissioner Fay Vincent, Vander Meer said he never forgot the feeling he got when the Brooklyn fans started cheering for him to complete the no-no. "He told me he was very taken by that," Vincent said. "I thought that was a very good baseball moment when the fans decided that this was certainly a very rare event."[137]

Vander Meer's rushed delivery in the ninth led to three straight one-out walks to load the bases, which prompted a mound visit by manager Bill McKechnie. "You are trying to put too much on the ball, John," his skipper said. "Just get it over there. Those hitters up there are scared to death."[138] Vander Meer settled down and pounced on a slow roller from Ernie Koy to force pinch runner Goody Rosen at home for out No. 2. He then got Leo Durocher to fly out to Craft in center to complete the amazing double no-no.

McKechnie reportedly ran onto the field singing, "Vander Meer bist du Schön," a play off the 1932 Yiddish song "Bei Mir Bist Du Schön" popularized by the Andrews Sisters.[139] ("Bei mir bist du schön" roughly translates to "You are beautiful," and it's unknown if [or how] McKechnie knew that.)

Among Vander Meer's most memorable postgame kudos was a "Nice going, kid" from the great Babe Ruth, who was a spectator in Brooklyn that night.[140]

Vincent said it's hard to envision anyone duplicating Vander Meer's feat. "You talk about a record in sports that's never going to be equaled, that's got to be it," Vincent said. "It certainly will never be broken because the only way you can break it is to throw three."

ODDLY, THE MARK was nearly equaled by one of Vander Meer's teammates nine years later. Ewell "the Whip" Blackwell had hurled a 6-0 no-hitter against the Boston Braves at Crosley Field on June 18, 1947, and had the opportunity to go for the double no-no four days later during the first game of a doubleheader against Brooklyn. The 6-foot-6, 185-pound sidearm hurler made it to the ninth and got the first out before Eddie Stanky drove a sharp grounder through Blackwell's legs and into center field for a base hit.[141]

Vander Meer watched from the Reds dugout. "I was up on the top step," Vander Meer told the *New York Times*. "I wanted to be the first one out there to congratulate him."[142]

NOLAN RYAN HOLDS another baseball record considered by many in baseball to be unbreakable—seven career no-hitters—and he came close to duplicating Vander Meer's feat in 1973. Four days after no-hitting the Tigers in Detroit on July 15, 1973, Ryan took a no-no into the eighth inning against the Orioles at home in Anaheim. He led off the inning by hitting Brooks Robinson with a pitch, and Mark Belanger followed by lining a fastball up the middle for a single.

The Baltimore shortstop didn't notice Ryan's glare, but his Orioles teammates did. "They told me that when I got to first base, Nolan looked at me," Belanger told *Times* columnist Dave Anderson. "Nolan tilts that head and then gives you that look."[143]

Such near misses always put Vander Meer on edge. "Every time somebody pitches a no-hitter, in a way I hold my breath to see if he'll pitch another one in his next start," he said. "I always thought Nolan Ryan or Sandy Koufax had a chance."[144] There would be no one else to congratulate, though, as the Dutch Master continues to occupy the only seat at the back-to-back no-hitter table.

Vander Meer pitched in the big leagues until 1951, building a 119-121 record with a 3.44 ERA over 11 seasons. He threw another no-hitter 14 years after his double no-nos in a 1952 minor league game in Texas. Tulsa's 12-0 victory came at the expense of Beaumont, a team managed by Vander Meer's old teammate Harry Craft.

A RAY OF LIGHT IN TAMPA

Matt Garza threw the first no-hitter in Tampa Bay Rays history. *(Photo by Dirk Lammers)*

The Tampa Bay Rays had been growing weary of no-hitters by the summer of 2010, having fallen victim over the previous 12 months to two perfect games (Mark Buehrle and Dallas Braden) and a walk-filled no-hitter (Edwin Jackson).

The Detroit Tigers' Max Scherzer was looking to make it four when he took the Tropicana Field mound for the sixth inning of a July 26, 2010, night game against the Rays, his no-no still intact. Scherzer loaded the bases on two walks and a catcher's interference call, giving designated hitter Matt Joyce a shot at breaking the 0-0 deadlock. The Tampa native jumped on a 3-2 pitch and slammed the fastball over the right-field fence in grand fashion for the game's first hit.

"Joyce hit it out, and everybody's ecstatic," said Matt Garza, the Rays' starting pitcher. "At that point I knew he had a no-hitter going, and I was like 'Oh, OK. Whew. We got some runs. Let's go.'"[145]

What Garza hadn't realized at the time was that *he*, too, had a no-hitter going—the Tigers' lone base runner reaching on a second-inning walk. Reenergized by his newfound 4-0 lead, Garza retired the next nine batters before returning to the dugout for the top of the ninth. As he tried to chat with teammates, all they returned were terse one-word answers, and that was when it dawned on him that he hadn't given up a hit.

"I was trying to talk to people, and no one would talk to me and I didn't know why," he said. "I looked up at the scoreboard and said, 'Oh, shoot. Let's finish it off.'" [146]

Garza retired the side, and teammates rushed to the mound to celebrate the first no-hitter in Tampa Bay Rays history.

"It was awesome, not only for the franchise but for myself," he said. "It was my first one ever. Words really can't explain the emotion."[147]

IF THROWING a team's first-ever no-hitter is a special achievement, imagine accomplishing the feat for two teams.

On June 2, 1990, Randy Johnson no-hit the Detroit Tigers for a 2-0 win at the Kingdome to post the Mariners' first-ever no-no. He walked six and struck out eight in what was also the 6-foot-10-inch lefty's first career shutout and complete game. Then, on May 18, 2004, at the age of 40, he tossed a perfect game against the Atlanta Braves on the road at Turner Field for the Diamondbacks' first no-hitter.

Johnson told a reporter that his 2004 perfect performance far exceeded his 1990 no-no, when he "didn't have any idea where the ball was going."[148]

Milt Pappas, who pitched for the Orioles before joining the Cubs, lost a perfect game on the 27th batter in 1972 but recovered to preserve his no-hitter. *(Photo by KeithAllisonPhoto.com)*

CHAPTER 13

JUUUST A BIT OUTSIDE

I'm still being recognized and still going out and signing auto-graphs, and I'm wondering to myself on numerous occasions, "If I would have done the perfect game, would I be getting this kind of adulation?"

—MILT PAPPAS

Veteran Cubs pitcher Milt Pappas threw up his arms à la Rocky Balboa as Padres pinch hitter Garry Jestadt popped a ball just behind Wrigley Field's infield grass. As second baseman Carmen Fanzone squeezed his glove around the ball, Pappas jumped into Ron Santo's arms to celebrate his first, and only, career no-hitter.

A jubilant moment? Sort of, but Pappas's mood on September 2, 1972, could best be described as mixed. The 6-foot-3 right-hander was seeking his 197th career victory that afternoon, and he plowed through San Diego's first 24 batters without allowing a walk, hit, or error before returning to the Chicago dugout.

"And of course no one was talking to me," Pappas recalled in a 2015 interview. "As I walked down to the bottom of the stairs I yelled out, 'Hey, guys, I'm pitching a no-hitter.' They all just started talking and yapping and just carrying on like it's nothing."[149]

Pappas, whose loose, nonsuperstitious demeanor came courtesy of a 4-0 lead, slipped away to the clubhouse corridor for a couple of cigarette puffs before a cadre of police officers, ushers, and security guards prepping for ninth-inning mayhem burst in out of nowhere, walkie-talkies blaring. "These guys made me more nervous than pitching," he said. "I turned around and said, 'Could you please turn your damn radios down so I don't have to hear it? Please!'"[150]

THE CUBBIES' BATS helped drown out the noise by scoring four insurance runs, and Pappas returned to the mound with an 8-0 lead, ready to complete the perfecto. Up stepped Johnny Jeter, and the Padres hitter lined a hard shot to left-center field that was about to be snagged by center fielder Billy North, but North slipped and fell to the grass. Billy Williams, who was sprinting over from left, lunged in to make a spectacular catch in front of North to save the perfect game.

"Oh, brother. Wooooooo!" belted Cubs TV play-by-play man Jack Brickhouse. "What a play. Man alive!"[151]

With rhythmic chants of "We want an out" bellowing from the scattered seats, Pappas got catcher Fred Kendall to ground out to shortstop Don Kessinger for out No. 2. He then worked a 1-2 count on the 27th batter, pinch hitter Larry Stahl.

Pappas's next pitch sailed near the outside of the plate, and second-year umpire Bruce Froemming called it a ball. Pappas again tried to paint the corner, and Froemming again called, "Ball," earning a lengthy glare from the pitcher as he snapped his glove on catcher Randy Hundley's return toss.

Brickhouse relayed the growing tension to those watching the WGN telecast: "Now here comes one of the most fateful pitches of the year," the announcer declared. "Ball three, strike two, two out; perfect game on the line; no-hitter on the line. Watch it."[152]

The 3-2 pitch touched the same inch of air, and Stahl checked his swing. "It's ... a ball! And Pappas is enraged," Brickhouse said. "Ball four. There's goes the perfect game. The no-hitter's still intact."[153]

Pappas slammed his fist into the air and marched a few steps toward home plate, jarring unidentified cuss words at Froemming. "It wasn't very nice," Pappas recalled.[154]

Froemming, speaking to MLB Network in a 2010 interview, defended his call that the 3-2 pitch was outside. "I've got a pitch to call, and I'm not a fan," he said. "I'm an umpire."[155]

Meanwhile, Stahl took first, and Pappas needed a reminder that a rare feat was still in the making. "Santo knew I was hot, so Ronny walked over and said, 'Hey, dummy. Don't forget you're pitching a no-hitter,'" Pappas said. "That sort of calmed me down a bit."[156] Pappas drew the pop-up from Jestadt, and Wrigley Field erupted in celebration.

ONLY TWO OTHER PITCHERS lost perfect games on the 27th batter yet escaped with no-hitters, but those perfecto bids were blown on hit batsmen.

On June 20, 2015, the Washington Nationals' Max Scherzer coaxed outs from the first 26 Pittsburgh Pirates whom he faced before engaging in a drawn-out battle with pesky pinch hitter José Tabata. Tabata fouled off several fastballs before Scherzer shook off his catcher to throw a slider, which grazed Tabata's elbow to give him first base. The right-hander then got Josh Harrison to fly out to left to complete the no-hitter.

More than a century earlier, the New York Giants' George "Hooks" Wiltse retired 26 Philadelphia Quakers during the first game of a July 4, 1908 doubleheader, and he would have been perfect through 27 if not for a questionable call by home-plate umpire Cy Rigler. The Giants southpaw was facing opposing pitcher George McQuillan in a 0-0 pitchers' duel, and Wiltse thought his 1-2 pitch retired the side. But Rigler called it a ball, and the next pitch hit McQuillan on the arm to end the perfect game.

Wiltse closed out the ninth, the Giants scored in the top of the 10th and Wiltse pitched a 1-2-3 bottom of the 10th to complete the 10-inning no-hitter.

"According to many spectators, had it not been for Rigler's poor judgment of a ball, Wiltse would have had the honor of retiring thirty men before they reached first," noted the *New-York Tribune*.[157]

Rigler later acknowledged the blown call, according to Gabriel Schechter's SABR biographical entry on Wiltse, and the umpire spent years giving Wiltse cigars to atone for the mistake.[158]

No CIGARS have been—or will be—exchanged between Pappas and Froemming. TV footage from Stahl's at-bat shows only the high-up behind-the-plate perspective, so it's hard for fans to weigh in on the enduring controversy. Both Pappas and Hundley were quoted after the game as saying that the pitches were outside but close enough to warrant a "strike three" punch-out.

"Those pitches to Stahl weren't that far off and I was hoping [Froemming] would sympathize with me and give me a call," Pappas told a reporter in a postgame interview. "But they were balls, no question about it."[159]

But decades later, Pappas still feels that he was robbed. He said the final pitch in Don Larsen's 1956 World Series perfect game missed by a mile, but the ump raised his arm because he knew what was at stake. "If I would have had a veteran umpire behind the plate, I don't think there would be a doubt in my mind that one of those pitches would have been called a strike," he said.[160]

Froemming, speaking to the *New York Times* in 2010, hasn't wavered. "I didn't miss the pitch; Pappas missed the pitch," he said. "You can look at the tape."

Pappas said he met Froemming years after the game and reminded the umpire that he could have cemented his place in history for calling just the ninth perfect game in nearly 100 years of major-league ball. Froemming wasn't impressed by the potential notoriety. "Name me one umpire that called a perfect game," he replied.

"I said, 'Bruce, you're missing the whole point of discussion. Umpires who have called a perfect game could go into a bar, at a party, at home sitting in their underwear watching a ball game, anywhere, and they can say, 'I called a perfect game.'"[161]

Pappas, now in his mid-70s, said he's gotten plenty of mileage out of his near-perfect no-no, and people still come up to him with comments such as "Man, you got screwed."

"I've gone through my whole life and people still remember that," he said.[162]

OTHER STREAKS OF NOTE

Yusmeiro Petit, seen here during the 2014 World Series championship parade, holds the major-league record of retiring 46 consecutive batters. *(Photo by E. M. During)*

You'd think that retiring more than 45 hitters in a row would get you a credit somewhere on the official no-hitters list, but that's not the case for the San Francisco Giants' Yusmeiro Petit. Petit retired a major league record 46 consecutive batters in the summer of 2014, but the reliever and spot starter accomplished the feat during 15 and one-third innings of work over more than a month's span.

The streak began in the fifth inning of a July 22 game against the Philadelphia Phillies in which Petit got the start. The Venezuelan righty gave up five earned runs in five innings of work, but he finished the frame and his day by getting Grady Sizemore to ground out to the mound. Sizemore was victim No. 1.

Petit continued to send batters back to the dugout during six relief assignments over the next month or so before earning an August 28 start at home against the Colorado Rockies. He downed the first seven batters he faced before setting the new major-league mark with a strikeout of Charlie Culberson. The next batter, opposing pitcher Jordan Lyles, lined a double to left to end the streak, but Petit had his consecutive-batter mark.

The record was a bit of redemption for Petit, who a season earlier had lost a September 6 perfect game on the 27th batter. Arizona Diamondbacks pinch hitter Eric Chavez worked the count full with two outs in the ninth inning of that game before blooping a base hit to right just out of the reach of a charging Hunter Pence.

After breaking the consecutive-batter record in 2014, Petit told reporters that he thought it was like a reward for all the work he puts into his pitching. "God gave me a second opportunity," he told the *San Francisco Chronicle* through an interpreter. "This time, I would not allow myself to not do it."[163]

PETIT'S NEW MARK edged Chicago White Sox starter Mark Buehrle out of the record books; Buehrle retired 45 batters in a row in 2009. The big difference was that Buehrle notched a perfect game in the process of his 2009 streak.

Buehrle began his streak by inducing a fly-out in the eighth inning of a July 18 start against the Orioles. The 6-foot-2, 240-pound southpaw extended his streak to 28 on July 23 by throwing a perfect game against the Tampa Bay Rays. The ninth inning of that contest featured a dramatic home run–robbing catch by center fielder Dewayne Wise.

During Buehrle's next start on July 28, he retired 17 consecutive Minnesota Twins before walking Alexi Casilla and then giving up a base hit to Denard Span.

Forty-five batters in a row down over three games for Buehrle. But he was also able to count the perfect game as his second no-no. Buehrle had thrown his first no-hitter in 2007 against the Texas Rangers.

JON LESTER, who tossed a no-hitter for the Boston Red Sox in 2008, also boasts a no-hit record from the other side of the plate. Lester spent the vast majority of his career in the American League, so his plate appearances from 2006 through 2014 were limited to occasional interleague games. But in 2015 he joined the Chicago Cubs, giving him enough at-bats to break—or avoid—the 0-for-57 record for poor-hitting pitchers set by the San Diego Padres' Joey Hamilton in the mid-1990s.

Facing the Nationals on May 27, 2015, Lester drilled a fly ball to deep center field, but the ball hovered just shy of the Wrigley Field ivy. Denard Span gloved it to brand Lester 0-for-58 and give him the major-league record.

Lester finally broke through a little over a month later in his 67th career at-bat, drilling opposing pitcher John Lackey in the leg to eke out an infield single. The southpaw's 0-for-66 streak represents the batting equivalent of nearly two and a half no-hitters.

".031 never looked so good!" Lester tweeted, hyping his midseason average.

A Topps "Big League Brothers" card shows Bob and Ken Forsch, the only sibling pair to throw no-hitters. *(Baseball card image used courtesy of The Topps Company, Inc., www.topps.com)*

CHAPTER 14

BROTHERLY NO-NOS

I want to find that spider that bit Kenny. Maybe it'll help me, too.

—Joe Niekro, after Ken Forsch joined
brother Bob Forsch in the no-no club

The Society for American Baseball Research notes that more than 60 sibling pitchers have stared down major-league batters since 1876, but just one pair of fraternal hurlers shares space on the official no-hitters list—Bob Forsch and Ken Forsch.

The Cardinals' Bob Forsch struck first on April 16, 1978, no-hitting the Philadelphia Phillies 5-0 at Busch Stadium.

Bob's brother, Houston Astros hurler Ken Forsch, followed up within a year. On April 7, 1979, just two days removed from a mysterious insect bite that swelled his nonpitching elbow, the elder Forsch tossed a 6-0 no-hitter against the Atlanta Braves in the Astrodome. "In my younger days, I probably couldn't have thrown a no-hitter," the 32-year-old told a reporter. "I mostly threw hard stuff and when you get into the seventh inning, it's hard to keep relying on fastballs every time."[164]

Bob Forsch added another no-hitter to the family list on September 26, 1983, tossing a second no-no at home against the Montreal Expos. He said his pitching performance was superior in No. 2, but the first no-no was a bigger thrill. "The first one set up the one Kenny got the next year," he said.[165]

. . .

EARLY ATTEMPTS AT sibling no-hitters date back to the summer of 1884, but the quests seemed to be based on mistaken assumptions by owners, scouts, and managers that no-no stuff must be in the genes.

Here is the fraternal fallout.

THE CHICAGO WHITE STOCKINGS' Larry Corcoran already had three no-hitters under his belt by June 1884, so the National League squad decided to give his older brother a try. It did not go well. Mike Corcoran surrendered 16 hits and walked seven during a complete-game 14-0 loss to the last-place Detroit Wolverines. The *Chicago Daily Tribune* noted the 25-year-old's "wild pitching and giving of bases, together with ragged fielding."

"Detroit slugged Corcoran's balls all over the field," the newspaper reported. "Chicago was completely demoralized."[166]

Mike Corcoran never pitched in the majors again.

CHRISTY "MATTY" MATHEWSON threw no-hitters for the New York Giants in 1901 and 1905, and manager John McGraw decided to give his 19-year-old brother, Henry, the start on the final day of the 1906 season.

The Boston Beaneaters silenced the Polo Grounds crowd by topping the Giants 7-1, with the result "principally due to the wildness of 'Christy's' brother,'" according to the *New York Times*. Henry Mathewson walked 14, which "broke the season's mark in the major leagues and probably made a new world's record for that kind of pitching."[167]

While Matty racked up 373 wins over a 17-year career, Henry pitched just one more inning for the Giants in May 1907 before being demoted to Wilmington of the Tri-State League.

. . .

JESSE AND VIRGIL BARNES, brothers from Jackson County, Kansas, spread out the pitching genes more evenly, and the two served as Giants teammates from 1919 through 1923. Jesse Barnes threw a no-no against the Philadelphia Phillies on May 7, 1922, and brother Virgil came close on July 10, 1927, yielding only a second-inning base hit to Cardinals catcher Bob O'Farrell during the Giants' 5-0 win over St. Louis in the first game of a doubleheader.[168]

OHIO-BORN KNUCKLEBALLERS Phil and Joe Niekro together amassed more wins (539) than any other major-league siblings, but only Phil could add the no-hitter to his résumé. He no-hit the San Diego Padres on August 4, 1973, for the Braves' first no-hitter after the franchise relocated from Milwaukee. "Knucksie" walked three and struck out four and told reporters that he stuck almost exclusively with the knuckleball after the sixth inning. He finished the feat by getting Cito Gaston to ground out to third.

"I admit I was nervous," he told a reporter after the game. "But I tried not to do anything different in the closing innings."[169]

Phil's brother Joe nearly preceded his sibling three years earlier. Pitching for the Detroit Tigers. Joe took a no-hitter against the New York Yankees into the ninth inning but couldn't retire Horace Clarke—who broke up an unprecedented three ninth-inning no-nos in the summer of 1970 (see Chapter 16). Second baseman Dick McAullife made a nice stop on Clarke's grounder, but McAullife's falling throw pulled the covering Joe Niekro off the first-base bag.

"It was my fault," the pitcher said after the game. "If I had stayed on the bag, I would have had it."[170]

Joe made one last attempt to join his brother in the no-no club as a 41-year-old member of the 1986 New York Yankees. He threw seven and

two-thirds innings of no-hit ball before yielding a two-out double to
Gary Pettis on his trademark knuckleball. "You can second guess your-
self," he told a reporter. "But if you throw a fastball and they get a hit,
it's not your best pitch. If they were going to get a hit, I wanted it to be
on my best pitch."[171]

GAYLORD AND JIM PERRY finished their careers just 10 wins short of
the Niekros with 529 victories, but only Gaylord earned a spot on the
no-no list. While pitching for the San Francisco Giants on September
17, 1968, he no-hit the St. Louis Cardinals for 1-0 victory.

Jim Perry, pitching for the Oakland Athletics on June 10, 1975, made
it through five and two-thirds innings against the Baltimore Orioles before giving up a two-out Al Bumbry single to center.

THE MARTÍNEZ BROTHERS, Pedro and Ramón, combined for 354
wins and nearly threw brotherly no-nos within six weeks of each other.
Pedro threw nine innings of perfect baseball against the San Diego Padres on June 3, 1995, but his Expos couldn't score a run, and the game
headed into extra innings. Montreal finally managed to bring a runner
home in the top of the 10th, but Martínez gave up a Bip Roberts leadoff
double in the bottom half of the frame to lose the no-no. Reliever Mel
Rojas was brought in to retire the final three batters, but the 1-0 victory
is credited as just a simple "W" for Pedro.

About six weeks later, on July 14, 1995, Ramón Martínez no-hit the
Florida Marlins and just missed perfection by issuing an eighth-inning
walk to Tommy Gregg. His no-no at least earned a spot in the record
books.

AL LEITER THREW his no-hitter for the Florida Marlins on May 11,
1996, but his older brother wasn't up to the task. The closest Mark Leiter

came to a no-no was a two-hit complete-game 4-1 victory over the Cincinnati Reds on July 26, 1995. Brett Boone led off the sixth inning with a single, and Leiter gave up an eighth-inning leadoff homer to Ron Gant.

THE LOS ANGELES ANGELS' Jered Weaver threw a no-hitter against the Minnesota Twins on May 2, 2012. A decade earlier, his older brother, Jeff Weaver, took a no-hitter into the eighth inning for the Detroit Tigers. Jeff made it through seven and two-thirds innings on May 22, 2002, before the Cleveland Indians' Chris Magruder doubled off Comerica Park's right-field wall, leaving Jeff to settle for the one-hit complete-game shutout.

GOING BACK TO the 1930s, there is a case of the much-less-famous brother getting the no-hitter. One got into the Hall of Fame; the other got the no-no.

St. Louis Cardinals great Jerome "Dizzy" Dean was pursuing his league-leading 27th victory of the year on September 21, 1934, when he got the start for the opening game of a doubleheader against the Brooklyn Dodgers. The Arkansas-born fastball ace pitched a three-hit complete-game shutout, noting he had no clue that he had held the Dodgers hitless for the first seven innings of his game.

"I should have known that," he told a reporter after the twin bill. "Then I'd have really breezed 'em in there and we'd both have had a no-hitter."[172]

The "both" referred to Dizzy and his younger brother Paul Dean, a 22-year-old Cardinals rookie going after his 18th win in the nightcap. The quieter and more serious Paul, whom the press corps inaccurately tried to nickname "Daffy," mowed down the Dodgers lineup for nine innings, yielding just a single walk en route to a 3-0 complete-game no-hitter.[173]

Paul Dean's no-hitter is also notable for ending the longest no-no drought in MLB history in terms of game days (535).

The boisterous and much-quoted Dizzy, whose Hall of Fame career was shortened by injury, never accomplished the feat.

To MAKE SURE the Forsches don't feel so alone, let's offer an honorable mention to the Pérez brothers, Pascual and Mélido, who threw rain-shortened no-hitters in the late '80s and early '90s. On September 24, 1988, the Montreal Expos' Pascual Pérez threw a five-inning, rain-shortened no-hitter at Veterans Stadium against the Philadelphia Phillies. A year and a half later, Chicago White Sox pitcher Mélido Pérez threw a six-inning, rain-shortened no-hitter against the New York Yankees at Yankee Stadium on July 12, 1990.

The outings were once considered brotherly no-nos, but the games are now relegated to footnotes in baseball's record books. Baseball's committee for statistical accuracy tossed rain- and darkness-shortened no-nos off the official list in 1991.

HALL OF FAME 300-GAME WINNERS *WITHOUT* A NO-HITTER

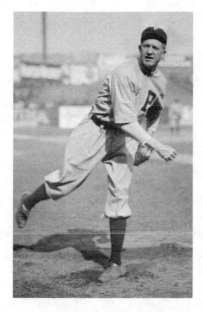

Grover Cleveland Alexander won 373 games over a 20-year career but never threw a no-hitter. *(Photo from Bain News Service Collection, Prints & Photographs Division, Library of Congress, LC-DIG-ggbain-12276)*

Baseball has seen many flash-in-the-pan hurlers toss a token no-hitter as the highlight of an otherwise unremarkable career.

Meanwhile, some of the game's greatest pitchers have reached the Hall of Fame without ever achieving one of its greatest feats.

Here is the list of 300-game winners in the Hall *without* a no-hitter.

Mickey Welch	1880–1892	307-210, 2.71 ERA
Tim Keefe	1880–1893	342-225, 2.63 ERA
Kid Nichols	1890–1906	361-208, 2.96 ERA

Eddie Plank	1901–1917	326-194, 2.35 ERA
Grover Cleveland Alexander	1911–1930	373-208, 2.56 ERA
Lefty Grove	1925–1941	300-141, 3.06 ERA
Early Wynn	1939–1963	300-244, 3.54 ERA
Steve Carlton	1965–1988	329-244, 3.22 ERA
Don Sutton	1966–1988	324-256, 3.26 ERA
Roger Clemens	1984–2007	354-184 3.12 ERA
Greg Maddux	1986–2008	355-227, 3.16 ERA
Tom Glavine	1987–2008	305-203, 3.54 ERA

Some other notable pitching greats *without* no-hitters include:

- Mordecai "Three Finger" Brown
- Dizzy Dean
- Robin Roberts
- Whitey Ford
- Don Drysdale
- Pedro Martínez

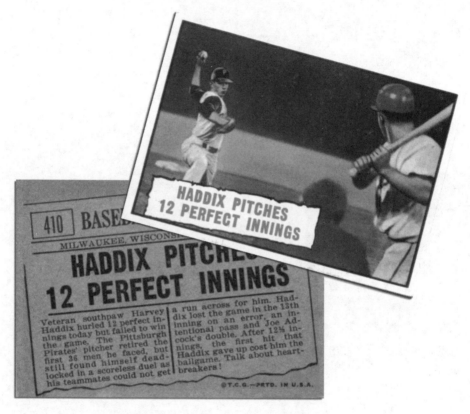

A 1961 Topps baseball card commemorates Harvey Haddix's
accomplishment of pitching 12 perfect innings. *(Baseball card image
used courtesy of The Topps Company, Inc., www.topps.com)*

CHAPTER 15

TWELVE SILVER GOBLETS

Why don't we add ol' Harvey to that list.

—The Baseball Project's "Harvey Haddix"

Harvey Haddix's two-out, ninth-inning strikeout of Milwaukee Braves pitcher Lew Burdette should have culminated in Pittsburgh Pirates catcher Smoky Burgess leaping into his batterymate's arms in a Don Larsen–Yogi Berra–esque moment.

Haddix on May 26, 1959, gained entry into an exclusive club of a half-dozen major-league pitchers to retire a lineup's first 27 batters without a hit, walk or error. Larsen, Lee Richmond, Monte Ward, Cy Young, Addie Joss and Charlie Robertson all got to brand their 27-up, 27-down performances as "perfect games." Haddix had duplicated those legends' dominance, but it would be premature for the 33-year-old hurler to claim such a title.

Rather than celebrate, Haddix fought off his lingering flu symptoms and returned to the Pirates dugout for a quick smoke before his 10th inning at-bat. The score at County Stadium in Milwaukee remained 0-0 heading into the 10th inning, as the Pirates' eight hits off Burdette over the nine innings had been fruitless in producing a run.

Pittsburgh threatened in the top of the frame when Don Hoak reached first on a one-out single to left, but the potential go-ahead run was left stranded when pinch hitter Dick Stewart flew out to center and Haddix—a paltry .145 hitter that season—grounded out with a come-backer for the third out.

The slender southpaw from Springfield, Ohio, took the mound again and kept perfection alive through 10, inducing fly-outs to center from pinch hitter Del Rice and Eddie Mathews before retiring Hank Aaron on a grounder to short. Haddix now boasted the sport's best pitching performance of all time, but it was back to the dugout for the 11th.

Pittsburgh shortstop Dick Schofield led off the top of the 11th with a single, but a Bill Virdon groundout and a double-play ball hit by Burgess squandered any chance for the Pirates to give Haddix a lead. The man who had retired 30 straight now settled in to face Joe Adcock, Wes Covington, and Del Crandall. Each stepped into the batter's box, and each was sent back to the dugout as Haddix extended his streak to 33 batters—an unprecedented 11 innings of perfection. But the Pirates still couldn't score. Bill Mazeroski reached base on a two-out, 12th-inning single, but he was forced out on the next play when Hoak hit a ground ball to short.

Andy Pafko and Johnny Logan each got their fourth at-bats in the bottom of the 12th, and each fell to 0-for-4 on the night. Burdette then stepped to the plate as Haddix's 36th opponent and grounded a ball deep into the hole between third and short. Hoak, the third baseman, lunged left and fielded the ball with his glove, made a half-pivot, and fired to first baseman Rocky Nelson to beat Burdette by a step.

"He got 'im," proclaimed KDKA radio commentator Jim Woods. "Thirty-six in a row for Haddix."[174]

Burdette, who had walked nary a batter during the marathon contest, continued to scatter his hits brilliantly. In the top of the 13th inning he yielded a two-out single to Schofield for the Pirates' 12th hit of the game, but Burdette turned Schofield into the 12th runner left on base by getting Virdon to ground out to second.

Haddix returned to the mound to face Felix Mantilla, who had subbed in to play second base for the Braves in the 11th. Mantilla hit a routine grounder to third that Hoak fielded cleanly, but the third base-man threw the ball into the dirt and Mantilla reached safely on an E-5.

"There isn't anybody right now sicker this moment than Don Hoak, I guarantee you that," noted KDKA play-by-play man Bob Prince. "He's stressed over this."[175]

The perfect game was over, but Haddix's no-hitter remained alive. Mathews laid down a sacrifice bunt to advance Mantilla to second, and the Pirates issued an intentional walk to slugger Hank Aaron to set up a potential double play while facing the cleanup hitter Adcock. The no-hitter was still alive.

Haddix hung a high slider, and Adcock pounced on it. Prince delivered the bad news to the growing legion of Pittsburgh fans who had gathered around their radios: "There's a fly ball, deep right center," Prince said. "That ball may be on through and over everything. It is ... gone! Home run!"

After a long pause, Prince added, "Absolutely fantastic."[176]

Haddix lost his no-hitter, and the Pirates lost the game. The Braves' base-running blunders kept the final score a mystery for a day. Aaron, who quit advancing after he saw Mantilla cross home plate with the winning run, strolled across the mound toward the dugout. An excited Adcock continued rounding the bases, then began backing up when he realized he had illegally passed Aaron. The game was recorded that night as a 2-0 Braves victory on an Adcock walk-off homer. National League officials the next day reclassified it as a 1-0 win on an Adcock walk-off double.

Haddix told sportswriter Joe Reichler after the game that all he knew was the Pirates had lost in 13 innings. "What's so historic about that?" Haddix asked. "Didn't anyone ever lose a 13-inning shutout?"[177]

Yes, but no one had ever pitched 12 *perfect* innings before losing a shutout in the 13th. And no one has since.

"You're kidding," Haddix said. "You mean nobody? Not even guys like Cy Young and Walter Johnson and Christy Mathewson or any of those old fellows? Well, what do you know about that."

Baseball officials gave Harvey Haddix an engraved silver tray and 12 goblets for his 12 perfect innings in 1959. *(Photo from Hunt Auctions, Inc., www.huntauctions.com)*

Haddix initially characterized the game as "just another loss" but later came to appreciate the masterpiece thought by many to be the greatest pitching performance in baseball history.[178]

National League president Warren Giles honored Haddix by sending a silver tray accompanied by 12 silver goblets, each engraved with the results of one of his perfect innings. The 22-inch circular tray's engraving, which was surrounded by the signatures of Haddix and his teammates, read:

TO HARVEY HADDIX

IN RECOGNITION OF HIS OUTSTANDING PERFORMANCE—

UNPRECEDENTED IN BASEBALL HISTORY

PITCHING 12 CONSECUTIVE PERFECT INNINGS

GAME OF MAY 26, 1959

	R H E
PITTSBURGH 000 000 000 000 0	0 – 12 – 1
MILWAUKEE 000 000 000 000 1	1 – 1 – 0

PRESENTED BY

NATIONAL LEAGUE OF PROFESSIONAL BASEBALL CLUBS

The set was auctioned off in 2010, but Haddix was honored in song more than 50 years after the triumph. The Baseball Project, an indie rock group featuring R.E.M. alums Peter Buck, Mike Mills, and Scott McCaughey; drummer Linda Pitmon; and her husband, Steve Wynn of the Dream Syndicate, penned "Harvey Haddix" in honor of the pitcher's accomplishment.

The tune lists the two dozen pitchers who've thrown credited perfectos with the catchy refrain "Why don't we add ol' Harvey to the list."

But baseball hasn't added ol' Harvey to the list, as his effort is considered neither a perfect game nor a no-hitter. That interpretation was cemented in 1991 when Major League Baseball's committee for statistical accuracy established an official definition for a no-hitter.

"It's disappointing to find out it's not a no-hitter, but it's still the record," Haddix told a reporter. "Most consecutive perfect innings, most consecutive batters retired."[179]

NO-HITTERS THROUGH
NINE LOST IN EXTRAS

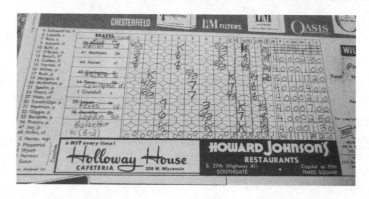

The May 26, 1959, game in which Harvey Haddix threw 12 perfect innings, shown in this scorecard, is the most famous of 13 nine-inning no-nos broken up in extras. *(Photo from Andy Sandler's All Sports Collectibles Auctions, www.allsportsauctions.com)*

Harvey Haddix's 12-perfect-inning game of 1959 is the most famous of baseball's 13 nine-inning no-nos lost in extras. In the most recent of these efforts, the Montreal Expos' Pedro Martínez threw nine innings of perfect baseball in 1995 only to lose the no-no in the 10th. Here is the full list chronologically.

- **Earl Moore:** Cleveland Blues (AL) / Thursday, May 9, 1901 / Cleveland Blues 2, Chicago White Sox 4 (10 inn.) / League Park (Cleveland) / Moore gave up a leadoff single in the 10th and allowed one more hit in a losing effort.
- **Bob Wicker:** Chicago Cubs (NL) / Saturday, June 11, 1904 / Chicago Cubs 1, New York Giants 0 (12 inn.) / Polo Grounds (New

York) / Wicker gave up just one single with one out in the 10th and got the victory.

- **Harry McIntire:** Brooklyn Superbas (NL) / Wednesday, August 1, 1906 / Brooklyn Superbas 0, Pittsburgh Pirates 1 (13 inn.) / Washington Park (Brooklyn) / McIntire gave up a single with two out in the 11th and allowed three more hits in a losing effort.
- **Red Ames:** New York Giants (NL) / Thursday, April 15, 1909 / New York Giants 0, Brooklyn Superbas 3 (13 inn.) / Polo Grounds (New York) / Ames gave up a single with one out in the 10th and allowed seven more hits in a losing effort.
- **Tom Hughes:** New York Highlanders (AL) / Tuesday, August 30, 1910 (second game of doubleheader) / New York Highlanders 0, Cleveland Naps 5 (11 inn.) / Hilltop Park (New York) / Hughes gave up a single with one out in the 10th and allowed six more hits and five 11th-inning runs in a losing effort.
- **Jim Scott:** Chicago White Sox (AL) / Thursday, May 14, 1914 / Chicago White Sox 0, Washington Senators 1 (10 inn.) / National Park (Washington) / Scott gave up a leadoff single in the 10th and allowed one more hit in a losing effort.
- **Hippo Vaughn:** Chicago Cubs (NL) / Wednesday, May 2, 1917 / Chicago Cubs 0, Cincinnati Reds 1 (10 inn.) / Weeghman Park (Chicago) / This is the only time in Major League Baseball history that both pitchers had no-hitters through nine innings. Vaughn gave up a single with one out in the 10th and allowed one more hit in a losing effort. The Reds' Fred Toney is credited with a no-hitter, completing the accomplishment in 10 innings.
- **Louis ("Buck" or "Bobo") Newsom:** St. Louis Browns (AL) / Tuesday, September 18, 1934 / St. Louis Browns 1, Boston Red Sox 2 (10 inn.) / Sportsman's Park (St. Louis) / Newsom gave up a single with two out in the 10th (the only hit against him) and lost the game.
- **Johnny Klippstein** (7 inn.), **Hersch Freeman** (1 inn.), **Joe Black** (3

inn.): Cincinnati Reds (NL) / Saturday, May 26, 1956 / Cincinnati Reds 1, Milwaukee Braves 2 (11 inn.) / Milwaukee County Stadium (Milwaukee) / Black, pitching in relief, gave up a double with two outs in the 10th and allowed two more hits for the loss.

- **Harvey Haddix:** Pittsburgh Pirates (NL) / Tuesday, May 26, 1959 / Pittsburgh Pirates 0, Milwaukee Braves 1 (13 inn.) / Milwaukee County Stadium (Milwaukee) / Haddix threw a perfect game through 12, retiring the first 36 batters he faced. He lost the perfect game, the no-no, and the game in the bottom of the 13th.

- **Jim Maloney:** Cincinnati Reds (NL) / Monday, June 14, 1965 / Cincinnati Reds 0, New York Mets 1 (11 inn.) / Crosley Field (Cincinnati) / Maloney gave up a leadoff home run in the 11th and allowed one more hit in the losing effort.

- **Mark Gardner** (9 inn.), **Jeff Fassero** (0 inn.): Montreal Expos (NL) / Friday, July 26, 1991 / Montreal Expos 0, Los Angeles Dodgers 1 (10 inn.) / Dodger Stadium (Los Angeles) / Gardner gave up a leadoff single in the 10th and allowed one more hit before Fassero took the ball. Fassero gave up the game-winning hit, but Gardner was charged with the loss, as he had responsibility for the base runner.

- **Pedro Martínez** (9 inn.), **Mel Rojas** (1 inn.): Montreal Expos (NL) / Saturday, June 3, 1995 / Montreal Expos 1, San Diego Padres 0 (10 inn.) / Jack Murphy Stadium (San Diego) / Martínez threw a perfect game through nine but gave up a leadoff double in the 10th. Rojas came in and retired the next three batters to secure the Expos' victory.

The New York Yankees' Horace Clarke broke up three
ninth-inning no-hit bids in 1970 within a month's span.
(Photo from National Baseball Hall of Fame and Museum)

CHAPTER 16

NO-HITTER KILLERS

I'm glad somebody got a hit, and it just happened it was me. Nobody likes to be in a no-hitter.

—Horace Clarke

Dock Ellis, Clyde Wright, Bill Singer, and Vida Blue all threw no-hitters during the 1970 season, and each should have immediately called and thanked a career .256 hitter named Horace Clarke.

Why?

Because they didn't face the no-hitter killer.

Clarke, the bespectacled, slightly bowlegged New York Yankees second baseman hailing from the U.S. Virgin Islands, crowned himself baseball's late-inning breakup king in the summer of 1970, ending three ninth-inning no-hit bids within a month's span. He didn't get to the four aforementioned pitchers, but Clarke and a few others made their names for being no-hitter killers.

3X Club

On June 4, 1970, at Yankee Stadium, the Kansas City Royals' Jim Rooker entered the bottom of the ninth nursing a 1-0 lead without yielding a Yankees hit. Horace Clarke led off and cracked a clean single into left field, killing Rooker's no-no. To add salt to the wound, Rooker lost the decision when Bobby Murcer doubled Clarke in, and to rub it in, Clarke won the game in the 12th with a sac fly off a reliever.

Fifteen days later against the Red Sox at Fenway, Clarke stood as the impediment to Sonny Siebert's second career no-hitter. Siebert, who had tossed his first no-no as a member of the Indians in 1966, held the Yankees hitless until Clarke led off the ninth by drilling a 2-0 fastball into right field for a single.

"It thought I had a chance for it," Siebert told a reporter. "But I cooled off in the last of the eighth when we had a long inning and scored two runs. I wasn't popping my fastball in the ninth."[180]

Siebert wound up giving up four earned runs before reliever Sparky Lyle put out the fire to secure the 7-4 win.

Thirteen days after Clarke's second no-no slaying, he did it again. Detroit Tigers knuckleballer Joe Niekro was dominating the Yankees lineup on July 2, 1970, holding his opponents to just a pair of walks. He opened the top of the ninth inning by getting Pete Ward to fly out and was just two outs away from history. Clarke stepped to the plate with one out and bounced a ball in the hole between first and second. Second baseman Dick McAullife made a nice stop, but his throw pulled the covering Niekro off the first-base bag. An infield hit, and a no-hitter no more. Clarke had broken the hearts of fans, teams, and, most important, pitchers three times in 28 days.

Clarke still reigns as king of ninth-inning no-no breakups in the same season, but the Minnesota Twins' Joe Mauer tied him for the career mark by breaking up three ninth-inning no-hitters over a six-year span:

- On May 6, 2008, facing the White Sox' Gavin Floyd, Mauer hit a one-out double. Bobby Jenks came in to retire the final two batters to complete the 7-1 victory.
- On August 23, 2010, facing the Rangers' Neftali Feliz with a runner on first, Mauer hit a one-out single to break up a potential combined no-no by Rich Harden (six and two-thirds innings), Matt Harrison (one-third inning), Darren O'Day (one inning),

and Feliz (one inning). Feliz followed with a wild pitch but recovered to get the two final outs for a 4-0 combined one-hitter.

- And on May 24, 2013, facing the Tigers' Aníbal Sánchez, Mauer hit a one-out single. Sánchez struck out the next two batters to secure the 6-0 one-hitter.

2X Club

In one week in 1989, the Blue Jays' Nelson Liriano broke up no-hitters in the ninth, including one against none other than Nolan Ryan. Ryan was working on what would have been his sixth no-hitter on April 23, 1989, when Liriano tagged him for a one-out triple in the ninth and scored on a groundout. Ryan had to settle for one of his record-tying 12 career one-hitters. (Ryan gets no sympathy, however, as he collected his sixth no-no in 1990 and his seventh in 1991.)

Six days later, Liriano did it again. On April 28, the Angels' Kirk McCaskill held the Blue Jays hitless through eight innings. Sent up as a pinch hitter to lead off the ninth, Liriano responded with a double, ending McCaskill's bid for the record books.

In the spring and summer of 1969, the Twins' Cesar Tovar tagged two Orioles pitching greats in the ninth. On May 15, Tovar nailed Dave McNally with a ninth-inning, one-out single. And on August 10, he killed Mike Cuellar's no-no attempt with a ninth-inning single.

The Angels' Wally Joiner broke up two ninth-inning no-hitters in 1986, frustrating the Rangers' Charlie Hough and the Tigers' Walt Terrell.

One Boston Braves veteran from the Dead Ball Era killed New York Giants no-hitters late in back-to-back games, if not in the ninth. Still, not too shabby.

On September 28, 1916, in the second game of a doubleheader, Ed Konetchy broke up a no-hitter being thrown by the Giants' Ferdie Schupp with a seventh-inning single. In the very next game, the opener of a September 30 Braves-Giants doubleheader, Konetchy killed Rube Benton's no-no with an eighth-inning single through the pitchers' box.

1X Club

The one-time no-hit-killer club may seem like an afterthought, but it feels as poignant and significant as the pitcher with one no-hitter. So near to greatness but not as remembered as so many others who achieved the feat multiple times. It matters more when the disparity between the quality of the hitter and pitcher is so great as to make the breaking up of the no-hitter that much more incredible. And even more so when the pitcher in question is two outs from breaking a team curse.

Exhibit A: Jim Qualls. Many old-time Mets fans know where they were July 9, 1969, when Qualls, a rookie batting just .234, ruined Tom Seaver's no-hitter with a weak single into the outfield.

Almost as dramatic, there's even been a father-son duo to break up ninth-inning no-hitters, albeit 20 years apart. On April 15, 1983, the White Sox' Jerry Hairston killed Milt Wilcox's perfect game for the Tigers with two outs in the ninth with a single to center. Nineteen years later, on September 3, 2002, the Orioles' Jerry Hairston Jr. led off the ninth with a single against Joaquin Benoit to end a Rangers' combined no-hitter.

HERE ARE SOME further notes on the matter of broken no-hitters.

First, two major-league hitters—Cesar Tovar and Eddie Milner— hold the distinction of having a complete game's lone hit five different times, though not all of those breakups happened in the latter innings, when such deeds are noteworthy.

As noted earlier, two of Tovar's feats were ninth-inning breakups, but he also broke up a no-hitter in the sixth in 1967 against the Senators and in 1975 with the Rangers against Yankees' Jim "Catfish" Hunter, also a sixth-inning single. Most oddly, when he was still with the Twins, his leadoff bunt single on August 13, 1970, was the only hit of the game against the Senators' Jim Bosman.

The Reds' Eddie Milner had one ninth-inning breakup. On August 24, 1983, the Chicago Cubs' Chuck Rainey was one out away from a no-hitter when Milner jumped on the first pitch and singled up the middle. But four other times, he had the lone hit of the game for Cincinnati: twice in 1982, once in 1984, and once in 1986.

As with all sports, a single throw, swing, run, shot, kick, or stroke can make the difference between immortality and a really bad day. Horace Clarke, we remember ye fondly, even as fans continue to link your name to an era of Yankee struggles.

EXTRA-INNING
NO-HITTERS (COMPLETED)

SPORTS AND PASTIMES.

An Unprecedented Base Ball Contest at Washington Park.

Ten Innings Without a Run—The Toledo and Brooklyn Nines Tie—Darkness Prevents a Settlement of the Match—Twelfth Annual Re-
the Pioneer Boat

The *Brooklyn Daily Eagle* called Kimber's 0-0 10-inning no-no an "unprecedented base ball contest." *(Image from* Brooklyn Daily Eagle*)*

Sam Kimber
Brooklyn Atlantics (AA)
Saturday, October 4, 1884
Brooklyn Atlantics 0, Toledo Blue Stockings 0 (10 inn.)
Washington Park (Brooklyn)

George "Hooks" Wiltse
New York Giants (NL)
Saturday, July 4, 1908 (first game of doubleheader)
New York Giants 1, Philadelphia Phillies 0 (10 inn.)
Polo Grounds (New York)

Fred Toney
Cincinnati Reds (NL)
Wednesday, May 2, 1917
Cincinnati Reds 1, Chicago Cubs 0 (10 inn.)
Weeghman Park (Chicago)
The Cubs' Hippo Vaughn threw nine no-hit innings in this game but lost in the 10th.

Jim Maloney
Cincinnati Reds (NL)
Thursday, August 19, 1965 (first game of doubleheader)
Cincinnati Reds 1, Chicago Cubs 0 (10 inn.)
Wrigley Field (Chicago)
Maloney's first of two official no-hitters; he also threw 10 innings of no-hit ball against the Mets on June 14, 1965, but lost in the 11th.

Francisco Cordova (9 inn.), Ricardo Rincon (1 inn.)
Pittsburgh Pirates (NL)
Saturday, July 12, 1997
Pittsburgh Pirates 3, Houston Astros 0 (10 inn.)
Three Rivers Stadium (Pittsburgh)

Umpire Jim Joyce apologized to Armando Galarraga for messing up the call
that cost Galarraga a perfect game. The pitcher said he appreciated
the gesture and gave Joyce credit for being a stand-up guy.
(Photo by KeithAllisonPhoto.com)

CHAPTER 17

THE IMPERFECT CALL

He probably feels more bad than me. Nobody's perfect. Everybody's human.

—Detroit Tigers pitcher Armando Galarraga

Detroit Tigers pitcher Armando Galarraga was dominating the Cleveland Indians lineup at Comerica Park on June 2, 2010, holding a 3-0 lead in the top of the ninth inning after retiring the first 26 batters he had faced. The 6-foot-3, 230-pound right-hander was one out away from the majors' 21st perfect game, and it seemed that only Cleveland shortstop Jason Donald stood between Galarraga and baseball immortality.

With 17,738 fans standing in expectation, Galarraga threw a 1-1 breaking ball and got Donald to hit a ground ball into the hole between first base and second base. First baseman Miguel Cabrera cut in front of Carlos Guillen to snag the ball, planted his feet, and threw a perfect feed to Galarraga, who had streaked over to cover first base. Galarraga squeezed his glove and stepped on the bag a full step ahead of Donald. The Tigers were about to break out in celebration, but the actual man standing between Galarraga and baseball immortality was first-base umpire Jim Joyce. The veteran arbiter swung out his arms and signaled, "Safe."

"He's out … no, he's safe!" said the puzzled FOX Sports Detroit play-by-play announcer Mario Impemba. "He is safe. He is safe at first base."[181]

A shocked Galarraga just stood there smiling, his thoughts unbetrayed by his expression. A bewildered Cabrera wrapped his hands around the back of his head. Tigers manager Jim Leyland rushed out to the field to confront Joyce, but his conversation was terse.

The verdict emerged as replays slowed down the action for television viewers: Donald was out, and he was out by a mile.

Fans continued booing, but Galarraga shook off the injustice and got Trevor Crowe to ground out to third base for the final out. He headed into the Tigers locker room with a complete-game, one-hit shutout.

Umpires seldom address the media, but Joyce had a chance to watch the replays and decided to acknowledge his mistake. He told reporters he had a great angle on the play and "just missed the damn call."

"This is a history call, and I kicked the shit out of it. And there's nobody who feels worse than I do," Joyce said. "I take pride in this job and I kicked the shit out of that and I took a perfect game away from that kid over there who worked his ass off all night."[182]

Joyce sought out the 27-year-old pitcher and asked him to come to the umpires' locker room so he could personally apologize. A gracious Galarraga said he appreciated the gesture and gave Joyce credit for being a stand-up guy.

"I give the guy a lot of credit for saying, 'I need to talk to you,'" Galarraga said. "You don't see an umpire tell you that after a game. I gave him a hug."[183]

IF THERE WAS one person who could empathize with Galarraga, it was retired Chicago Cubs pitcher Milt Pappas, who was watching the Tigers-Indians game on TV from his home in Illinois. Pappas had retired the first 26 batters during his September 2, 1972, bid for a perfect game before losing it on a walk when umpire Bruce Froemming called three straight pitches outside.

Pappas said he at least got to salvage a no-hitter; Galarraga had no such consolation prize. "The whole world could see he was out," Pappas said of Joyce's call at first. "It should have been a perfect game."[184]

THE MORNING AFTER Galarraga's near perfecto, Michigan Governor Jennifer Granholm issued a proclamation stating that Galarraga had retired 27 straight batters and thus pitched a perfect game. That's fine, but it's MLB's declarations that matter in the record books.

Eyes turned to Commissioner Bud Selig. Would he use his "best interests of baseball" power to step in and award Galarraga the perfect game? Selig's answer was no, though he pledged to look into expanding replay, which at the time was used only to determine home runs. "While the human element has always been an integral part of baseball, it is vital that mistakes on the field be addressed," Selig said in a statement. "Given last night's call and other recent events, I will examine our umpiring system, the expanded use of instant replay and all other related features."[185]

Selig's remarks drew the ire of *Detroit Free Press* columnist Mitch Albom, who called Selig the "latest commissioner to resist technology available to any guy with a black-and-white television."

"You can't say baseball doesn't want instant replay because it *already has it*," Albom wrote. "It's on every TV broadcast. It's on most stadium scoreboards. The only people not using instant replays are the umpires. And that's insane."[186]

Pappas agreed. "Everybody has seen the play. Everybody knows that the man was out," he said. "Why didn't he step in and reverse the call?"[187]

The controversy even reached White House press secretary Robert Gibbs, a Tigers fan, who responded to a reporter's question about Selig's refusal to reverse the call. Gibbs joked that the White House was "going to work on an executive order," then praised Galarraga and Joyce for their respectful handling of the situation. "I think it's tremendously heartening to see somebody understand that they made a mistake and somebody accept the apology from somebody who made that mistake," Gibbs said. "I think that's a good lesson in baseball. It's probably a good lesson in Washington."

Figuring that fans might have some lingering hostility toward Joyce when he took the field the next day for the finale of the three-game series, Leyland sent Galarraga out to deliver the Tigers lineup card with a handshake. A tearful Joyce gave Galarraga a pat on the back, and the pitcher returned to the Detroit dugout to applause.

Leyland said he couldn't be prouder of his team and their fans for showing so much class. "To accept that was tough," he told MLB.com. "But they did it like champions and I'm proud of them."[188]

GALARRAGA'S GAME might not be in baseball's record books, but it does have a book of its own. Galarraga and Joyce joined forces in 2012 to tell their tale in *Nobody's Perfect: Two Men, One Call, and a Game for Baseball History.* The pairing carried the unintended consequence of preventing Galarraga and Joyce from ever again appearing at the same time on a baseball diamond, as Major League Baseball now viewed the two as business partners.

PERFECT GAMES LOST ON THE 27TH BATTER

The New York Giants' George "Hooks" Wiltse hit 27th batter George McQuillan with a pitch in the ninth inning to kill the perfect game but finished with a 10-inning no-hitter. *(Photo from Bain News Service Collection, Prints & Photographs Division, Library of Congress, LC-DIG-ggbain-12047)*

It's never easy losing a perfect game on the 27th and supposedly final batter, but George "Hooks" Wiltse, Milt Pappas, and Max Scherzer at least preserved their no-hitters and their spots in the record books. The other 10 pitchers on this list have only the memories of their 26-out accomplishments. Here are 13 potential perfect games zapped by the 27th batter.

- **George "Hooks" Wiltse:** New York Giants (NL) / Saturday, July 4, 1908 (first game of doubleheader) / New York Giants 1, Philadelphia Phillies 0 (10 inn.) / Polo Grounds (New York)

  Wiltse hits George McQuillan with a pitch in the ninth inning to kill the perfect game. He finishes with a 10-inning no-hitter.
- **Tommy Bridges:** Detroit Tigers (AL) / Friday, August 5, 1932 / Detroit Tigers 13, Washington Senators 0 / Navin Field (Detroit)

Dave Harris's clean single to left breaks up the perfect game. Bridges retires Sam Rice on a bouncing grounder to first to preserve the one-hit shutout.

- **Billy Pearce:** Chicago White Sox (AL) / Friday, June 27, 1958 / Chicago White Sox 3, Washington Senators 0 / Comiskey Park (Chicago)

  Ed Fitz Gerald, swinging at the first pitch, lines a double down the right-field line to break up the perfecto. Pierce strikes out Albie Pearson for the one-hit shutout.

- **Milt Pappas:** Chicago Cubs (NL) / Saturday, September 2, 1972 / Chicago Cubs 8, San Diego Padres 0 / Wrigley Field (Chicago)

  Pappas walks Larry Stahl, jaws with umpire Bruce Froemming, then retires Garry Jestadt for the win and the nonperfect no-no.

- **Milt Wilcox:** Detroit Tigers (AL) / Friday, April 15, 1983 / Comiskey Park (Chicago) / Detroit Tigers 6, Chicago White Sox 0

  Jerry Hairston breaks up the perfect game with a pinch-hit single. Wilcox gets Rudy Law to ground out for the one-hit shutout.

- **Ron Robinson:** Cincinnati Reds (NL) / Monday, May 2, 1988 / Riverfront Stadium (Cincinnati) / Cincinnati Reds 3, Montreal Expos 2

  Wallace Johnson singles to left to kill the perfecto, and Tim Raines follows with a two-run home run. John Franco relieves and gets the save to preserve at least a "W" for Robinson.

- **Dave Stieb:** Toronto Blue Jays (AL) / Friday, August 4, 1989 / Toronto Blue Jays 2, New York Yankees 1 / SkyDome (Toronto)

  Roberto Kelly tags Stieb for a double to left to kill the perfect game, and Steve Sax follows with an RBI single to right to kill the shutout.

- **Brian Holman:** Seattle Mariners (AL) / Friday, April 20, 1990 / Seattle Mariners 6, Oakland Athletics 1 / Oakland–Alameda County Coliseum (Oakland)

  Pinch hitter Ken Phelps launches a homer to end Holman's bid for a perfect game. Holman strikes out Rickey Henderson to finish out the win.

- **Mike Mussina:** New York Yankees (AL) / Sunday, September 2, 2001 / New York Yankees 1, Boston Red Sox 0 / Fenway Park (Boston)

   Pinch hitter Carl Everett kills the perfect game by singling to left. Mussina gets Trot Nixon to ground out to preserve the one-hit shutout.

- **Armando Galarraga:** Detroit Tigers (AL) / Wednesday, June 2, 2010 / Detroit Tigers 3, Cleveland Indians 0 / Comerica Park (Detroit)

   Jason Donald hits a ground ball between first base and second base. First baseman Miguel Cabrera cuts in front of Carlos Guillen to snag the ball and throws a perfect feed to Galarraga covering first. Umpire Jim Joyce rules him safe.

- **Yu Darvish:** Texas Rangers / Tuesday, April 2, 2013 / Texas Rangers 7, Houston Astros 0 / Minute Maid Park (Houston)

   Marwin Gonzalez singles to center to break up the perfect game. Jose Altuve takes over on the mound and gives up another hit before preserving the shutout for Darvish.

- **Yusmeiro Petit:** San Francisco Giants / Saturday, September 6, 2013 / San Francisco Giants 3, Arizona Diamondbacks 0 / AT&T Park (San Francisco)

   Eric Chavez singles to right to zap the perfecto. Petit retires A. J. Pollock to preserve the one-hit shutout.

- **Max Scherzer:** Washington Nationals / Saturday, June 20, 2015 / Washington Nationals 6, Pittsburgh Pirates 0 / Nationals Park (Washington, D.C.)

   Scherzer hits pinch hitter José Tabata in the elbow with a slider but recovers to get Josh Harrison to fly out to left to complete the no-hitter.

Hall of Fame broadcaster Mel Allen knew that neither his words nor his actions influenced the on-field action, but he followed the practice of not mentioning a no-hitter in progress out of respect for the dugout tradition.

(Photo from New York World Telegram & Sun *Newspaper Photograph Collection, Prints & Photographs Division, Library of Congress, LC-USZ62-112027)*

CHAPTER 18

MUM'S THE WORD

It's one of the great things that separate it from the other sports,
like the seventh-inning stretch or Take Me Out to the Ball Game.

—HALL OF FAME SPORTSCASTER MEL ALLEN
ON BASEBALL SUPERSTITION

Baseball has long embraced superstition, and what happens in the dugout often seeps into the press box. The sport's early traditions dissuaded ballplayers from a mere mention of a no-hitter in progress after the fifth inning to spare their pitcher any added pressure. Renowned Brooklyn Dodgers broadcaster Red Barber said "this hoodoo" quickly spread to baseball writers and eventually to broadcasters such as the Yankees' Mel Allen.[189]

"This superstition infected most of the radio booths when radio play-by-play arrived on scene," Barber said. "Mel Allen was a hoodoo medicine man of the most violent order. I never had paid any attention to it."[190]

Allen knew that neither his words nor his actions influenced the on-field action, but the Hall of Fame broadcaster said he followed the practice out of respect for the dugout tradition. He noted, "It's part of the romance of the game."[191]

Mutual Broadcasting paired Allen and Barber to call the 1947 World Series between the Yankees and Dodgers, and the play-by-play men's contrasting no-no styles took center stage when the Bronx Bombers' Bill

Bevens took a no-hitter into the final inning of Game 4. The historic contest is known in baseball circles as "the Cookie Game."

Allen, who called the first half of the game, consistently danced around the phrase "no hits." Barber, who took over the microphone in the middle of the fifth, immediately gave listeners the raw numbers: one run, no hits, no errors for the Dodgers.

"Mel gasped alongside me," Barber recalled. "The rest of the men in the booth were smitten."[192]

Barber stayed the course into the ninth inning as Bevens nursed a 2-1 lead despite yielding 10 bases on balls: "No hits by Bevens, eight and two-thirds innings."

Pinch hitter Cookie Lavagetto then stepped to the plate with two runners on and killed the no-hitter and ended the game with an opposite-field double off the right-field wall. Lavagetto's hit scored the tying and winning runs.

Red Barber, a Hall of Fame broadcaster for the Reds, Dodgers, and Yankees, believed you should tell listeners what's happening on the field, even if a pitcher is throwing a no-hitter. *(Photo from New York World Telegram & Sun Newspaper Photograph Collection, Prints & Photographs Division, Library of Congress, LC-USZ62-112032)*

"Several announcers on various sports programs said I had done the most unsportsmanlike broadcast in radio history," Barber recalled in his book on the 1947 season. "Yankee fans telephoned the papers and radio stations complaining that I had jinxed Bevens. It was a real rhubarb around my red head."[193]

Though several radio and television broadcasters continue to pay homage to the tradition of no-no silence, the days of television camera operators slowly panning the scoreboard's "0 R, 0 H, 0 E" to communicate the impending feat seem to be fading, albeit slowly. Major League Baseball's Twitter account religiously sends out alerts after a pitcher throws seven innings of no-hit ball. There's even an iPhone app to tip fans of no-hitters in progress when they reach a certain threshold. And Fox Sports TV networks commonly add a "No-hitter through X innings" line over the corner scoreboard graphic when a no-no begins to look possible.

Robert Ford, the Houston Astros' radio play-by-play man, said he's glad that broadcasting has evolved beyond the silence. "If you're flipping around the channels and see that, you're going to stop and watch," Ford said. "If guys are talking in code or no one says anything, you're less likely to stop at that."[194]

Legendary broadcaster Vin Scully is adamant that announcers should call 'em as they see 'em. But as a 27-year-old play-by-play man playing second fiddle to Allen for Game 5 of the 1956 World Series, he deferred to the 43-year-old veteran's protocol. Don Larsen was throwing a perfect game when Scully took over in the fifth inning, and Allen was simply stating, "That's the 15th man he's retired."

"So I picked right up, 'That's the 16th man, that's the 18th, that's the 20th,'" the Dodgers' play-by-play man told *GQ* magazine. "Today I would say, 'Call your friends, this fella is pitching a perfect game!'"[195]

But Scully, who has called more than 6 percent of the league's no-hitters over his 65-year storied career, said it insults listeners to withhold information based on the fallacy that what an announcer says affects the game. "You see, no one expects a listener to hang on every word for three hours," Scully told the *Los Angeles Times*. "They leave the radio from time to time and this service must be rendered."[196]

Carl Erskine, who threw two no-hitters in his Dodgers playing days before doing a little broadcast work, sees no harm in mentioning an ongoing no-no. "Actually, the pitcher certainly knows it all the time," Erskine said. "It's always obvious that the other team is trying to break it up. So why not tell the fans about the no-hitter?"[197]

If ever there was a team with good cause to buy into the no-hitter jinx, it was the New York Mets. The team spent 50 years desperately seeking its first no-no until Johan Santana accomplished the feat on June 1, 2012. Mets WFAN radio announcer Howie Rose had commonly uttered "no-hitter" during his previous radio broadcasts, but the native New Yorker decided to take a different tack while calling the team's 8,020th regular-season game. "I said let me try something a little different tonight, and I said, 'The Mets have all the hits and all the runs,' and, you know, all things like that," Rose noted in a postgame radio chat with *SportsNet New York* television announcer Gary Cohen.[198]

Cohen, who shuns the jinx concept, said he uttered "no-hitter" regularly in the TV booth from the fifth inning on, and "somehow it happened nonetheless."[199]

Bob Uecker, longtime radio play-by-play man for the Milwaukee Brewers, said on-air no-no silence is part of baseball lore, but to him it means nothing.

"Everybody knows it," Uecker said. "That stuff about jinxing, I think if you ask guys who have thrown no-hitters, it doesn't bother them. They know it. They're looking at the scoreboard all the time."[200]

When the Los Angeles Angels' Jered Weaver threw his 2012 no-hitter a month before Santana's effort, Angels play-by-play announcer Victor Rojas and color analyst Mark Gubicza stuck to the unwritten code. Rojas told the *Los Angeles Times* that he made no mention of the no-no and refused to alter his booth routine. "Some people say jinxes have no place in sports, but that's just how I am," said Rojas, whose dad, Cookie Rojas, played 16 seasons in the majors. "I didn't move from my position after the third inning. I didn't move any paper. I put my pens back in the same spot."[201]

The Tampa Bay Rays' TV crew didn't want to jinx Matt Garza on July 26, 2010, when the right-hander was on the verge of throwing that franchise's first-ever no-no. Sun Sports play-by-play announcer Dewayne Staats framed the situation in every way possible without actually saying "no-hitter." Viewers can see the box score at the end of each inning noting that a team has no hits, he said. "At one point, I said, 'Garza has faced the minimum and has allowed only one base runner and that came on a walk,'" Staats told a reporter. "So I'm essentially saying it without saying it."[202]

Steve Busby, TV play-by-play man for the Texas Rangers, says he doesn't make a big deal out of a no-hitter but isn't opposed to saying it.
(Photo by Dirk Lammers)

Ford, who has called two minor-league no-hitters, was broadcasting his second Astros game on April 2, 2013, when the Texas Rangers' Yu Darvish lost a perfect game in the ninth. He made no effort to conceal what Darvish was doing, and he said the reason why no-hitters and perfect games often fall short is because they're difficult to complete. "It's not because the broadcaster said there was a no-hitter," he said.[203]

Steve Busby threw two no-hitters for the 1970s Kansas City Royals before settling into the Rangers' TV booth as a play-by-play man. He said he doesn't dance around a no-no in progress, and Darvish has never accused him of jinxing his near misses. "I don't make a big deal out of it, but I'm not opposed to saying there's a no-hitter going," Busby said. "I don't go out of my way to say it, but I don't avoid it, either."[204]

Allen, best known nationally for his longtime stint as *This Week in Baseball* host and his "How about that?" catchphrase, continued to honor the "hoodoo" tradition late into his career. The Voice of the Yankees danced around the "no hits" phrase into the ninth inning of Dave Righetti's July 4, 1983, no-hitter against the Boston Red Sox. "And they'll roar on every pitch here now if Dave Righetti can turn the trick," Allen said. "There have been eight hits in the game; the Yankees have had 'em all.[205]

ONE PITCHER WHO wanted to hear some chatter during his no-hitters was the Philadelphia Phillies' Jim Bunning. Bunning was working on a no-hitter in the seventh inning of a May 29, 1964, day game at Connie Mack Stadium, nursing a 5-0 lead over the Houston Colt .45s. The Kentucky-born right-hander was no stranger to the no-no. As a Detroit Tigers starter in 1958, Bunning no-hit a talented Boston Red Sox lineup that featured batting champions Ted Williams and Pete Runnels. And he completed his Tigers no-no by following the superstitious baseball tradition of not talking to his teammates, manager, or coaches. Bunning said he felt like collapsing from tension after it was over, but the superstition worked, so he followed the same protocol in '64 against Houston.

"Nobody is saying anything, and everyone is staying away from me," he recalled in a 2015 interview. "And I blew it."[206]

Bunning lost the no-no and the shutout in the top of the seventh inning, then lost the lead in the top of the eighth inning on an error and four more Colt .45s' hits—so much for superstition. "I said if I ever get close again, I'm going to talk about it to anybody who will listen," Bunning said. "And that's what I did in New York."[207]

Weeks later at Shea Stadium, Bunning was mowing down a string of Mets batters during the first game of a Father's Day doubleheader and reached the fifth inning with the no-no still intact. He threw a straight changeup to Jesse Gonder, who hit the ball in the hole between first base and second base. Second baseman Tony Taylor dove at the ball and threw from his knees to nab the slow-footed Gonder by two steps.

When Bunning returned to the dugout after getting the third out, he kept his promise and broke protocol to lighten the mood. "I said, 'Hey, guys, five perfect innings. Now let's start diving at the ball.'"[208]

Bunning hit a two-RBI double to help his cause, then returned to the mound to continue to retire Mets batters. And he continued talking. "The manager got away from me," he said. "He walked off the bench when I was on it. He stayed completely away from me."[209]

But Bunning completed the National League's first perfect game in 84 years by striking out pinch hitter John Stephenson and got to celebrate Father's Day with a kiss from his 12-year-daughter, Barbara, who had been cheering him on from behind home plate.

SAVED BY THE GLOVE

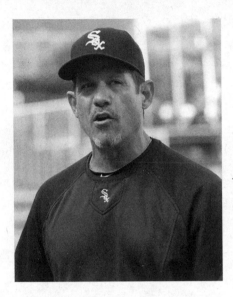

Juan Nieves threw the first no-hitter for the Milwaukee Brewers franchise, thanks in part to a diving catch by Robin Yount for the final out. *(Photo by KeithAllisonPhoto.com)*

Pitchers typically get the glory from no-hitters, but most efforts are aided and abetted by at least one stellar defensive play over the course of a nine-inning game. Such saves draw more excitement when they're made with two outs in the ninth.

The Milwaukee Brewers' Juan Nieves was mixing a few sharp curveballs into a plethora of cutting and sinking fastballs on April 15, 1987, holding the Orioles hitless through eight innings. Brewers catcher Bill Schroeder said the seven guys behind Nieves were all doing their part.

"Jim Paciorek made a diving catch," Schroeder said. "Paul Molitor stabbed one down the line. Dale Sveum got a bad hop at short but got an out."[210]

Nieves took the mound for the top of the ninth inning and quickly put himself one out from history, enticing a pair of first-pitch groundouts before issuing his fifth walk of the night to Cal Ripken Jr. Up stepped Eddie Murray, who had been robbed of a base hit in the second inning by Paciorek. Murray swung at the first pitch and drove the high fastball deep to right-center field, but the wind-drifting ball popped into the glove of a diving Robin Yount.

"To watch Robin make the belly-flop catch to preserve it, I think that's the one thing you remember about that whole game—the last out." said Brewers radio announcer Bob Uecker. "It was one of those games where everything was right."[211]

Some memorable ninth-inning no-no-saving plays from this decade:

- On October 6, 2010, in the first National League Divisional Series, the Philadelphia Phillies' Roy Halladay was one out away from completing baseball's second postseason no-hitter when the Reds' Brandon Phillips dribbled a ball just in front of the plate. Catcher Carlos Ruiz maneuvered around the dropped bat to field the ball before throwing from his knees to nab Phillips at first.
- The Washington Nationals' Jordan Zimmermann was working a no-hitter during the final regular-season game of 2014 when Christian Yelich hit a deep fly ball to left-center field. Nats rookie Steven Souza, a late-inning defensive replacement, chased down the ball and made a diving catch to save Zimmermann's no-no.
- This one was with no outs in the ninth, but White Sox outfielder Dewayne Wise saved Mark Buehrle's July 23, 2009, perfecto by running back to the wall and robbing what had been destined to be a home run off the bat of the Rays' Gabe Kapler.

Dock Ellis says he was tripping on LSD when he threw his no-hitter in 1970. *(Photo from National Baseball Hall of Fame and Museum)*

CHAPTER 19

THE ACID-WASHED NO-NO

It was a lovely summer's morning, an off day in L.A. / So thought one Dock Ellis, as he would later say.

—CHUCK BRODSKY, *Dock Ellis's No-No*

The date was June 10, 1970, and the Pittsburgh Pirates had just finished a Wednesday-afternoon game in San Francisco. The Pirates boarded a plane bound for San Diego to enjoy a scheduled day off ahead of a four-game series against the Padres. Dock Ellis, a 25-year-old Pirates pitcher who had grown up in Los Angeles, got permission to head home to visit childhood friend Al Rambo.

It was the '70s, and the free-spirited Ellis liked to kick back on his off days. He rented a car at the airport, dropped some acid, and started driving north, figuring the hallucinogen's effects wouldn't fully kick in until he reached L.A. He arrived at the home of Rambo's girlfriend, Mitzi, "high as a Georgia pine."[212]

According to his account in the *Dallas Observer*, Ellis spent Wednesday night downing screwdrivers, smoking pot, and popping amphetamines before dozing off early Thursday morning. He awoke sometime after noon and dropped another tab of LSD, and as the partying continued, Thursday evolved into Friday.[213]

Thinking he had a full day of partying ahead of him, Ellis took another hit of acid. But Friday's newspaper had arrived, and Mitzi was reading the sports page when an item caught her eye: Ellis was to start Game 1 of a doubleheader 120 miles south in San Diego—in four hours.

No way, Ellis said; he wasn't scheduled to pitch until Friday.

"It *is* Friday," Mitzi informed him. "You slept through Thursday."[214]

"I said, 'Ah, wow, what happened to yesterday?'" Ellis told American Public Media's *Weekend America*. "She said, 'I don't know, but you've got to get to that airport.'"[215]

Ellis rushed to LAX, boarded a $9.50 shuttle flight, and arrived in San Diego 22 minutes later. He hailed a cab to San Diego Stadium and headed to the dugout, where a female acquaintance clutching a gold pouch awaited with a fix of Benzedrine. Ellis popped a handful of "bennies" in an attempt to regain his wits.

A misty rain hovered over the ball field, and Ellis hoped it would erupt into a downpour so he wouldn't have to take the mound while still tripping. Then the national anthem singer belted out, "Oh, say, can you see ..."

"Damn. Looks like I'm gonna have to pitch," Ellis thought.[216]

The 6-foot-3, 205-pound right-hander said the ball sometimes felt as large as a volleyball and sometimes seemed to shrink into a golf ball. Ellis walked two batters in the first inning and one in the third, contributing to a base-on-balls tally that would eventually reach eight. In the fourth inning, he plunked Ivan Murrell.

"I didn't see the hitters," Ellis said. "All I could tell was if they was on the right side or the left side. The catcher put tape on his fingers so I could see the signals."[217]

Ellis's recollections of the game are spotty. He remembers diving out of the way of one ball that he thought was a hard-hit line drive. It was actually a slow roller, and third baseman Bob Robertson grabbed the ball and threw it to first for the out. He remembers rookie Dave Cash turning to him in the dugout sometime in the middle innings and breaking baseball code by uttering, "You've got a no-no going."

Chuck Brodsky, a singer-songwriter who has penned numerous baseball-related tunes, describes what Ellis must have been feeling in his song "Dock Ellis' No-No":

Sometimes he saw the catcher, sometimes he did not
Sometimes he held a beach ball, other times it was a dot
Dock was tossing comets that were leaving trails of glitter
At the seventh-inning stretch, he still had a no-hitter[218]

A ticket stub from Dock Ellis's no-hitter in San Diego
(Photo from Robert Edward Auctions, www.robertedwardauctions.com)

Ellis wasn't paying attention to the score, but if he had glanced at the stadium display, he would have discerned that he was nursing a 2-0 lead compliments of Willie Stargell's solo homers in the second and seventh innings. Ellis said he was simply concentrating on getting the batters out. "And I'm throwin' a crazy game," he told *Weekend America*. "I'm hittin' people, walkin' people, throwin' balls in the dirt. They going everywhere!"[219]

Ellis somehow made it to the ninth inning, and the team mobbed him in celebration after he caught Ed Spiezio looking at a curveball for the final out. "I didn't think I had good enough stuff to throw a no-hitter," Ellis told a reporter after the game. "The ball I was throwing was moving and I walked so many because I was throwing away from the hitter."[220]

ELLIS MADE NO MENTION of the drugs in game-day accounts, and his original no-no tale revealed six years after the game was far tamer. The

1976 book *Dock Ellis in the Country of Baseball*, cowritten by Ellis and poet Donald Hall, said that Ellis had been drunk on vodka and tried to sober up by drinking coffee before throwing his no-no. That was a lie, Hall later said.

Ellis, who had been traded to the Yankees at the end of the 1975 season, feared repercussions from George Steinbrenner, so the authors sanitized the story. After Bob Smizik of the *Pittsburgh Press* broke the LSD angle of Ellis's no-no story in 1984, Ellis and Hall revised their book with the now outed story. The 1989 second edition of *Dock Ellis in the Country of Baseball* got rid of the vodka and coffee to tell the tale with LSD and bennies.

Ellis, who once drew a fine for wearing hair curlers during batting practice and once began a game by plunking the first three Cincinnati Reds batters, gave up drugs after his baseball career and later became a prison drug counselor.

New York Yankees pitcher David Wells made his own no-no-under-the-influence revelation decades later, acknowledging in his 2004 autobiography that he was half-drunk when he threw a perfect game on May 17, 1998. Wells retired each of the 27 Minnesota Twins hitters at Yankee Stadium that day while battling a wicked hangover spurred by an overnight *Saturday Night Live* cast party.[221]

There's a good chance that Wells is not the only pitcher to have tossed down a few potent potables prior to throwing a no-no, but it's doubtful that anyone has—or will want to—duplicate Ellis's accomplishment.

The late Robin Williams expressed amazement at Ellis's feat during an HBO comedy special, wondering how someone who was tripping could stay on task for that long. "If I took LSD, I'd be talking to every blade of grass like, 'Sorry … sorry … sorry," Williams said. "He should have his own black-light room at the Hall of Fame."[222]

NO-NOS, WITH OR WITHOUT THE K'S

Earl Hamilton (pictured), "Sad" Sam Jones, and Ken Holtzman all threw no-hitters without a single strikeout. *(Photo from Bain News Service Collection, Prints & Photographs Division, Library of Congress, LC-USZ62-98946)*

A pitcher who throws a no-hitter typically dominates the opposing team's lineup, often striking out quite a few batters along the way. Nolan Ryan holds several of the top spots for batters gunned during a no-no, sharing the No. 1 record of 17 strikeouts with Max Scherzer.

But not every no-hitter is rich in strikeouts, as evidenced by three no-hit games thrown without a single "K" on the scorecard. Here are the lists for both ends of the no-no strikeout spectrum (We flesh out our "most" list to third place to celebrate some additional great games).

0—FEWEST STRIKEOUTS IN A NO-HITTER

Earl Hamilton
St. Louis Browns (AL) / Friday, August 30, 1912 / St. Louis Browns 5, Detroit Tigers 1 / Navin Field (Detroit)

"Sad" Sam Jones
New York Yankees (AL) / Tuesday, September 4, 1923 / New York Yankees 2, Philadelphia Athletics 0 / Shibe Park (Philadelphia)

Ken Holtzman
Chicago Cubs (NL) / Tuesday, August 19, 1969 / Chicago Cubs 3, Atlanta Braves 0 / Wrigley Field (Chicago) *(His first of two no-hitters)*

17—MOST STRIKEOUTS IN A NO-HITTER

Nolan Ryan
California Angels (AL) / Sunday, July 15, 1973 / California Angels 6, Detroit Tigers 0 / Tiger Stadium (Detroit) *(His second of seven no-hitters)*

Max Scherzer
Washington Nationals (NL) / Saturday, October 3, 2015 (second game of doubleheader) / Washington Nationals 2, New York Mets 0 / Citi Field (New York) *(His second of two no-hitters)*

16—SECOND-MOST STRIKEOUTS IN A NO-HITTER

Nolan Ryan
Texas Rangers (AL) / Wednesday, May 1, 1991 / Texas Rangers 3, Toronto Blue Jays 0 / Arlington Stadium (Texas) *(His seventh of seven no-hitters)*

15—THIRD-MOST STRIKEOUTS IN A NO-HITTER

Warren Spahn
Milwaukee Braves (NL) / Friday, September 16, 1960 / Milwaukee Braves 4, Philadelphia Phillies 0 / Milwaukee County Stadium *(His first of two no-hitters)*

Nolan Ryan
California Angels (AL) / Saturday, September 28, 1974 / California Angels 4, Minnesota Twins 0 / Anaheim Stadium *(His third of seven no-hitters)*

Don Wilson
Houston Astros (NL) / Sunday, June 18, 1967 / Houston Astros 2, Atlanta Braves 0 / Astrodome (Houston) *(His first of two no-hitters)*

Clayton Kershaw
Los Angeles Dodgers (NL) / Wednesday, June 18, 2014 / Los Angeles Dodgers 8, Colorado Rockies 0 / Dodger Stadium

The St. Louis Browns' Ernie Koob, left, and Bob Groom threw no-hitters on consecutive days in 1917, but the pitchers had their accomplishments separated by the first game of a doubleheader. *(Photos from Bain News Service Collection, Prints & Photographs Division, Library of Congress, LC-DIG-ggbain-22607)*

CHAPTER 20

WET AND WILD, BACK-TO-BACK

When a pitcher's throwing a spitball, don't worry and don't complain, just hit the dry side like I do.

—STAN "THE MAN" MUSIAL

Nineteen sixty-eight and 1969 were tumultuous years in American political and social history. From antiwar riots to the assassinations of Martin Luther King Jr. and Robert Kennedy, from muddy Woodstock to the moon landing, America and the world seemed to be unraveling in anger and reaching new heights.

America's game certainly gave fans a break from the daily news, and they witnessed some firsts. In 1968, the Detroit Tigers' Denny McLain notched 30 victories, the first pitcher to do so in over 30 years, and the two leagues would play the season as the last one before breaking into divisions, introducing the additional League Championship Series round in '69.

Also in '69, baseball dropped the pitching mound height by one-third to 10 inches, made saves an official stat, and watched the Amazin' Mets capture the team's first world championship.

ON THE NO-HITTER FRONT, '68 and '69 saw one-third of all the no-hitters tossed in the '60s: 11 out of 34. In May of '68, the Oakland

Athletics' Catfish Hunter became the first American League pitcher to throw a perfect game since Don Larsen's perfecto in Game 5 of the '56 World Series.

This momentous pair of years—'68 and '69—also witnessed a pair of rare back-to-back no-hitters between opposing teams.

THE 1968 CARDINALS clinched the team's second straight National League pennant in mid-September, making the remaining regular season a mere formality ahead of the World Series, the last time the series would be played by the regular-season league leaders with no preliminary matchups.

St. Louis was making its first postclinch stop in San Francisco, and the Cards took the field at Candlestick Park on September 17, 1968, to face the team they had just eliminated from contention.

The San Francisco Giants were a strong team with a veteran pitching staff led by Juan Marichal (who'd had a no-no in '63), Gaylord Perry, and sluggers such as Willie Mays and Willie McCovey. But the Cardinals boasted a lineup of future Hall of Famers: Lou Brock, Steve Carlton, Orlando Cepeda, and an All-Star rookie pitcher named Bob Gibson. (Gibson would get his no-hitter three years later, in '71.)

Cardinals manager Red Schoendienst sent Gibson to the mound to battle Perry, a seven-year veteran who had developed a reputation for throwing the spitball. It was only considered cheating if you got caught—and he actually did get ejected for tossing a moist orb in 1984.

Giants second baseman Ron Hunt led off the game by launching a Gibson inside fastball over the left-field fence to give San Francisco a 1-0 lead. The lone run was all Perry needed as he proceeded to—literally, perhaps—slip and slide his way through the Cardinals lineup without yielding a single hit.

Perry "caught the Cards in a festive mood" and "knocked the pins out from under them," penned UPI writer Joe Gergen.[223] Perry issued walks in the second and eighth innings but retired 18 consecutive batters between them. "Was it my best stuff?" Perry pondered after the game. "You've got to say so when you pitch a no-hitter. The most important thing was my control."[224]

Reporters asked the Cardinals' Curt Flood, who was caught looking at a called strike three for the game's final out, if Perry was doctoring the baseball. The center fielder didn't take the bait. "You saw it," Flood said. "The guy pitched a great game. What else is there to say?"[225]

If there was nothing else to say, there was certainly plenty to do. And soon.

THE NEXT DAY, on September 18, the Cardinals' Ray Washburn turned the tables on the Giants with his own no-hitter, the first time in major-league baseball history that a no-hit victim responded with one of its own the very next game.

The 30-year-old Washburn walked five batters and needed 138 pitches to complete the task. His catcher, John Edwards, said Washburn was a little wild with his fastball. "As a result, he got behind an awful lot of hitters," Edwards told a reporter. "What saved him was his breaking ball."[226]

Washburn said he started thinking of the no-hitter in the sixth inning, but his teammates stayed focused on breaking a scoreless tie. "By then, the boys were saying 'Let's get some more hits' or 'Let's get some more runs,'" Washburn said. "But nobody said anything about a no-hitter."[227] The Cardinals scored a run each in the seventh and eighth innings, and Washburn completed the 2-0 victory to join the list of elites. Perry popped over to the Cardinals dugout to congratulate his counterpart.

BASEBALL'S SECOND back-to-back no-hitters arrived early the next season, but this exchange wasn't nearly as gentlemanly. The spring 1969 games between the Cincinnati Reds and Houston Astros at Crosley Field carried through the theme of doctored baseballs while adding a twist of nastiness.

The Reds' Jim Maloney was already a no-no veteran. His official no-hitter was a 10-inning, 1-0 victory over the Chicago Cubs in 1965. (Months earlier that same season, he threw 10 innings of no-hit ball against the Mets, but his Reds couldn't score a run, and the Mets' Johnny Lewis tagged Maloney for a leadoff homer in the 11th to ruin the effort.)

But nine innings was enough on April 30, 1969, as the curveball specialist struck out 13 and walked five as he toiled through the Houston lineup without allowing a single hit. The Reds emerged as 10-0 victors. "I wasn't nervous—I've been there before," Maloney said after the game.[228]

Astros manager Harry Walker thought Maloney was a little *too* dominant. The Houston skipper speculated that an unknown greasy substance had aided Maloney's trademark curveball. "He didn't go to his mouth," Walker said, "but he's getting grease on the ball. Back of the neck? I don't know. But he's getting it up there some way."[229]

Maloney's no-no caught Houston in a bad slump. It was the team's eighth straight loss and 15th defeat in 16 games. The Astros were already mad. It took them just nine innings to get even.

Don Wilson, Houston's 24-year-old flamethrower, already had his first no-hitter in hand, having thrown fastball after fastball to no-hit a 1967 Atlanta Braves lineup that included Felipe Alou and Hank Aaron. Come the dawn of a new day—May 1, 1969—and the Astros had slept on being no-hit and were generally ticked off at the Reds. But Wilson was especially mad. The right-hander was still stewing over Cincinnati's 14-0 walloping of Houston at the Astrodome during his previous start against the Reds on April 22. Wilson griped that players in the Reds dugout were laughing at the struggling ball club, and he questioned catcher Johnny Bench's calling for breaking balls on 3-1 counts with such a large lead. Wilson was clear: "They embarrassed us. I was pretty strongly motivated not only for the win but to get the no-hitter. I wanted to prove to them that we're professionals, too."[230]

The fiery Wilson jawed with Reds players throughout the first half of the game. Cincinnati starter Jim Merritt plunked Wilson with a pitch during Wilson's third-inning at-bat, and Wilson returned the favor to Bench in the fifth. No one at Crosley Field that night thought either was an accident.

Wilson was a tad wild, walking six during the game, but he struck out 13 without yielding a base hit. The Astros had their revenge for Maloney's no-hitter the day before, and Wilson had his revenge for the April debacle.

The Reds' manager wasn't exactly congratulatory. "I'm not a Don Wilson fan," said Cincinnati skipper Dave Bristol. "I don't think many of our guys think much of Wilson either."[231]

ONLY ONE OTHER TIME in baseball history had no-hitters been thrown on consecutive days—in 1917—but the two St. Louis Browns pitchers had their accomplishments separated by the first game of a doubleheader.

The Browns' Ernie Koob threw a no-hitter against the Chicago White Sox on May 5. The teams were scheduled for a Sunday-afternoon doubleheader the following day at Sportsman's Park, and the Browns topped the White Sox in the opener 8-4.

Then Bob Groom, who had actually pitched the last two innings of the first game in relief, kept the ball for the nightcap and threw nine hitless for his very own no-hitter and a 3-0 victory. Counting his two innings of relief in the opener, Groom threw 11 consecutive innings of no-hit ball that day.

These 1917 consecutive-day no-hitters by the Browns helped avenge a no-hitter heaped on them just weeks earlier by White Sox pitcher Eddie Cicotte, best remembered as one of the *Eight Men Out*.

. . .

A FUN FOOTNOTE to the end of the '60s: In '63, manager Alvin Dark supposedly joked that there'd be a man on the moon before light-hitting Gaylord Perry would hit a home run. Perry hit the first home run of his career on July 20, 1969, the same day that Neil Armstrong and Buzz Aldrin made their lunar landing.

Technically, Dark was right. The astronauts' steps on the moon beat Perry's launch over the fence by about 20 minutes.

PITCHERS TO NO-HIT
THE SAME TEAM TWICE

The Cleveland Naps' Addie Joss no-hit the Chicago White Sox in 1908 and 1910. *(Photo from Bain News Service Collection, Prints & Photographs Division, Library of Congress, LC-DIG-ggbain-08196)*

Addie Joss
Cleveland Naps (AL) vs. Chicago White Sox (AL)

Friday, October 2, 1908
Cleveland Naps 1, Chicago White Sox 0 (perfect game)
League Park (Cleveland)

Wednesday, April 20, 1910
Cleveland Naps 1, Chicago White Sox 0
South Side Park (Chicago)

Tim Lincecum
San Francisco Giants (NL) vs. San Diego Padres (NL)

Saturday, July 13, 2013
San Francisco Giants 9, San Diego Padres 0
Petco Park (San Diego)

Wednesday, June 25, 2014
San Francisco Giants 4, San Diego Padres 0
AT&T Park (San Francisco)

Larry Corcoran, shown in a 1987 Old Judge Cigarettes baseball card, was the first pitcher to toss three no-hitters. *(Baseball card photo from the Benjamin K. Edwards Collection, Prints & Photographs Division, Library of Congress, LC-DIG-bbc-0207f)*

CHAPTER 21

THREE FOR THREE

I heard Feller pitch his third no-hitter on the radio. I was glad he did it.

—84-YEAR-OLD CY YOUNG, AFTER FELLER
TIED HIS CAREER NO-NO RECORD

No-hitters are considered one of baseball's most rare feats, but 33 major-league pitchers have managed to add more than one no-no to their résumés. The list narrows quickly when raising the bar to three. In fact, it contains just five names.

Two of the pitchers are familiar to every baseball fan of almost any age: Sandy Koufax and Nolan Ryan. Sandy Koufax has four no-hitters, and Nolan Ryan has the likely never-to-be-matched mark of seven.

Following are the three other great pitchers who each threw three no-hitters.

Larry Corcoran

Brooklyn-born Lawrence J. Corcoran made his pro debut in 1880 with the National League's Chicago White Stockings at the age of 20. Corcoran and catcher Silver Flint are believed to have developed base-ball's first signal system, with the pitcher shifting the tobacco in his mouth to indicate the grip of his upcoming throw.

The 5-foot-3, 127-pound right-hander posted a 43-14 record with a

1.95 ERA in his rookie season, splitting the starting duties in tandem with Fred Goldsmith. Corcoran, who could also throw lefty when his right arm was sore, struck out a league-leading 268 batters while also issuing a league-leading 99 walks. His dominance helped the White Stockings capture the 1880 pennant.

On August 19 of that year, Corcoran held the Boston Red Caps hitless during a 6-0 home victory at Lakefront Park. The only base runners reached first on a pair of errors by second baseman Joe Quest and one flub each by shortstop Tom Burns and third baseman Ned Williamson.

"Corcoran was never in such form before, and Flint caught him superbly," the *Chicago Daily Tribune* reported. "It is true that the ball was mushy and shapeless for the greater part of the play but that did not prevent the White Stockings from making eleven hits and thirteen totals off [Tommy] Bond and [Curry] Foley."[232]

Corcoran tossed his second no-no on September 20, 1882, in front of 1,500 fans who braved a raw and disagreeable day to watch the White Stockings take on Worcester. He held the club without a hit during a 5-0 shutout thanks to phenomenal pitching and phenomenal fielding behind him, the *Tribune* said: "This result was partly due to bad luck, as several very good hits were made by Worcester, but each one of them was grabbed by either Williamson, Quest, Burns or (King) Kelly in time to put a man out."[233]

Corcoran's third no-hitter came two years later during a grueling season that destroyed his arm. The hurler no-hit the Providence Grays on June 27, 1884, for a 6-0 win, with the White Stockings scoring two runs each in the seventh and eighth innings.

But in August of that season, manager Cap Anson cut Corcoran's rotation partner, Goldsmith, and Corcoran's tired arm bore the brunt of the work. He ended the season having thrown 516 innings, depleting the gas in his tank. Chicago released Corcoran midway through the 1885 season, and the pitcher made an unsuccessful bid to earn a permanent job with the New York Metropolitans. (To think that Corcoran could have actually thrown the first Mets no-hitter in the 19th century!)

Corcoran played just 14 more games before transitioning to the position of umpire. He died of Bright's disease on October 14, 1891, leaving behind a widow and four children in Newark, New Jersey.

Cy Young

Denton True "Cy" Young pitched his first major-league game for the Cleveland Spiders at the age of 23 on August 6, 1890, and the three-hit, 8-1 victory in the opening game of a doubleheader over the Chicago Colts turned out to be Young's first of a record-setting 511 wins over a 22-year career.

Cy Young warms up for the Boston Red Sox in 1908. *(Photo from Bain News Service Collection, Prints & Photographs Division, Library of Congress, LC-DIG-ppmsca-18467)*

"The new phenomenon is named Young," noted a special telegram in the *Inter Ocean*. "He comes from the Canton Tri-State League club, and his ability will be recognized when it is learned that he is the man who not many moons ago struck out eighteen in a game."[234]

The 6-foot-2, 210-pound right-hander held opponents hitless in three of those 511 wins, with the first no-hitter coming in his eighth season. On September 18, 1897, at the age of 30, Young no-hit Cincinnati with just one base on balls as the Spiders topped the Reds 6-0. "That Cy's arm was in old form this result shows, and nobody ever saw better ball pitching since ball pitching began," noted a *Cincinnati Enquirer* special dispatch.[235]

Young's second no-hitter, at age 37, was a Boston Americans perfect game thrown on May 5, 1904, against the Philadelphia Athletics "without a run, without a hit and without a single runner reaching first base," noted one wire report.

"It was a remarkable exhibition of ball playing, and it will go down in history as the best ever seen on the local grounds," the report said. "One after another of the Athletics stepped up to bat and one after another retired to the bench."[236]

Four years later, on June 30, 1908, Young tied Corcoran with his third no-hitter, an 8-0 Red Sox win over the New York Highlanders that "made hitless Yankees out of the whole outfit," according to the *New York Times*.[237] The then 41-year-old hurler allowed just one base runner on a walk as the Red Sox played error-free baseball. Young helped his cause with three hits that drove in four of Boston's eight runs, and he once crossed the plate himself.

"Even aside from his pitching proclivities, this gay old blade was the life of that party," the *Times* said. "He galloped around the bases like he was out for the Swift Stakes."[238]

A plaque hanging at the Bob Feller Museum in Van Meter, Iowa, celebrates Feller's three no-hitters. *(Photo by Dirk Lammers)*

Young, an Ohio native, returned to Cleveland in 1909 as a member of the American League's Naps. He earned his 500th victory for that squad before being released in August 1911. Young signed with the National League's Boston Rustlers to finish out the final chapter of his storied career.

Bob Feller

Iowa-farm-boy sensation Robert William Andrew Feller had already done about as much damage as he could to high school and American Legion lineups by the summer of 1935, when the Cleveland Indians quietly signed him to a $1 minor-league contract with the Fargo-Moorhead Twins.

The Indians had no plans to send him to North Dakota, but a year later the 17-year-old Feller got the opportunity to pitch three innings of the Indians' All-Star break exhibition game against the St. Louis Cardinals. He struck out eight consecutive Cardinals. "The kid's a natural," Cardinals' star pitcher Dizzy Dean told a reporter. "He can't miss."[239]

Veteran umpire "Red" Ormsby was equally impressed. "I don't care how old the boy is," Ormsby said. "He showed me more speed than I've ever seen uncorked by an American Leaguer, and that doesn't except Walter Johnson when he was in his prime."[240]

Feller's first no-hitter was the famed Opening Day no-no of 1940 (see Chapter 10). His second came early in 1946—his first full season after losing nearly four years of baseball to U.S. Navy duty during World War II. On April 30, Feller carried a 1-2 record into Yankee Stadium and was "amused and slightly peeved about reports he was 'slipping,'" according to sportswriter Jack Hand.[241]

So "Rapid Robert" used baseball's biggest stage to prove critics wrong, throwing the legendary ballpark's first no-hitter. Feller used his fastball and wove in curves and sliders to mow down 11 New York Yankees for a 1-0 victory. "I believe I had better stuff than when I pitched my other no-hitter against the White Sox in the 1940 opener," he said after the game.[242]

By the end of the 1946 season, Feller had zapped any speculation about whether he could successfully return to form from his extended wartime absence. He posted a 26-15 record with a 2.18 ERA while striking out a league-leading 348 batters.

On July 1, 1951, Feller tied the record shared by Young and Corcoran by throwing his third and final no-hitter in the first game of a home doubleheader against the Detroit Tigers. Then 32 years old, Feller called the accomplishment a "marvelous thrill" but said he had better stuff during his second no-no against the Yankees. He had retired every batter he faced by the third inning, but something odd in Feller's delivery prompted pitching coach Mel Harder to visit the mound, according to UP.

"You don't look right. Is anything wrong?" Harder asked.

"The only thing wrong with me is I don't have a damn thing," Feller replied.[243]

But Harder left him in, and Feller completed the 2-1 no-hit victory, striking out five while walking three. A pair of fourth-inning errors by Cleveland led to the Tigers' unearned run.

The postgame celebration was marred a bit when the Indians learned that Yankees manager Casey Stengel had picked his own Bob Lemon over Feller for the American League All-Star team. Lemon's record was 8-6; Feller's was 11-2.

Feller shrugged and guessed he'd "go fishin'."[244]

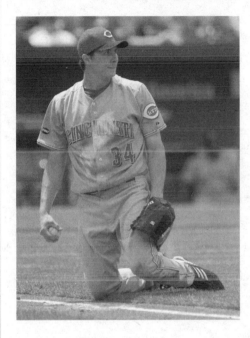

The Cincinnati Reds' Homer Bailey threw no-hitters in 2012 and 2013. *(Photo by KeithAllisonPhoto.com)*

Pud Galvin: For the Buffalo Bisons (NL) in 1880 and 1884

Al Atkinson: For the Philadelphia Athletics (AA) in 1884 and 1886

Adonis Terry: For the Brooklyn Grays/Bridegrooms (NL) in 1886 and 1888

Ted Breitenstein: For the St. Louis Browns (NL) in 1891 and the Cincinnati Reds (NL) in 1898

Christy Mathewson: For the New York Giants (NL) in 1901 and 1905

Frank Smith: For the Chicago White Sox (AL) in 1905 and 1908

Addie Joss: For the Cleveland Naps (AL), a perfect game in 1908 and a no-hitter in 1910

Hubert "Dutch" Leonard: For the Boston Red Sox (AL) in 1916 and 1918

Johnny Vander Meer: For the Cincinnati Reds (NL) in back-to-back starts in 1938

Allie Reynolds: For the New York Yankees (AL) in 1951

Virgil Trucks: For the Detroit Tigers (AL) in 1952

Carl Erskine: For the Brooklyn Dodgers (NL) in 1952 and 1956

Jim Bunning: For the Detroit Tigers (AL), a no-hitter in 1958, and for the Philadelphia Phillies (NL), a perfect game in 1964; first pitcher in modern era to throw no-hitter in both leagues

Warren Spahn: For the Milwaukee Braves (NL) in 1960 and 1961

Jim Maloney: For the Cincinnati Reds (NL) in 1965 and 1969; also threw 10 innings of no-hit ball against the Mets on June 14, 1965, but lost in the 11th

Don Wilson: For the Houston Astros (NL) in 1967 and 1969

Bill Stoneman: For the Montreal Expos (NL) in 1969 and 1972

Ken Holtzman: For the Chicago Cubs (NL) in 1969 and 1971

Steve Busby: For the Kansas City Royals (AL) in 1973 and 1974

Bob Forsch: For the St. Louis Cardinals (NL) in 1978 and 1983

Randy Johnson: For the Seattle Mariners (AL), a no-hitter in 1990, and for the Arizona Diamondbacks (NL), a perfect game in 2004

Hideo Nomo: For the Los Angeles Dodgers (NL) in 1996 and the Boston Red Sox (AL) in 2001

Mark Buehrle: For the Chicago White Sox (AL) in 2007 and 2008

Justin Verlander: For the Detroit Tigers (AL) in 2007 and 2011

Roy Halladay: For the Philadelphia Phillies (NL), a perfect game in the 2010 regular season and a no-hitter in the 2010 NLDS

Homer Bailey: For the Cincinnati Reds (NL) in 2012 and 2013

Tim Lincecum: For the San Francisco Giants (NL) in 2013 and 2014, both against the San Diego Padres

Max Scherzer: For the Washington Nationals (NL) in 2015

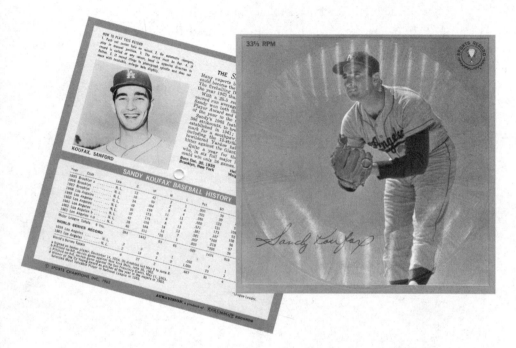

Dodgers pitcher Sandy Koufax, who set a major-league mark by throwing
four career no-hitters, discusses pitching on a 1964 "talking baseball card"
produced by Auravision. *(Photo by Dirk Lammers)*

CHAPTER 22

A SHORT REIGN OF SHEER DOMINANCE

I tried to pitch a no-hitter every time I went out. It seemed like the safest way to try and get everybody out.

—SANDY KOUFAX

There's one easy way to make a left-handed major-league baseball pitcher uncomfortable: Ask him how he compares to Sandy Koufax.

ESPN's Buster Olney brought up the legend during an interview with L.A. Dodger Clayton Kershaw, who had recently no-hit the Colorado Rockies during his stellar 21-3, 1.77 ERA 2014 season. Kershaw, a seven-year veteran, told Olney that he doesn't even want to be in the same category as Koufax, as he's never going to throw 300 innings or strike out 300 batters in a season. "The numbers that he put up are ridiculous," Kershaw said in the *SportsCenter* interview. "I'm not trying to compete with him there. I'm just trying to be me."[245]

Even Nolan Ryan, the Hall of Fame ace who tied Koufax's career record of four no-hitters in 1975 and later broke it by three more no-nos, eschewed comparisons with Koufax. "I'm the only one since Koufax to have a chance at this record, but I don't compare myself to him," Ryan—a righty—told a reporter in 1981. "He was the most over-powering pitcher I've ever seen."[246]

Koufax's career spanned 12 years, beginning in Brooklyn in 1955, but batters say he was practically unhittable between 1962 and 1966, the year he retired due to persistent arm pain.

Koufax was born as Sanford Braun on December 30, 1935, and raised in the New York City borough of Brooklyn by his mother, Evelyn, and stepfather, attorney Irving Koufax. Koufax took great pride in his Jewish faith, which was thrust into the national spotlight in 1965 when he chose not to pitch the opening game of the World Series because it fell on Yom Kippur, Judaism's holiest day.

Koufax played just a couple of years of sandlot ball before transitioning to more-formal fields for four years of high school baseball and a year of college. In a 1964 interview for Auravision's phonographic talking baseball cards, sports announcer Marty Glickman asked Koufax if he had always aspired to be a pitcher. "No, I didn't, but I found out I couldn't hit at a very young age, and that was the only place to go," quipped Koufax, displaying his usual wit.[247]

The Brooklyn Dodgers signed Koufax ahead of the 1955 season, but the left-hander struggled with control in those early years and walked

nearly as many batters as he struck out. Koufax used his 1972 Hall of Fame speech to thank those who had "a lot more faith than I did to be honest" during what began as a "very inglorious career."[248]

"And I had times I would be possibly tempted to go look for a job somewhere for those first six years," Koufax told the Cooperstown crowd.[249]

Two baseballs representing Sandy Koufax's first two no-hitters sit on display at the National Baseball Hall of Fame. *(Photo by Dirk Lammers)*

Koufax's fortunes began to change after the team moved out to Los Angeles, thanks in part to a 1960 Spring Training conversation in the skies over Florida with backup catcher Norm Sherry. The Dodgers were flying from Vero Beach to Orlando for an exhibition match against the Washington Senators when Sherry offered him a bit of advice, according to UPI. "Why don't you take something off your fastball and see what happens?" Sherry suggested. "You throw so hard, few guys can hit you anyway."[250]

Koufax threw seven innings of no-hit ball that afternoon, and the pitcher began shifting his philosophy. On June 30, 1962, he threw his first no-hitter against the expansion New York Mets.

Koufax told the AP's Charles Maher that he had become a pitcher instead of just a thrower. "I finally decided I wasn't going to try to throw the ball past every hitter," he said. "I discovered I could throw pretty well to spots."[251]

Koufax dominated the National League in 1963, capturing the Cy Young Award by leading the league in wins (25), ERA (1.88), shutouts (11), and strikeouts (306). On May 11, 1963, Koufax threw his second no-no against the San Francisco Giants, allowing just two base runners on walks. Giants manager Alvin Dark, who faced Koufax as a batter from 1956 through 1960, said the lefty's fastball just overpowered hitters. "Koufax is the only pitcher I ever played against that I couldn't get a line drive off," Dark told Maher.[252]

Another year brought another great season (19-5 record, 1.74 ERA) and another no-no. On June 4, 1964, Koufax tied Larry Corcoran, Cy Young, and Bob Feller for the league career record by tossing his third no-hitter, striking out 12 Philadelphia Phillies while issuing just one fourth-inning base on balls to Dick Ward. Catcher Doug Camilli threw out Ward as he tried to steal second, allowing Koufax to face the minimum 27 batters during his 3-0 near-perfect win.

In a 1969 interview with sportswriter Lee Mueller, Koufax offered some insight into a pitcher's mentality when he's tossing a no-no. "You begin counting down," Koufax said. "Six more outs, five more, four …

the pressure is always there, although I think after your first no-hitter there's no real increase."[253]

Koufax would finally achieve perfection on September 9, 1965, tossing a perfect game against the Chicago Cubs in front of 29,000 Dodger Stadium fans. His catcher that night, Jeff Torborg, said Koufax was struggling early in the game with his normally dominant curveball. "It was rolling instead of the big snapper that he really could break," Torborg said.[254]

But Koufax proceeded to mow down the Cubs lineup with his fastball, which seemed to get stronger as the game progressed. "As the exceptional pitchers oftentimes do late in the game, it's almost like they sniff something special, and they kick it up a notch," Torborg said. "He started to really pop the ball late in the game, and then his curveball got sharp, too."[255]

Torborg, who was just 23 years old and still "in awe of Sandy," decided that he was not going to make a mistake in the late innings and call for a breaking ball if Koufax was looking to throw fastballs. The only way a Cubs hitter would see a curve would be if Koufax shook off Torborg's sign and called for it himself. "Sandy was well into one of the greatest careers ever when I got there," he said. "I just didn't want to get in the way."

Koufax called for that curve against pinch hitter Joey Amalfitano with one out in the ninth inning, and Torborg jumped as Amalfitano tapped it foul. "I tell you what, the adrenaline was flying, and I got the ball in foul ground," Torborg said. "I was thinking, 'Boy, I'm not taking any chances on that.'"

Koufax crowned his perfect game by fanning pinch hitter Harvey Kuenn, his sixth straight strikeout, to become the first major-league pitcher to throw four no-nos. Dodgers play-by-play man Vin Scully marked the time of the historic moment: 9:46 p.m. PDT. "He has done it four straight years, and now he capped it on his fourth no-hitter—he made it a perfect game," Scully called.[256]

Torborg was likely more nervous than Koufax. "I knew I had the no-hitter all along," Koufax told UPI's George Langford. "But it never entered my mind that it might be a perfect game."[257]

Koufax ended the 1965 season with 382 strikeouts, retiring after the 1966 season as sole owner of the career record for most no-hitters as well as the single-season strikeout record. Both records would eventually fall to "the Ryan Express."

Kevin Millwood threw his own no-hitter with the Philadelphia Phillies and six innings of a combined no-no with the Seattle Mariners. *(Photo by KeithAllisonPhoto.com)*

Five major-league pitchers have thrown their own no-hitters *and* participated in a combined no-no.

Vida Blue
Oakland Athletics (American League)
- **Solo**
  Monday, September 21, 1970
  Oakland Athletics 6, Minnesota Twins 0
  Oakland–Alameda County Coliseum, Oakland
- **Vida Blue** (5 inn.), **Glenn Abbott** (1 inn.), **Paul Lindblad** (1 inn.), **Rollie Fingers** (2 inn.)
  Sunday, September 28, 1975
  Oakland Athletics 5, California Angels 0
  Oakland–Alameda County Coliseum, Oakland

Mike Witt
California Angels (American League)
- **Solo (perfect game)**
  Sunday, September 30, 1984
  California Angels 1, Texas Rangers 0
  Arlington Stadium, Texas
- **Mark Langston** (7 inn.), **Mike Witt** (2 inn.)
  Wednesday, April 11, 1990
  California Angels 1, Seattle Mariners 0
  Anaheim Stadium

Kent Mercker
Atlanta Braves (National League)
- **Solo**
  Friday, April 8, 1994
  Atlanta Braves 6, Los Angeles Dodgers 0
  Dodger Stadium (Los Angeles)
- **Kent Mercker** (6 inn.), **Mark Wohlers** (2 inn.), **Alejandro Peña** (1 inn.)
  Wednesday, September 11, 1991
  Atlanta Braves 1, San Diego Padres 0
  Atlanta–Fulton County Stadium (Atlanta)

Kevin Millwood
Philadelphia Phillies (NL) and Seattle Mariners (AL)
- **Solo**
  Philadelphia Phillies
  Sunday, April 27, 2003
  Philadelphia Phillies 1, San Francisco Giants 0
  Veterans Stadium (Philadelphia)
- **Kevin Millwood** (6 inn.), **Charlie Furbush** (2/3 inn.),
  Stephen Pryor (1/3 inn.), Lucas Luetge (1/3 inn.), **Brandon**

League (2/3 inn), **Tom Wilhelmsen** (1 inn.)
Seattle Mariners (AL)
Friday, June 8, 2012
Seattle Mariners 1, Los Angeles Dodgers 0
Safeco Field (Seattle)

Cole Hamels
Philadelphia Phillies (National League)
- **Solo**
  Saturday, July 25, 2015
  Philadelphia Phillies 5, Chicago Cubs 0
  Wrigley Field (Chicago)
- **Cole Hamels** (6 inn.), **Jake Diekman** (1 inn.), **Ken Giles** (1 inn.), **Jonathan Papelbon** (1 inn.)
  Monday, September 1, 2014
  Philadelphia Phillies 7, Atlanta Braves 0
  Turner Field (Atlanta)

A circle of seven baseball caps at the National Baseball Hall of Fame celebrates Nolan Ryan's seven career no-hitters. *(Photo by Dirk Lammers)*

CHAPTER 23

THE RYAN EXPRESS

Nolan Ryan is pitching much better now that he has his curve ball straightened out.

—SPORTSCASTER JOE GARAGIOLA

When Nolan Ryan threw his second no-hitter in 1973 within two months of his first, UPI sportswriter Fred Down predicted great things from the fast-throwing Texan:

NEW YORK—Nolan Ryan has done it again and most baseball experts think he's capable of doing it again ... and again ... and again.[258]

Down's bold prediction would fall two "and agains" short. Ryan threw an unprecedented seven no-hitters during his 27-year Hall of Fame career, shattering the mark set by the great Sandy Koufax by three.

But it took "the Ryan Express" a few years to get on track. The New York Mets drafted Ryan in the 12th round of the 1965 amateur draft, but the 6-foot-2, 170-pound right-hander never settled into the squad's rotation and was traded to the California Angels before the start of the 1972 season. And his transition to the American League was complicated by baseball's first players' strike, which delayed the start of the season for a week and a half. "When he first came over from the Mets, we spent a lot of time working on his delivery," said the Angels' veteran catcher Jeff Torborg. "We weren't even at a ballpark. We were at a field on State College Boulevard not far from Anaheim Stadium."[259]

Ryan said in his 1999 Hall of Fame induction speech that Angels pitching coach Tom Morgan took him on "as a special project" and vowed that he "wasn't going to allow me to stumble and fall."

"If Tom was here today I would walk up to him and tell him that it was one of the best things that ever happened to me," he said.[260]

Ryan posted his first winning season in 1972 with a 19-16 record and a 2.28 ERA while throwing 329 strikeouts, the best in the AL. But he continued to struggle with control issues, topping the league in both walks (157) and wild pitches (18).

No one was seeing seven no-hitters inside the crystal ball, but it was clear that Ryan was about to blossom, Torborg said. "You knew he was special, and if he was able to harness everything that he had, you could project greatness for Nolan," he said.[261]

RYAN WAS JUST three innings into what would become his first no-hitter on May 15, 1973, when Kansas City Royals manager Jack McKeon put the game under protest. McKeon told the umpires that Ryan's right foot was not keeping contact with the pitching rubber, but his plea had little effect. Ryan struck out 12 and walked three en route to a 3-0 no-hitter.

He hadn't planned on throwing a second no-hitter on July 15, 1973, until he struck out 12 of the first 14 Detroit Tigers he faced.

"I wanted it," he told a reporter.

Ryan continued plowing through the lineup, striking out five more batters while walking four. Norm Cash, a Tigers slugger known as a jokester, tried to break up the no-no with comedy in the ninth. Cash, the final batter, had one strike on him before home-plate umpire Ron Luciano noticed that Cash was holding not a bat but a leg from a clubhouse table. When Luciano told him he couldn't use it, Cash reportedly replied, "Why not? I won't hit him anyway."

After the 6-0 win, Ryan noted that his pitching had been better a year earlier. "So I've thrown two good games," he told a reporter. "But look at my record. I'm 11-11. I can't look back and say 1973 was my best year just because I pitched two no-hitters."[262]

Ryan's mother, Martha Lee Ryan, called the accomplishment "wonderful" but said she had six kids and didn't "get too excited about the things they do anymore."

"What I'm waiting for Nolan to do now is pitch a perfect game," she said.[263]

Ryan would never get his perfect game, but four days after his second no-no he nearly duplicated a more elusive accomplishment—Johnny Vander Meer's back-to-back no-hitters. Ryan was no-hitting the Baltimore Orioles through seven innings when Mark Belanger led off the eighth inning with a bloop single to center.

Torborg said Ryan's third no-hitter should have been awarded on August 29, 1973. The Angels were facing the New York Yankees at Anaheim Stadium that night when Thurman Munson hit a first-inning pop-up right over second base. "Rudy Meoli, the shortstop, and Sandy Alomar Sr. came together, looked at one another, and it dropped on the dirt and they called it a base hit," Torborg said. "It was the only hit of the game, and the official scorer's comment was 'Well, it took the pressure off.'" But according to Torborg, "Nolan never felt that pressure."[264]

No-hitter No. 3 would instead come during Ryan's final start of the 1974 season, when the Angels were 24 games out of first place in the AL West. Ryan told catcher Tom Egan that he was going to "let it all out," and he struck out 15 batters while walking eight. "I just knew one thing," he said. "If they were going to get it a hit, it was going to be on my best pitch, my fastball."[265]

Nolan Ryan
California Angels
July 15, 1973
California   6
Detroit   0

A baseball from Nolan Ryan's first no-hitter is displayed in the Hall of Fame. *(Photo by Dirk Lammers)*

A half-season later, on June 1, 1975, against the Baltimore Orioles, Ryan tied Koufax with his fourth no-no, striking out nine while issuing four bases on balls.

Koufax, who announced his retirement just months after Ryan made his first major-league start, expected Ryan to break his record. He predicted that Ryan could pitch 10 or 12 no-hitters with that blazing fastball. "There was no doubt he was going to do it," Koufax told AP sportswriter Mike Rubin. "The only question is how many more he's going to pitch."[266]

Ryan's fourth no-hitter was his last with the Angels, as he returned to his home state of Texas before the start of the 1980 season to join the National League's Houston Astros.

ON SEPTEMBER 26, 1981, Ryan broke Koufax's 16-year-old mark with a 5-0 no-hitter against, as irony would have it, the Dodgers. He struck out 11 and walked three, making great use of his breaking ball. "I've seen him throw harder, but I've never seen him throw better," said Dusty Baker, who made the final out.[267]

Ryan shied away from comparisons with Koufax, but Dodgers manager Tommy Lasorda said Ryan's dominance was on a par. "When Nolan Ryan gets his breaking ball over the plate to go along with his tremendous fastball, he's just awesome," Lasorda said. "It's really hard to imagine pitching five no-hitters. I saw two of Sandy Koufax's, and I'd compare them with what I saw today."[268]

. . .

IT WOULD BE nearly a decade before Ryan would finish out his record tally with two no-hitters thrown well into his 40s.

Ryan returned to the American League in 1989 with a ride up I-45 to join the Texas Rangers, and on June 11, 1990, he no-hit the Oakland Athletics for a 5-0 victory. The then 43-year-old veteran was battling persistent back problems and was just looking to endure the pain beyond the sixth inning. "Then I got through seven innings and I decided I'm not going to give in to it, because I just needed six more outs," he told AP sportswriter Dick Brinster.[269]

Ryan was still battling that aching back a year later. Prepping for his May 1, 1991, start against league-leading Toronto, Ryan did some extra stretches, wore a heating pack, and popped a generous dose of Advil. But the 44-year-old pitcher, reaching 93 mph on the speed gun, struck out 16 batters as he no-hit the Blue Jays for a 3-0 complete-game victory.

Rangers pitching coach Tom House told the *Dallas Morning News* that Ryan went into a zone where normal people don't go. Shortstop Jeff Huson said the Blue Jays "just got in the way of a train."[270]

The train nearly added another stop to its 27-year route two months later. Ryan was working on his eighth no-hitter against his old team, the California Angels, on July 6, 1991, when Dave Winfield broke it up with an eighth-inning single. Ryan had been perfect through six in that game but walked Luis Polonia to lead off the seventh.

THE ODDITY THAT none of Ryan's no-nos was a perfect game is not entirely surprising given a look at his career stats. He is baseball's all-time strikeout leader with 5,714 K's, but he's also the sport's leader in walks issued with 2,795.

OLDEST AND YOUNGEST PITCHERS TO THROW NO-HITTERS AND PERFECT GAMES

The New York Giants' Amos Rusie is the youngest pitcher to throw a no-hitter at 20 years, 2 months, and 1 day. *(Baseball-card photo from the Benjamin K. Edwards Collection, Prints & Photographs Division, Library of Congress, LC-DIG-bbc-0597f)*

Whoever coined the phrase "The age of miracles is past" clearly isn't a baseball fan, as two of baseball's dominant pitchers of their eras threw no-hitters after turning 40. Other major-league hurlers were able to accomplish the feat barely into their 20s.

Here are the youngest and oldest pitchers to throw no-hitters and perfect games.

Oldest pitcher to throw a no-hitter:

Nolan Ryan
Age: 44 years, 3 months, 1 day
Texas Rangers (AL)
Wednesday, May 1, 1991
Texas Rangers 3, Toronto Blue Jays 0
Arlington Stadium (Texas)
His seventh of seven no-hitters

Oldest pitcher to throw a perfect game:

Randy Johnson
Age: 40 years, 8 months, 8 days
Arizona Diamondbacks (NL)
Tuesday, May 18, 2004
Arizona Diamondbacks 2, Atlanta Braves 0
Turner Field (Atlanta)
His second of two no-hitters

Youngest pitcher to throw a no-hitter:

Amos Rusie
Age: 20 years, 2 months, 1 day
New York Giants (NL)
Friday, July 31, 1891
New York Giants 6, Brooklyn Grooms 0
Polo Grounds (New York)

Youngest modern-era pitcher to throw a no-hitter:

Vida Blue
Age: 21 years, 1 month, 24 days
Oakland Athletics (AL)

Monday, September 21, 1970
Oakland Athletics 6, Minnesota Twins 0
Oakland–Alameda County Coliseum (Oakland)

Youngest pitcher to throw a perfect game:

John Montgomery Ward
Age: 20 years, 3 months, 14 days
Providence Grays (NL)
Thursday, June 17, 1880
Providence Grays 5, Buffalo Bisons 0
Messer Street Grounds (Providence)

Youngest modern-era pitcher to throw a perfect game:

Jim "Catfish" Hunter
Age: 22 years, 1 month
Oakland Athletics (AL)
Wednesday, May 8, 1968
Oakland Athletics 4, Minnesota Twins 0
Oakland–Alameda County Coliseum (Oakland)

The Dodgers' Fernando Valenzuela, honored in this bobblehead, and Dave Stewart, honored on this card, joined the no-hit club on the same day in 1990. *(Photo by Dirk Lammers)*

CHAPTER 24

POGO FOR THE FANS: PITCH ONE, GET ONE FREE

It is a remarkable performance to shut out an opposing team without a hit of any kind in a game, and when two pitchers in one
league do the trick in the same day, it is still more remarkable.

—*Harrisburg Telegraph*, APRIL 23, 1898

Game time was approaching at Dodger Stadium on June 29, 1990,
but veteran left-hander Fernando Valenzuela figured he could
catch a few innings of ESPN baseball before his evening start against the
St. Louis Cardinals. The clubhouse TV was tuned to a game being played
2,200 miles to the northeast, and Valenzuela and his fellow Dodgers
huddled around the screen to watch former teammate Dave Stewart in
action against the Toronto Blue Jays. Stewart, now anchoring the Oakland Athletics rotation, walked a couple of batters in the first inning but
quickly gained his control and proceeded to mow down the Blue Jays
lineup.

"I had a real crisp fastball, good movement and I thought my location was good," the 33-year-old right-hander told a reporter.[271]

Stewart had retired 20 straight batters when Fred McGriff, Toronto's
power-hitting first baseman, gave him a scare in the bottom of the eighth
inning. McGriff blasted a fastball nearly 400 feet into deep center, but
outfielder Dave Henderson snagged the fly just shy of the SkyDome

fence. "I was thinking that he [McGriff] got it," Stewart said. "I was fortunate that it didn't go out."[272]

Stewart retired four more batters before walking Junior Felix with two outs in the ninth. He recovered to get Tony Fernandez to fly out to center, completing his 5-0 no-hit victory. "I never thought about pitching a no-hitter," Stewart told a reporter after the game. "I've had people mention it to me any number of times. I always said, 'Heck, I'll probably be the last guy to throw a no-hitter.'"[273]

BACK IN LOS ANGELES, Valenzuela was readying his arm for his start when someone ran up to him with the news from Toronto: Stewart had thrown a no-no. "I said, 'Well you guys are watching one on TV; now you're gonna watch one live,'" Valenzuela declared to his teammates.[274]

Valenzuela later said he was joking, but the Mexican-born southpaw brought his best stuff for the contest televised as the late game of ESPN's Friday-night doubleheader. Valenzuela, known for a unique quirk in his delivery—that odd skyward glance at the top of his leg kick—juxtaposed his fastball and screwball to keep the Cardinals off base.

Valenzuela's scare came with two outs in the eighth inning on a long drive off the bat of pinch hitter Craig Wilson. Center fielder Stan Javier's early jump on the ball allowed him to chase it down on the edge of the warning track, as told by Dodgers' play-by-play man Vin Scully. "The left-hander deals, and there's a drive into left center and deep; Javier on a dead run … picks it off," bellowed Scully.[275]

Valenzuela issued a one-out walk to Willie McGee in the ninth inning before facing his former teammate Pedro Guerrero. Guerrero poked a dribbler up the middle past Valenzuela's glove, but second baseman Juan Samuel fielded the ball on top of the bag for the force-out and then threw to first to complete the double play that cemented Valenzuela's no-hitter.

"If you have a sombrero, throw it to the sky," proclaimed Scully.[276]

. . .

THE SAME-DAY PERFORMANCES of Stewart and Valenzuela mark the only time since the turn of the 20th century that no-hitters have been thrown on the same day, and the national broadcasts helped put the games in front of millions of viewers.

A far tinier sum of 4,358 combined fans got to witness baseball's first same-day no-nos, thrown on April 22, 1898, by the Reds' Ted Breitenstein in Cincinnati and the Orioles' Jim Hughes in Baltimore. Breitenstein, a 29-year-old veteran, already had one career no-no after throwing an 8-0 no-hitter for the St. Louis Browns in his first career start in 1891. On this day he faced the Pittsburgh Pirates, and the *Chicago Daily Tribune* reported that he pitched one of the most remarkable games on record, and his defensive support was "brilliant."

"Not a semblance of a hit was made off of his delivery, and only twenty-eight men faced him in the nine innings," the paper said. "Not a man got as far as second base."[277]

Meanwhile, in another National League matchup 425 miles to the east in Maryland, Hughes was dominating the world champion Boston Beaneaters. "Pitcher Hughes was a problem today which the Bostons could not solve, and no hits and no runs was their portion," the *Chicago Daily Tribune* said. "The Orioles at times played magnificent ball, but two of their errors were very yellow."[278]

The *Harrisburg Telegraph* rated Hughes's performance above Breitenstein's no-no. "The Baltimorean's feat is more creditable inasmuch as this is his first season in the big league and the Bostons are harder hitters than the Pirates," the paper noted.[279]

Hughes's 8-0 blanking was a tough game for Boston, who a year earlier had defeated Baltimore to capture the Temple Cup, the predecessor to the World Series trophy.

. . .

THE 1990 STEWART-VALENZUELA NO-NOS were thrown in a month that saw a record four no-hitters. An unprecedented seven no-hitters were tossed that year, establishing a new major-league record that would be duplicated in 1991.

The glut in back-to-back years had baseball purists thinking that a previously rare feat was becoming too commonplace, and the heightened awareness led baseball to establish a committee to look into the issue. As a result, changes would soon be on the horizon.

NO-HITTERS BY DECADE

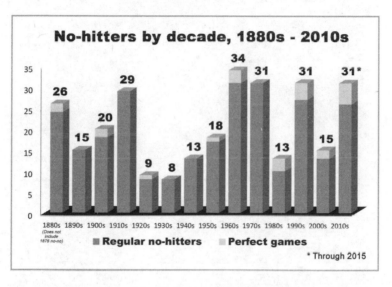

The 2010s are on pace to break the record for most no-hitters in a decade.

(Graphic by NoNoHitters.com)

No major-league pitcher battled the no-no gods more than Dave Stieb, who finally pitched a no-hitter in 1990 after four ninth-inning misses.

(Photo from National Baseball Hall of Fame and Museum)

CHAPTER 25

FIFTH TIME A CHARM

If at first you don't succeed, try, try again. Then quit. There's no point in being a damn fool about it.

—W. C. FIELDS

Toronto Blue Jays pitcher Dave Stieb had already suffered more than his share of no-hit heartbreaks by 1989, losing a pair of no-hitters with two outs in the ninth inning during back-to-back starts the previous season.

But on August 4, 1989, the 32-year-old right-hander from Santa Ana, California, stood on the SkyDome pitcher's mound one out from perfection, having yielded not a hit, walk, nor error to the visiting New York Yankees.

Center fielder Roberto Kelly, the potential 27th and final out, stepped up to the plate and drove a 2-0 slider over third base for a double to left for the Yankee's first hit. The crowd of nearly 49,000 already standing in anticipation of a celebration shook off their shock and showered Stieb with applause.

"I've told you before, I don't care," Stieb told *Toronto Star* sportswriter Allan Ryan after the game. "No-hitters are bonuses. It's all luck anyway."[280]

Stieb then had a moment to reconsider. "Okay, don't let me kid you," he said. "It was exciting and it'll probably bother me a lot more tomorrow."[281]

. . .

PLENTY OF PITCHERS have let late-inning no-hitters slip through their fingertips. Hall of Famer Tom Seaver lost three no-nos in the ninth for the 1970s New York Mets before finally getting his due as a member of the 1978 Cincinnati Reds. The Texas Rangers' Yu Darvish lost ninth-inning no-hitters in 2013 and 2014, although a postgame official scoring change later credited David Ortiz with an earlier hit in the 2014 contest.

Cy Young, Dazzy Vance, Grover Cleveland Alexander, and Curt Schilling all lost no-hit games with two outs in the ninth.

BUT NO MAJOR-LEAGUE PITCHER battled the no-no gods more than Stieb. His string of stings began on August 24, 1985, when he took a no-hitter into the ninth inning at Chicago's Comiskey Park. Stieb stepped onto the mound for the final frame and gave up back-to-back home runs to White Sox hitters Rudy Law and Bryan Little. Manager Bobby Cox took the ball from Stieb and called in reliever Gary Lavelle.

Blue Jays catcher Ernie Whitt said Stieb was throwing his best fastball since joining Toronto in 1979. He guessed that Stieb's arm might have tightened up in the ninth. "I knew he had a no-hitter going," Whitt told *Chicago Tribune* sportswriter Steve Nidetz. "I wanted to get it for him. They hit fastballs. I called them."[282] Stieb said he didn't have a good fastball in the ninth and was simply going on guts.[283]

Perhaps foreshadowing the growing intensity of his relentless quest for a no-hitter, Stieb released his autobiography, titled *Tomorrow I'll Be Perfect*, in 1980.

Stieb wasn't perfect on September 24, 1988, in Cleveland, but he was holding the Indians hitless through eight and two-thirds innings. This time it was Julio Franco who stood between Stieb and his elusive no-no. Franco poked a 2-2 pitch toward the right side of the infield for what appeared to be a routine chopper, but the ball's second bounce pinpointed the edge of the infield between the grass and dirt. The ball

launched over the lofty leap of second baseman Manuel Lee and dribbled into center field for Cleveland's first hit. Whitt strolled to the
mound to console his pitcher before giving Stieb five pats on the tummy
and returning to his position behind the plate. "It wasn't a bad feeling,"
Stieb told a reporter. "I just had to laugh."[284] He got Dave Clark to fly
out to center to secure a 1-0 one-hit, complete-game victory for the Blue
Jays.

Stieb got the opportunity to avenge that bad hop six days later during
his next start at home against the Baltimore Orioles. He appeared poised
to make history, sending each of the first 26 batters back to the dugout.
He plunked Joe Orsulak with a pitch in the fourth and walked Pete
Stanicek in the seventh, but the Blue Jays retired both batters on double
plays.

Orioles manager Frank Robinson sent Jim Traber up to bat for pitcher
Jeff Ballard with two outs in the ninth, and Traber popped a broken-bat
single above a valiant jump by first baseman Fred McGriff.

Stieb got Orsulak to ground out to third for his 4-0 complete-game
victory and his third one-hitter, but teammates and coaches couldn't
help but mourn Stieb's loss of two ninth-inning no-hitters in less than a
week's span. "Never seen anything like it," pitching coach Galen Cisco
said. "The other one [in Cleveland] was worse because of the bad hop.
This one was bad because it was so close to the other one."[285]

BUT THE FIFTH TIME was the charm for Stieb, who finally accomplished the feat on September 2, 1990.

With two out in the bottom of the ninth inning, Jerry Browne pulled
a hanging liner to right, and it appeared that Stieb might again be headed
for heartbreak. But right fielder Junior Felix took a few steps back and
caught the ball with one hand at his chest and pumped his fists to re-
joice. Stieb had just thrown the first no-hitter in Toronto Blue Jays history.

The smiling pitcher put his hand to his head in amazement before catcher Pat Borders greeted him with a hug. Moments later in a post-game television interview with CTV, Stieb said he still didn't believe it. "I was thinking about getting it, of course, but I remember sitting here last time thinking about the same thing," he said. "I didn't want to jinx myself, but I already thought about it and that was that and I just kept going at it."[286]

ANOTHER BLUE JAYS PITCHER tapped into Stieb's no-no hoodoo during back-to-back starts in June 2015.

Marco Estrada was no-hitting the Orioles on June 19 when he yielded an eighth-inning broken-bat bloop single to Jimmy Paredes.

Five days later, Estrada again reached the eighth without allowing a hit before his no-no was spoiled by a one-out Logan Forsythe infield single.

NO-HITTERS WITH FEWEST OFFICIAL AT-BATS

Bob Groom holds the record of the no-hitter thrown with the fewest official at-bats—23. *(Photo from Bain News Service Collection, Prints & Photographs Division, Library of Congress, LC-DIG-hec-02493)*

The at-bat is a statistical oddity in the sports world, as a player who is up at bat is not credited with an official at-bat if he reaches first on a base on balls, is hit by a pitch, or sacrifices himself to advance a runner with a fly ball or bunt. (Note that reaching first on a catcher's interference is another rare way to get on base without an at-bat.) So a player who made four plate appearances in a game with a single, a walk, a ground-out, and a sacrifice fly is considered to have gone 1-for-2 on the day.

That convention allows a full nine-inning baseball game to have fewer than 27 at-bats even though it has to have at least 27 plate appearances. In a nine-inning no-hitter, a low at-bat count is usually the sign of a pitcher issuing an abundance of walks and those runners being retired on double plays, sacrifices, steal attempts, or pickoffs.

The record for fewest at-bats in a no-hitter is 23, accomplished by Bob Groom in 1917. Six major-league pitchers have thrown no-hitters with 24 at-bats, sharing the second-place position. Here are the details.

Bob Groom
St. Louis Browns (AL)—23 at-bats
Sunday, May 6, 1917 (second game of doubleheader)
St. Louis Browns 3, Chicago White Sox 0
Sportsman's Park (St. Louis)

Groom walked three, hit one batter with a pitch, and allowed another to reach first base on a sacrifice, but only one of the White Sox runners was left on base during the game. The Browns turned one double play, and although the box score printed in newspapers doesn't specify how the other runners were retired, they were likely caught stealing.

Dick Fowler
Philadelphia Athletics (AL)—24 at-bats
Sunday, September 9, 1945 (second game of doubleheader)
Philadelphia Athletics 1, St. Louis Browns 0
Shibe Park (Philadelphia)

Fowler walked four batters during the game. A sacrifice bunt advancing one of those runners accounted for another non-at-bat. Two others who reached first on walks were retired on double plays.

Cliff Chambers
Pittsburgh Pirates (NL)—24 at-bats
Sunday, May 6, 1951 (second game of doubleheader)
Pittsburgh Pirates 3, Boston Braves 0
Braves Field (Boston)

Chambers walked eight batters during the game. Two sacrifice bunts advancing runners accounted for two non-at-bats. Another runner who reached first on a walk was retired on a double play.

"Toothpick" Sam Jones
Chicago Cubs (NL)—24 at-bats
Thursday, May 12, 1955

Chicago Cubs 4, Pittsburgh Pirates 0
Wrigley Field (Chicago)

Jones walked seven batters during the game. One of them was caught stealing, and two of the others were retired on double plays.

Burt Hooton
Chicago Cubs (NL)—24 at-bats
Sunday, April 16, 1972
Chicago Cubs 4, Philadelphia Phillies 0
Wrigley Field (Chicago)

Hooton walked seven batters during the game. One of the runners was caught stealing, and one of them was retired on a double play. A sacrifice bunt advancing a runner who had walked accounted for the other non-at-bat.

Joe Cowley
Chicago White Sox (AL)—24 at-bats
Friday, September 19, 1986
Chicago White Sox 7, California Angels 1
Anaheim Stadium (Anaheim)

Cowley walked seven batters during the game, and one of them was caught stealing. An RBI sacrifice fly scoring a runner who had walked accounted for another other non-at-bat, and another runner who reached on a base on balls was retired on a double play.

Francisco Liriano
Minnesota Twins (AL)—24 at-bats
Tuesday, May 3, 2011
Minnesota Twins 1, Chicago White Sox 0
U.S. Cellular Field (Chicago)

Liriano walked six batters during the game, but three of those runners were retired on double plays.

Padres fans, seen here watching a game at Petco Park, have been waiting more than 46 years for the team's first no-hitter. *(Photo by Dirk Lammers)*

CHAPTER 26

FRIARS' CLUB

When I try to look at the logic behind it, I don't see it. We were 20 or 30 games behind and we needed something to drum up interest in the ball club. A no-hitter would have given the franchise a much bigger boost than one more victory.

—The Padres' Clay Kirby to the *Los Angeles Times*

Four major-league franchises entered the 2010s seeking their first no-hitters, but baseball's no no-no society quickly downsized into the Friars' club, a.k.a. the San Diego Padres.

Ubaldo Jiménez threw the Colorado Rockies' first no-hitter on April 17, 2010, and Matt Garza followed with the Tampa Bay Rays' first no-no on July 26, 2010. The New York Mets ended more than 50 years of futility two years later when Johan Santana no-hit the St. Louis Cardinals on June 1, 2012. Santana's gem branded the circa 1969 San Diego Padres as the only major-league team that has failed to accomplish the feat.

Many Padres fans trace the team's curse back to July 21, 1970, the night that Padres manager Preston Gómez pinch hit for Clay Kirby despite the Padres starter tossing eight innings of no-hit ball. The Padres lost the no-hitter and the game to the visiting Mets, and San Diego is still seeking its first no-no.

"I don't play for fans; I knew they'd be upset," an unapologetic Gómez said after the game. "I play to win. That's what the game is about."[287]

Kirby, a 22-year-old right-hander, had fallen behind at the game's onset. He walked Mets' leadoff batter Tommie Agee, and the speedy center fielder stole second base. Ken Singleton also walked, and the pair pulled a double steal to put Agee 90 feet from home plate. Agee then scored on an Art Shamsky groundout to give the Mets a 1-0 lead. Kirby settled down and held the Mets hitless through eight innings while scattering three more walks through his eight innings of work. He said it was probably the best game he had ever pitched.[288]

But Mets starting pitcher Jim McAndrew was even better, stifling the Padres offense by striking out nine batters and walking none. McAndrew allowed just three base runners on two doubles and a single, but he prevented those runners from advancing.

Gómez's Padres trailed 1-0 in the bottom of the eighth inning, and the manager needed to generate some runs. With two outs and nobody on base, Gómez sent Cito Gaston to the plate to pinch hit for Kirby. The move drew the ire of 10,373 San Diego Stadium fans, who showered the skipper with jeers and catcalls.

Kirby wasn't thrilled, either. "Sure I was a little mad and a little surprised that he would take me out but he's the manager and we wanted to win the game," Kirby said after the game.[289]

Gaston struck out, and the boo-birds upped their intensity. One fan jumped onto the field and darted toward the Padres dugout before being ejected by security officers.

Padres reliever Jack Baldschun took the ball for the top of the ninth and immediately gave up a single to the Mets' Bud Harrelson, killing the no-hitter. Cleon Jones and Joe Foy followed with singles to give the Mets a 3-0 lead and seal the win for McAndrew. Kirby took the loss. "I'll have a lot more chances to throw a no-hitter," Kirby said. "I would rather have won the game than throw a no-hitter."[290]

Kirby had two more chances in 1971, but he couldn't convert on either attempt. On September 13, 1971, he was no-hitting the Houston

Astros with a 2-0 lead when John Edwards doubled with one out in the eighth. The Astros scored two runs in the eighth to tie the game, and Kirby lost the contest in the ninth when Padres third baseman Garry Jestadt let a grounder slip through his legs.

Five days later, at San Francisco's Candlestick Park, Kirby was perfect through seven innings when slugger Willie McCovey homered to lead off the eighth. Kirby held on for a 2-1 complete-game one-hitter.

KIRBY'S WOES set off a series of near misses for the Padres. On July 18, 1972, at home against Philadelphia, Steve Arlin was leading 5-0 and was one out away from throwing the Padres' first no-hitter when Denny Doyle stepped to the plate. Padres manager Don Zimmer, looking to guard against a potential bunt, signaled third baseman Dave Roberts to creep in onto the grass. Doyle poked a single over Roberts's head and the no-hitter was kaput.

"I messed up," said Zimmer. "I had Roberts playing in. If he plays back, he fields the ball."[291]

A flustered Arlin balked Doyle to second and allowed him to score on a Tom Hutton single before salvaging the complete-game one-hitter.

More near misses would follow. Andy Ashby, Chris Young, and a five-pitcher committee all fumbled Padres no-hitters in the ninth inning. Randy Jones, Greg Harris, Andy Benes, Sterling Hitchcock, and Adam Eaton each lost a no-no in the eighth inning. San Diego rosters have featured the likes of Gaylord Perry, Jake Peavy, Kevin Brown, and Greg Maddux, but none has been able to complete the task while wearing a Padres uniform.

Jones, the 1976 Cy Young Award winner, is amazed that no Friar has been able to cross the no-no finish line. "It's crazy that we don't have a no-hitter," Jones told sportswriter Mel Antonen in a piece for *Sports Il-lustrated*. "We've had great pitchers and a lot of stories of near no-hit-ters."[292]

Further opening the wound, the Padres' National League expansion partner exited the no no-no club in that franchise's ninth game. On April 17, 1969, Montreal Expos reliever turned starter Bill Stoneman no-hit the Philadelphia Phillies for a 7-0 win. The 25-year-old right-hander, who was making his second career start, was in such unfamiliar territory that he didn't feel any pressure. "I wasn't as nervous as I should have been," Stoneman said. "I had good stuff and I was getting the ball where I wanted it."[293]

Meanwhile, Gómez moved on to manage in Houston, where he repeated his infamous eighth-inning move. The Astros' Don Wilson was no-hitting the Cincinnati Reds on September 4, 1974, but trailed 2-0 due to a pair of fifth-inning walks followed by a Roger Metzger throwing error.

Houston had trimmed the score to 2-1 by the bottom of the eighth when Gómez called on Tommy Helms to pinch-hit for Wilson. Helms grounded out to short, the Astros couldn't score, and rookie reliever Mike Cosgrove took the ball for the top of the ninth. "It didn't make me feel good to go out there and pitch with all the fans booing," Cosgrove said.[294]

Tony Pérez led off the inning with a single, killing the no-hitter. The Astros went down 1-2-3 in the bottom of the ninth for the loss. Wilson said he respected Gómez "more than ever" for his decision and praised him as "consistent."[295]

Across the field in the visitors' dugout was Kirby, who had been traded to the Reds from the Padres in the off-season. Kirby could just watch with empathy. "I understand how Don feels, but I understand now how Preston felt," he said. "I understand because I watched from the other side, from the side of a team trying to win a pennant. He had to try to beat us."[296]

ANOTHER BASEBALL RARE FEAT that's just slightly more common than a no-hitter had eluded the Padres until midway through the 2015 season.

From the team's first game on April 8, 1969, until a Coors Field matchup against the Colorado Rockies on August 14, 2015, no Padres player was able to hit for the cycle (a single, double, triple and home run in the same game, not necessarily in that order). Even the no-no-starved Mets were able to notch 10 hits-for-the-cycle during the team's years of no-hitter futility.

But in the Padres franchise's 7,444th game, Matt Kemp hit a first-inning homer, a third-inning single, a seventh-inning double and a ninth-inning triple to leave the circa-1993 Miami Marlins as the only club still seeking its first cycle.

A NO-NO GOES FOWL
IN SAN DIEGO

It was expected to be a night of non-sense, and it almost ended with a no-no. Yet what happened in between was due to the horse sense of a man named Horton.

In my guise as the San Diego Chicken on June 29, 1984, my 10th birthday was being celebrated before a sellout crowd at Jack Murphy Stadium as the Padres faced the St. Louis Cardinals. As I cavorted with irreverent aplomb during every inning break, goofing with fans, umpires, coaches, and players in a variety of chicken-shtick bits, the stands erupted in raucous laughter.

By TED GIANNOULAS
The San Diego Chicken

On the mound, though, serious business was in play. The Cards' rookie left-hander, Ricky Horton, was pitching the game of his life, making his own punch line of the powerful Padres.

Horton was upstaging the levity with a no-hitter—and then came the eighth inning.

As the Cardinals southpaw took to his warm-ups on the mound, I undertook the most outrageous sketch ever—*Indiana Chicken and the Ballpark of Doom*—a takeoff on that summer's blockbuster film.

Adorned with the same Harrison Ford leather jacket, hat, and bullwhip, I challenged the Redbirds' bullpen in the right-field corner to a duel. Instead, four team members (all actors, unbeknownst to the crowd) bull-rushed me in a chase. I hopped into the stands, and their pursuit continued, to the fans' astonishment.

Up the aisle, onto the plaza runway, into the right-field bleachers; it was a helter-skelter dash. Suddenly, from a service entrance to those seats, four more Cardinals players mysteriously emerged, trapping me between eight oncoming enemies, high above the outfield fence. There was only one way out: to jump off the nineteen-foot-high wall.

I hurdled its railing and plunged like a cliff diver to three tiers of audience screams, disappearing behind the right-field fence and landing on a pole-vault cushion placed there.

Meanwhile, a nonplussed Horton continued his warm-ups.

But then the outfield gate whipped open. There, in a flash amid the delirium, 45,468 people suddenly saw me, the Chicken, on horseback, bolting in a full gallop straight across the acres of outfield. The fowl had flabbergasted everyone—or just about.

Horton had concluded his practice tosses and readied himself for the eighth inning, seemingly oblivious of the extra 30 seconds it took to corral the horse beneath the left-field pavilion.

The Padres' first batter, Carmelo Martínez, struck out, and Terry Kennedy popped out to third base. Then came Kevin McReynolds, who whacked a line-drive double off the left-field fence, cracking Horton's no-hit goose egg.

On the St. Louis bench, manager Whitey Herzog seethed. Upstairs in the Padres general manager's suite, Jack McKeon stewed in his cigar cloud. Even San Diego manager Dick Williams smoldered.

They were all convinced I had distracted Ricky Horton from his masterpiece. When the media swarmed him after a complete-game, 5-0 two-hitter, Horton silenced them as quickly as the Padres' bats in a night's work that only took 2:10.

"I've seen Teddy's show many times and love it, but honestly, I had no time to watch tonight," he said. "I was locked in and focused on what I was doing."

The media were incredulous: "What about that horse on the field?"

"Horse?" Ricky said. "There was a horse on the field?"

End of a would-be controversy? Not quite.

Ricky would personally tell me months later of just how many times media members would continue to bring up the escapade, trying to get him to 'fess up that the Chicken had ruined his concentration for the gem. He merely laughed them off, he said.

But Jack McKeon, bless his smokescreen, wouldn't let it go. Still, years later, his embellishment to the press was so colorful that I've adopted it as the official Chicken version, too: that the colt crashed over the fence; that he almost trampled the Cards' outfielders; and—best of all—that he even stopped in center field for a steaming dump before continuing onward. McKeon was adamant: Horton had to have been rattled!

Shovel, please, indeed.

Boston Red Sox catcher Jason Varitek has caught four no-hitters,
tied for the most in the majors. *(Photo by KeithAllisonPhoto.com)*

CHAPTER 27

THE UNSUNG HEROES

Baseball is ninety percent mental and the other half is physical.

—YOGI BERRA

When the Montreal Expos' Dennis Martínez threw his perfect game against the Los Angeles Dodgers on July 28, 1991, the spotlight shone brightly on the Nicaraguan right-hander. Martínez had just joined an elite group of 15 pitchers by retiring 27 straight batters without yielding a hit, walk or error.

Far less attention that day was paid to Martínez's veteran battery-mate, but Ron Hassey entered a class of his own. Hassey, who had caught Len Barker's perfect game against the Toronto Blue Jays a decade earlier, became the only major-league catcher behind the plate for two perfectos. "We had a game plan, and we went out and did it," Hassey told a reporter. "You give the credit to Dennis. He's the guy who had to throw the pitches. I'm just the guy who's catching him and helping him."[297]

HASSEY'S GRACIOUS COMMENTS are indicative of the postgame generosity shown by those who suit up in the mask, chest protector, and shin guards dubbed the "tools of ignorance." The no-hitter is an odd instance in which an athlete who plays an integral part in a rare feat receives so little public credit.

But there'd be no Penn without Teller, no Han Solo without Chewbacca, no Maverick without Goose. Few understood the role of sidekick better than Ed McMahon, who built a career playing second fiddle to Johnny Carson. In a 1988 AP interview McMahon compared his role with that of those who squat behind home plate. "It's like a pitcher who has a favorite catcher," McMahon said. "The pitcher gets a little help from the catcher, but the pitcher's got to throw the ball. Well, Johnny Carson had to throw the ball, but I could give him a little help."[298]

Don Larsen, who threw the only perfect game in World Series play in 1956, said he couldn't have made history without the leadership of Yogi Berra. "I think the catcher runs all the game, no matter who's managing," Larsen said. "He's on the field all the time. Everything's in front of him."[299]

Catching is baseball's most challenging position. Squatting each day for nine innings over the course of a 162-game season is a grueling task, and it's the catcher's side job to jump up, run down the line, and back up first base on every routine infield grounder hit when the bases are empty. When a runner on first takes off to steal second, the catcher must quickly snag the ball, jump up, and gun an accurate throw 127 feet into the fielder's glove.

The position is no less taxing on the brain. Catchers must possess encyclopedic knowledge of the opposing team's lineup, cataloging which pitches each batter likes, where he likes them, and in which situations he likes to swing. "If a guy's had much experience at all, or even the backups, they know the hitters as well as anybody," Larsen said.[300]

THE PRESSURE ONLY INCREASES when a pitcher takes a no-hitter into the latter innings. Alan Ashby, who caught three Houston Astros no-hitters tossed by Nolan Ryan, Ken Forsch, and Mike Scott, said no catcher wants to be the one who makes a mistake and costs his pitcher a piece of history. "I think I was more nervous than they were," Ashby told *Chicago*

Tribune sportswriter Steve Rosenbloom. "I felt like it was on my shoulders to make sure I didn't mess up what this guy was accomplishing."[301]

RED SOX CATCHER Jason Varitek and the Phillies catcher Carlos Ruiz share the record for most no-hitters caught with four.

Varitek caught his over an eight-year period beginning in 2001:

- Hideo Nomo's April 4, 2001, no-hitter against the Baltimore Orioles
- Derek Lowe's April 27, 2002, no-hitter against the Tampa Bay Devil Rays
- Clay Buchholz's September 1, 2007, no-hitter against the Baltimore Orioles
- Jon Lester's May 19, 2008, no-hitter against the Kansas City Royals

Buchholz was a 23-year-old, wide-eyed rookie when he and Varitek teamed up for a no hitter in the right hander's second major-league start. Buchholz said everyone knew the studying and preparation that Varitek put into every game, so he just "threw the pitches that 'Tek' put down."[302]

The Orioles' scouting report on Buchholz had him throwing a 95- to 96-mph heater, a big curveball, and a slider. But Varitek knew that Buchholz also had a solid changeup, and he called for them liberally to keep Baltimore off guard.

"Pitchers put a lot of trust in their catchers, whether it'd be knowing you can bounce a curve ball with a runner on third and know if they're going to block it or pitch calling," Buchholz said in a 2015 interview. "That was really early in my career, so I didn't really have any idea who I was throwing to, what they hit well, what they didn't hit well."[303]

Red Sox manager John Farrell, who was the team's pitching coach

when Varitek caught his fourth no-no, heaped praise on Varitek after
Lester's gem. He told the *New York Times* that Varitek has a photographic
memory and true feel for what the hitter is doing in the batter's box.
"Second, third, fourth time through the lineup, he's well aware of the
sequences that he's called in the previous at-bats," Farrell said. "If adjust-
ments are needed with pitch selection, he has the recall to make that on
the fly."[304]

Ruiz caught his no-nos over a six-year period beginning in 2001:

- Roy Halladay's May 29, 2010, perfect game against the Florida
  Marlins
- Halladay's October 6, 2010, no-hitter against the Cincinnati Reds
  in Game 1 of the National League Division Series
- A September 1, 2014, no-hitter by the Phillies tandem of Cole
  Hamels (6 inn.), Jake Diekman (1 inn.), Ken Giles (1 inn.) and
  Jonathan Papelbon (1 inn.) thrown against the Atlanta Braves
- Cole Hamels's July 25, 2015, no-hitter against the Chicago Cubs

Hamels, speaking to reporters after his 2015 no-hitter, praised his
batterymate's knowledge of the game and ability to sense what he wants
to throw, sometimes without even exchanging signs.

"When you're able to get that, it's special," Hamels said. "That's
tough to develop. He's a tremendous catcher and it just shows."[305]

FEW CASUAL BASEBALL FANS have heard of Lou Criger, but the catcher
for the Cleveland Spiders and Boston Americans/Red Sox caught most
of Cy Young's 511 record-setting career victories. He also was behind the
plate for two of Young's three no-hitters. Young said Criger was a great
student of the game who knew the weaknesses of every batter. When
Boston traded Criger to the Cleveland Naps in 1908, Young noted that
he was going to have to start paying attention to batters and features "to
which I had heretofore paid no attention."

"I've pitched to him so long he seems a part of me, and I'm confident no one will suffer from the departure more than I," Young told the *St. Louis Post-Dispatch*.[306]

Ray Schalk is a Hall of Fame catcher who participated in three officially recognized no-hitters for the Chicago White Sox from 1914 to 1917. He would share record-book space with Varitek and Ruiz had Major League Baseball's committee for statistical accuracy not zapped his fourth caught no-no. On May 14, 1914, the White Sox's Jim Scott held the Washington Senators hitless through nine innings but gave up a leadoff single in the 10th and allowed one more hit in a losing effort.

Jeff Torborg, who caught no-hitters from Sandy Koufax, Nolan Ryan, and Bill Singer, said Schalk more than anyone

Ray Schalk caught three no-hitters for the Chicago White Sox between 1914 and 1917. *(Photo from Bain News Service Collection, Prints & Photographs Division, Library of Congress, LC-DIG-ggbain-25390)*

appreciated the catcher's role in a no-no. Until his death in 1970, Schalk made an effort to send a wire to every catcher who caught a no-hitter indicating that he was aware of the batterymate's importance in the feat. "I still have it in the scrapbook," Torborg said. "That was nice. It made you feel a part of a unique fraternity."[307]

TWO OF THE MOST recognizable names to catch a hat trick of no-nos are the Brooklyn Dodgers' Roy Campanella and the New York Yankees' Berra.

Campanella caught Sal Maglie's 1956 no-hitter and both of Carl Erskine's no-nos in 1952 and 1956. In the '56 game, Erskine knew he was pitching a no-no at the midpoint but had to keep thinking about winning the game, as the Dodgers had just a 1-0 lead until the seventh inning. The pitcher praised both Campanella and first baseman Gil Hodges for helping him keep focused. "Campanella and Hodges both were wonderful in slowing me down when I started pressing," Erskine told a reporter.[308]

Berra was behind the plate for both of Allie Reynolds's 1951 no-hitters before catching Larsen's World Series perfecto. In his 1996 book, *The Perfect Yankee*, Larsen said that despite being known for his quirky Yogi-isms, Berra was a fierce competitor who knew how to call a game. Any pitcher who could consistently pitch where Berra told him could surely win 20 games every year, Larsen surmised.

"Contrary to published reports, never once did I ever shake him off or change the pitch he asked me to throw," Larsen wrote. "I trusted his judgment too much. Berra's sign was the final word as far as I was concerned."[309]

CATCHERS SELDOM RECEIVE the glory, but they are certainly eligible in fans' eyes to become the goat.

Ernie "Schnozz" Lombardi felt he never received the respect he deserved even though he caught Johnny Vander Meer's back-to-back no-hitters in 1938. The 6-foot-3, 230-pound ballplayer boasted a .306 lifetime average over a 17-year career and played in seven All-Star games despite being one of baseball's slowest runners. But in 1939 he became best known for a World Series blunder branded the "Lombardi Snooze."

Down three games to none, the Reds were locked in a 4-4 tie with the Yankees in the 10th inning of Game 4 when Joe DiMaggio lined a single to right with two runners on base. Frank Crosetti scored easily, and Charlie "King Kong" Keller barreled into Lombardi as he crossed the plate, rendering the catcher motionless. DiMaggio, who had reached third, hustled home before Lombardi could recover. Sportswriters blasted Lombardi for snoozing on the play, but umpire Babe Pinelli later shared what the press didn't report: Lombardi was reeling in pain after Keller unintentionally kicked him in the groin.

The Reds were already well on their way to losing that series, but the magnified misstep helped keep Lombardi out of baseball's Hall of Fame until nine years after his death. Lombardi operated a liquor store and worked in the San Francisco Giants' press box after retiring but disappeared from the public eye in the mid-1970s.

In his book *Beyond DiMaggio: Italian Americans in Baseball,* Lawrence Baldassaro said Lombardi was by all accounts a gentle giant who later became embittered and depressed by the slight. "Perhaps the indignities he had quietly endured throughout his career, together with the stigma of the 'snooze,' had done more damage than he knew or was willing to admit," Baldassaro wrote.[310]

The Hall of Fame veterans committee finally gave Lombardi his proper recognition in 1986, describing him on his induction plaque as a "skilled receiver and handler of pitches" with an "outstanding arm from the crouch position, rifling throws with side-arm release." However, the plaque does also note his "slowness afoot."

There is one major-league record that Ernie "Schnozz" Lombardi continues to hold alone: He's the only catcher who was behind the plate for back-to-back no-hitters, and it's highly unlikely that that record will ever be broken.

CATCHERS OF MULTIPLE NO-HITTERS

Lou Criger, who was Cy Young's favorite catcher, caught two of Young's three no-hitters. *(Photo from Bain News Service Collection, Prints & Photographs Division, Library of Congress, LC-DIG-ggbain-01981)*

As noted, Jason Varitek and Carlos Ruiz hold the major-league lead for no-hitters caught with four. (Varitek also caught an unofficial five-inning rain-shortened no-hitter by Devern Hansack in 2006.) Here are the other catchers with multiple official no-nos from behind the plate.

CATCHERS WITH THREE NO-HITTERS

Silver Flint[1]	Luke Sewell	Jeff Torborg[4]
Ray Schalk[2]	Jim Hegan	Alan Ashby
Ed McFarland	Yogi Berra	Charles Johnson
Bill Carrigan	Roy Campanella	Buster Posey
Val Picinich[3]	Del Crandall	Wilson Ramos

1. Flint was removed in the ninth inning of one of those no-hitters—the 1880 no-no by Larry Corcoran.
2. Schalk also caught a May 14, 1914, game in which Jim Scott held Washington hitless for nine innings and lost in the 10th.
3. Picinich caught his no-nos for three different teams (Philadelphia Athletics, Washington Senators, and Boston Red Sox).
4. Torborg is the only catcher behind the plate for no-nos by both Nolan Ryan and Sandy Koufax.

Note: The Philadelphia Athletics' Ossee Schreck caught three rain- or darkness-shortened no-hitters from 1905 through 1907, but his official no-no tally is zero.

CATCHERS WITH TWO NO-HITTERS

Jack Rowe	Jay Justin Clarke	Johnny Roseboro
Dan Sullivan	Art Wilson[4]	Jim Pagliaroni
Rudy Kemmler	Hank Gowdy	John Bateman
Charlie Ganzel[1]	Hank Severeid	Johnny Edwards[6]
Jimmy Peoples	Ernie Lombardi[5]	Joe Azcue
Wilbert Robinson	Walker Cooper	Tim McCarver
Chief Zimmer	Buddy Rosar	Ted Simmons
Heinie Peitz[2]	Gus Triandos	Randy Hundley
Lou Criger[3]	Bob Tillman	Fran Healy

Darrell Porter   Terry Steinbach   Joe Girardi
Ron Hassey   Mike Scioscia   Miguel Olivo
Lance Parrish   Ivan Rodriguez   A. J. Pierzynski
Ron Karkovice   Mike Piazza   Ryan Hanigan
Miguel Montero

1. In addition to his two official no-nos, Ganzel was behind the plate for an 1892 five-inning no-hitter called by mutual consent.
2. Peitz caught a six-inning darkness-called no-hitter in 1906 by the Pittsburgh Pirates' Al "Lefty" Leifield.
3. Criger, Cy Young's longtime batterymate, also caught New York Highlanders pitcher Tom Hughes's 1910 no-hitter through nine. Hughes lost that no-no in the 10th and the game in the 11th.
4. Wilson was behind the plate for the Cubs in the Cubs-Reds double no-no of 1917. His pitcher, Hippo Vaughn, threw nine no-hit innings but gave up a hit and a run in the 10th. The Reds' Fred Toney completed the 10-inning no-hitter.
5. Lombardi caught Johnny Vander Meer's back-to-back no-hitters in 1938.
6. Edwards also shared catching duties with Don Pavletich when Jim Maloney of the Reds tossed 10 hitless innings against the New York Mets before giving up a game-winning homer in the 11th.

Andy Hawkins threw a complete-game no-hitter for the New York Yankees in 1990 but lost 4-0 on walks and errors. He's not credited with an official no-no. *(Photo by Dirk Lammers)*

CHAPTER 28

AND THE LEAGUE TAKETH AWAY

I think one of the great events in sports is to have a no-hitter in the seventh or eighth inning and realize the odds are still enormously high that you're not going to make it. I get caught up in it.

—Former MLB Commissioner Fay Vincent

The New York Yankees' Andy Hawkins was pitching brilliantly at Chicago's Comiskey Park on July 1, 1990, holding the White Sox hitless through seven and two-thirds innings in a 0-0 game. In any other Yankees era, Hawkins might have been destined for celebration. But this was not a typical Bronx Bombers squad; the 1990 Yankees were carrying the worst record in baseball through a seemingly endless streak of blunders and bad breaks.

With two out in the eighth inning, Yankees third baseman Mike Blowers bobbled Sammy Sosa's chopper, allowing the White Sox slugger to reach first on the error. Hawkins then walked Ozzie Guillen and Lance Johnson to load the bases for Robin Ventura, who launched a deep fly ball to left fielder Jim Leyritz.

Leyritz, who typically played third base, positioned himself under the fly as the ball glanced off his glove. Sosa, Guillen, and Johnson hustled home. Iván Calderón then hit a fly ball to right field that Jesse Barfield lost in the sun, allowing Ventura to score. Hawkins returned to the Yankees dugout down 4-0 without yielding a single base hit.

"I had a couple walks—that was my doing, and that was part of it," Hawkins said in a 2015 interview. "We had three errors that inning and tough wind out there. We had a guy out there playing in a position he never played before, so it was a combination of things. Everything that could have gone wrong in that one inning did."[311] The Yankees couldn't stage a comeback in the top of the ninth, and the White Sox escaped with a 4-0 hitless victory.

Hawkins's performance at the time was considered a no-hitter, albeit a rare type not seen for a hundred years. The situation arises only when a visiting team's pitcher holds the home squad hitless with the road team trailing in runs; the pitcher doesn't get the opportunity to pitch a ninth frame because the home team has no reason to bat when it has already won the game.

So Hawkins and Silver King—a Chicago Pirates pitcher who held the Brooklyn Ward's Wonders hitless on June 21, 1890, during a 1-0 loss— had earned their spots in the exclusive no-hitter club ...

... until September 4, 1991.

Major League Baseball Commissioner Fay Vincent, chairman of the committee that established an official no-hitter definition in 1991, says he felt that a pitcher should have to throw a full nine innings to be eligible for a no-hitter, as many no-nos in progress are lost in the final frame. *(Photo from National Baseball Hall of Fame and Museum)*

Fifty rain-shortened, darkness-shortened, and eight-inning-loss no-hitters were torn out of the record books on that day as Major League

Baseball's committee for statistical accuracy established the first official definition of a no-hitter. The committee's declaration, which arose amid a sudden spike in no-hitters, declared: "A no-hitter is a game in which a pitcher or pitchers complete a game of nine innings or more without allowing a hit."

Major League Baseball Commissioner Fay Vincent, the committee's chairman, said he felt that a pitcher should have to throw a full nine innings to be eligible for a no-hitter, as many no-nos in progress are lost in the final frame. "I was a traditionalist, and I wanted the standard to be very high," he said in a 2014 interview.[312]

SEYMOUR SIWOFF, a renowned Elias Sports Bureau statistician who served on the committee, noted at the time that *The Elias Book of Baseball Records* still mentions accomplishments such as Hawkins's game, even though they're not considered official no-hitters. They're listed under "No-Hit Games: Regular Season, Fewer Than Nine Innings."[313]

"Hawkins is in the record book," Siwoff said. "Years from now, he can tell people, 'I'm in the record book. I'm in the no-hit section.'"[314]

Hawkins said the designation—or lack thereof—is "just a formality." "Everybody knew what happened that day," Hawkins said. "It was a no-hitter. It just happened that it was on the road and I lost it. Not too many people really envision that kind of thing happening."[315]

New York Times baseball writer Murray Chass took issue with the committee's inconsistent parsing of baseball terminology. "If [a pitcher] gives up one hit, we say he pitched a one-hitter," Chass wrote in 1992. "So if he allows no hits, we should say he pitched a no-hitter. If rain ends the game after five innings, it doesn't change the terminology: He pitched a three-hitter, he pitched a one-hitter, he pitched a no-hitter."[316]

Vincent said he and Chass, both retired, continue to discuss the committee's designation a quarter-century after it was established. "He's an old friend, and we're good friends," Vincent said. "He says I was wrong about some parts of it."[317]

. . .

BEFORE THE COMMITTEE established an official definition of the no-hitter, news organizations had been free to make their own judgment on what constituted a no-no. The *Sporting News* record book had considered a pitcher who threw a nine-inning no-no but yielded a hit in extra innings part of the elite club.

But the committee's 1991 ruling was unabashedly strict, and it relegated baseball's finest pitching performance to a mere historical footnote. In 1959, the Pittsburgh Pirates' Harvey Haddix threw 12 perfect innings before yielding a hit and losing the game in the 13th inning (see Chapter 15). Haddix's unprecedented gem suddenly was just another loss, although Elias lists it and others like it under "No Hits through Nine Innings, Allowed Hit in Extra-Inning."[318]

"I'd probably say it wasn't a no-hitter because it wasn't a complete game," Haddix told a reporter in 1991 after the decision. "When you think about it, that would be correct."[319]

The definition also downgraded 11 other extra-inning breakups thrown by such hurlers as Bobo Newsom, Jim Maloney, Mark Gardner, and James "Hippo" Vaughn, who was on the losing end of baseball's only double no-hitter in 1917. In that contest, both Vaughn and Fred Toney held their opponents hitless through nine innings, but Vaughn gave up a hit and a run in the 10th inning for the loss. Toney held his spot in the books while his longtime rival got the boot.

Red Ames, Rube Waddell, Walter Johnson, "Toothpick Sam" Jones, Dean Chance, and 31 others lost no-nos called short of nine innings due to rain or darkness. They're now relegated by Elias to the "No-Hit Games: Regular Season, Fewer Than Nine Innings" section.[320]

That part of the committee's ruling was particularly harsh for the Pérez family, which began the day with two official no-hitters and went to bed with zero. The Montreal Expos' Pascual Pérez threw a five-inning rain-shortened no-hitter against the Philadelphia Phillies on September 24, 1988. Brother Mélido Pérez threw a six-inning rain-shortened no-hitter for the Chicago White Sox against the New York Yankees on July 12, 1990. Both lost their no-no status. "I have the tape and I have the ball, and I'll keep the no-hitter in my heart," Mélido Pérez told a reporter.[321]

One century-old baseball oddity survived the no-no bloodletting of 1991—Brooklyn Atlantic pitcher Sam Kimber's 10-inning no-hitter against the Toledo Blue Stockings that ended in a 0-0 tie.

Three ineligible non-no-nos have been thrown since the committee's ruling:

- On June 3, 1995, Pedro Martínez threw nine perfect innings, but his Montreal Expos couldn't score a run until the top of the 10th. The Padres' Bip Roberts led off the bottom of the 10th with a double, and San Diego had its first hit. Reliever Mel Rojas entered the game and retired the next three batters to secure the 1-0 win, but a no-hitter through nine was no longer eligible.
- On April 12, 1992, Boston Red Sox pitcher Matt Young lost a 2-1 no-hitter on the road to the Cleveland Indians but pitched just eight innings.
- On June 28, 2008, the Los Angeles Angels' Jered Weaver and Jose Arredondo lost a 1-0 no-no on the road to the Los Angeles Dodgers, but the pair combined to pitch just eight innings.

Pedro Martínez threw nine perfect innings against the Padres in 1995, but his Expos couldn't score a run, and Martínez wound up giving up a hit in the 10th. The game is not considered a no-hitter. *(Photo by Dirk Lammers)*

Chass, who wrote his *Times* column shortly after Young threw his eight-inning non-no-no, can't understand why the game is not considered a no-hitter. "It seems like a rather simple term, meaning an absence of hits," he wrote. "Why should anyone have trouble with that concept?"[322]

"Salida" Tom Hughes lost a no-hitter in extras for the 1910 New York Highlanders but finally got one for the Boston Braves in 1916. *(Photo from Bain News Service Collection, Prints & Photographs Division, Library of Congress, LC-DIG-ggbain-22481)*

These pitchers would have joined the roster of those throwing two career no-hitters, but rules about no-nos broken up in extra innings and games shortened by rain, darkness, or other reasons keep them off the official two-timers list.

Matt Kilroy

Kilroy threw an official no-hitter for the American Association's Baltimore Orioles in 1886. He followed it up with an unofficial seven-inning darkness-shortened no-hitter in 1889.

Jack Stivetts

Stivetts, of the Boston Beaneaters, tossed an official National League no-hitter against the Brooklyn Grooms in August 1892. Two months later, he threw an unofficial seven-inning no-hitter against the Grooms in the nightcap of a doubleheader. The game was called by mutual consent.

Red Ames

Ames, of the New York Giants, threw a five-inning rain-shortened no-hitter in 1903. Then, in 1909, he threw nine innings of no-hit ball only to give up a single in the 10th and lose the game in the 13th. He's officially credited with zero no-nos.

Rube Waddell

The Philadelphia Athletics' Waddell threw a five-inning rain-short-ened no-hitter in 1905 and relieved for the final two innings of a five-inning rain-shortened no-hitter in 1906. Neither counts in the books.

Johnny Lush

Lush threw an official no-hitter for the Philadelphia Phillies in 1906 and an unofficial six-inning rain-shortened no-hitter for the St. Louis Cardinals in 1908.

Ed Walsh

Walsh tossed an unofficial five-inning rain-shortened no-hitter for the Chicago White Sox in 1907. He got his official nine-inning no-no in 1911.

Tom Hughes

Hughes, of the New York Highlanders, threw nine innings of no-hit ball in 1910 but gave up a hit in the 10th and lost the game in the

11th. He got his official no-hitter in 1916 as a member of the Boston Braves.

Walter Johnson

Johnson, of the Washington Senators, threw an official no-hitter in 1920 and an unofficial seven-inning no-hitter shortened by rain in 1924.

"Toothpick" Sam Jones

Jones tossed an official no-hitter for the Chicago Cubs in 1955 and followed it in 1959 with an unofficial seven-inning rain-shortened no-hitter for the San Francisco Giants.

Dean Chance

Chance, of the Minnesota Twins, threw an unofficial five-inning rain-shortened perfect game on August 6, 1967. He followed it up with an official nine-inning no-hitter 20 days later.

An autograph seeker gets too close to Los Angeles Angels pitcher
Bo Belinsky, center, who threw a no-hitter in 1962.

(Photo from National Baseball Hall of Fame and Museum)

CHAPTER 29

HOLLYWOOD HUSTLE

How come Bo Belinsky's in a slump? Simple story: Bo Meets Girls!

—Gossip columnist Walter Winchell

No one expected greatness from Bo Belinsky when the perennial minor-league pitcher strutted nine days late into the Los Angeles Angels' training camp in the spring of 1962. Actually, one person did—Bo Belinsky.

The pool-hustling playboy informed Angels GM Fred Haney that his six years of small-ball experience warranted more than the league's $6,500 minimum salary. He wanted a couple of grand more. Haney's response? Sign or leave.

The two split the difference, and Haney's lack of excitement seemed merited in early March when the expansion Houston Colt .45s pounced on Belinsky for seven runs in the first three innings of an exhibition. But the 6-foot-2, 190-pound southpaw bounced back, earning a job in the Angels' rotation thanks to starter Ted Bowsfield's sore arm.

Belinsky won his first three regular-season starts, and Hollywood began taking notice of the tanned thrower from Trenton, who arrived in Tinseltown with a well-established reputation for late-night carousing. The ride was destined to grow wilder after he took the ball for a May 5, 1962, night game at Dodger Stadium.

Belinsky fell into a bit of trouble in the second inning, plunking Baltimore Orioles leadoff batter Jim Gentile with a pitch and walking Gus Triandos, but he cleaned up the mess without allowing a run. A walk and an error by Angels shortstop Felix Torres allowed another Baltimore runner to reach third in the fourth inning, but Belinsky again retired to the dugout unscathed.

He walked three more batters and hit another batsman but struck out nine and held the Orioles without a hit to become the first left-handed rookie in modern baseball history to throw a no-hitter. "No, I don't think I'll ask for a raise. I hate to push fate," he told sportswriter Charles Maher. "I'll let them come to me and ask me to take a raise."[323]

THE NO-NO THRUST the cocky Belinsky into instant stardom. He bought himself a candy-apple-red Cadillac convertible and began partying with Hollywood's elite. He showed up acting on the set of *77 Sunset Strip*. Gossip columnist Walter Winchell began to take notice, making Bo a frequent focus of his columns.

Unfortunately, Belinsky also caught the eye of Beverly Hills police. At a party for singer Eddie Fisher about a month or so after the no-no, officers held the Angels pitcher for questioning after a woman accused him of hitting her. Belinsky insisted that the woman had cut her eye getting out of his car, and police released the ballplayer after teammate Dean Chance and another witness corroborated his story.[324] Manager Bill Rigby fined Belinsky $250 for breaking curfew.

On June 26, 1962—perhaps foreshadowing an impending shift in fortunes—Belinsky watched Boston Red Sox pitcher Earl Wilson throw a no-hitter against his Angels as the two pitchers battled at Fenway Park on June 26. His win-loss record after that defeat sat at a still respectable 7-3.

But Belinsky continued showing up at late-night Hollywood parties, and tabloid photos and columns placed him with Ann-Margret, Tina Louise, Juliet Prowse, Connie Stevens, and blonde bombshell Mamie Van Doren. "He has a distorted view of life," commented Ignacio Lopez, a sportswriter for Riverside's *Press-Enterprise*. "Everything today—don't wait for the future. That's why he's trying to get everything he can now."[325]

As baseball slipped on Belinsky's priority list, so did his record. Belinsky learned in early September that the Angels planned to send him to the Kansas City Athletics as a player to be named later from an earlier deal to obtain pitcher Dan Osinski. Belinsky grumbled publicly to quash the pending trade, prompting Los Angeles to anoint Bowsfield instead of Belinsky as the player to be named later.[326]

Belinsky finished the season with a 10-11 record, issuing a league-leading 122 walks. He acknowledged that if he wanted to continue in the profession of baseball and regain fans' early-season respect, he had to improve his win-loss ratio. "I overdid the night clubs and the bright lights in every town we hit last season," Belinsky told UPI's Vernon Scott. "In each city it was a different story about Belinsky living it up."[327]

The 1963 season began with Belinsky presenting Van Doren with an engagement ring, but the bliss did little to help his struggles on the mound. Belinsky went 2-9 with a 5.75 ERA in his sophomore effort, his performance earning him a months-long demotion to class AAA minor-league affiliate Hawaii. At least in Honolulu, he could carouse outside the limelight.

Belinsky and Van Doren parted ways by October, never reaching the altar, and the pitcher seemed baseball-focused heading into the 1964 season. He posted a 9-8 record with a 2.86 ERA—his only winning season—but an incident in August ended his tenure in California. Braven Dyer, the *Los Angeles Times*'s 64-year-old beat writer, showed up at Belinsky's Washington hotel room to get a comment on a report that the pitcher was about to retire. Dyer said Belinsky just opened the door and slugged him. Belinsky said he was defending himself from Dyer's aggression.[328] The details didn't matter, as the report gave the Angels' management its excuse to part ways with Belinsky. The team suspended him indefinitely, then dealt him to the Philadelphia Phillies before the start of the 1965 season.

Belinsky couldn't muster success in Philadelphia, and his attempts at major-league comebacks with the Houston Astros, the Pittsburgh Pirates, and the Cincinnati Reds also fell short. He retired in 1970.

Meanwhile, he sank deeper into the bottle, and marriages to *Playboy* playmate Jo Collins and paper-company heiress Janie Weyerhaeuser ended in divorce.

He briefly recaptured the media spotlight in 1973 by teaming with sportswriter Maury Allen to chronicle his adventures in the 1973 biography, *Bo: Pitching and Wooing*. "He has moved on from Malibu," sportswriter Murray Olderman wrote at the time of the book's release. "He hangs around Las Vegas these days shooting pool, playing cards, picking up a buck or a broad with equal diffidence, subsisting on coffee and cigarettes and vodka."[329]

BELINSKY HIT BOTTOM in 1976 when he awoke under a freeway bridge outside Akron, Ohio, clutching an empty sake bottle.[330] That was his last drink. Belinsky settled in Las Vegas and built a second career working in customer relations for a car-dealership chain. He became a born-again Christian in 1998.

When the AAA Las Vegas 51s chose to honor the former major leaguer on June 1, 2001, by staging a "Bo Belinsky Night," the 64-year-old Belinsky insisted that the event raise money for his Trinity Life Church. "We spend the first 40, 50 years satisfying our egos and the next 20 or 10 trying to wipe the slate clean," Belinsky said after that honor. "I'm at that second stage."[331]

Five months after "Bo Belinsky Night," the pitcher succumbed to a heart attack. His 28-51 career record is already forgotten, but his May 5, 1962, accomplishment and his numerous off-the-field stories live on.

TWINS' FARM CLUB HURLS 18-DAY, TWO-STATE NO-NO

Rochester Red Wings pitcher Logan Darnell and catcher Dan Rohlfing celebrate the completion of a combined no-hitter that was started 18 days earlier. *(Photo by Bare Antolos, Rochester Red Wings)*

The Minnesota Twins franchise boasts seven no-hitters including the team's 60 years spent in the nation's capital as the Washington Senators. Walter Johnson and Bobby Burke threw the Senators' no-hitters, and Jack Kralick threw the Twins' first no-no in the team's second season in Minneapolis.

Kralick reigned over the Kansas City Athletics on August 26, 1962, just missing a perfect game on a one out ninth inning walk. Pinch hitter George Alusik typically hit Kralick well, the pitcher noted, and it was a better option to walk Alusik than to give him a good pitch to hit.

"I suppose that it's a little nicer to be a perfect game, but it really makes no diffrence to me," Kralick said. "I'm plenty satisfied."[332]

Dean Chance, Scott Erickson, Eric Milton, and Francisco Liriano threw Minnesota's other no-hitters, but it's the Twins' AAA minor-league affiliate that notched one of the oddest no-nos on record.

Rochester Red Wings right-hander Trevor May threw three innings of no-hit ball against the Durham Bulls in North Carolina on July 24, 2014, but the game was suspended due to rain in the middle of the fourth inning. When the game was finally resumed 18 days later in Rochester, New York, May couldn't take the mound because he had been called up to the show as a member of the Minnesota Twins.

Red Wings southpaw Logan Darnell took the Frontier Field mound and threw six innings of no-hit ball to finish the game. Darnell immediately texted May. "I told him what happened," Darnell told MiLB.com. "He was pretty pumped."[333]

Pitcher Jim Abbott, who was born with one hand, threw a no-hitter for the New York Yankees in 1993. *(Photo from National Baseball Hall of Fame and Museum, Michael Ponzini)*

CHAPTER 30

AGAINST ALL ODDS

From the seeds of doubt, from a place where there could have been little, along came something out of the ordinary.

—JIM ABBOTT, *Imperfect: An Improbable Life*

Overcoming a disability to succeed at any level of athletic play can seem like a challenge befitting long-shot odds. Pitcher Jim Abbott, who was born with one hand, shattered those odds and repeatedly doubled down at every level of his baseball career. The left-hander not only reached the majors but carved out a 10-year professional career accentuated with a 1993 no-hitter in the game's most storied setting.

Abbott conveyed his amazing story in his 2012 autobiography, *Imperfect: An Improbable Life*, inspiring a generation of kids to live for their dreams regardless of the obstacles. Retired from the game since 1999, Abbott continues to share his inspiring message through motivational speeches throughout the country.

Abbott wrote in his book that people's low expectations of him, especially in new situations, drove him toward success. Bolstered by a father who wouldn't let him quit and a mother who inspired through her work ethic and resilience, Abbott excelled at every level—Little League, high school, college ball, the Olympics, and ultimately the pros.

Simply playing ball with one hand required resourcefulness, but the necessity of having to pitch, field, and throw as part of the game's premier position became the mother of invention. As a young boy grow-ing up in Flint, Michigan, Abbott developed a clever way to deliver his pitch and then transfer his glove from his right wrist onto his left hand, readying himself for a bunt or comebacker. He could field the hit, drop his glove, and grab the ball in a fluid motion before throwing out the runner.

Abbott led the University of Michigan to two Big Ten champion-ships, prompting the California Angels to select the pitcher in the June 1988 amateur draft. Just a few months later, Abbott helped propel the U.S. Olympic team to a demonstration-sport gold medal in Seoul.

Abbott skipped the minor leagues and made his major-league debut against the Seattle Mariners on April 8, 1989, in front of 47,000 fans at Anaheim Stadium. The ballpark that night also drew 150 credentialed reporters keyed on the unique story of the one-handed pitcher, a label Abbott spent his career trying to shake.

The outing didn't go well (he gave up six runs in four and two-thirds innings during a 7-0 loss), but Abbott persevered to post a 12-12 record with a 3.92 ERA. Abbott hit his stride by 1991, improving to 18-11 with a 2.89 ERA. He lowered his ERA to 2.77 the next season, but a slip in run support led to a 7-15 record. His agent had been discussing a contract extension with the Angels when the club traded him to the Yankees in December 1992.

ABBOTT STRUGGLED in the Big Apple with a 9-11 record when he got the ball for a September 4, 1993, start against the Cleveland Indians at Yankee Stadium. He began the game by walking leadoff batter Kenny Lofton but followed by inducing a 5-4-3 double play from Felix Fermin. He walked four additional batters, but a strong Yankees defense kept a handful of hard-hit balls from resulting in a single base hit.

Lofton tried to break up the no-hitter in the ninth with a bunt at-tempt, drawing boos from the Yankee Stadium crowd of 27,000, but the effort went foul, and Lofton grounded out to second. Abbott got Fermin to fly out to center before enticing a grounder-to-short out of Carlos Baerga.

"He did it! He did it!" bellowed Yankees announcer Dewayne Staats. "No-hitter for Jim Abbott."[334]

Teammates rushed the mound as Abbott pounded his right arm into his glove and reached out to embrace catcher Matt Nokes. Abbott said the feeling was "unreal." "I'm just thrilled to death," he told a reporter. "I never thought about pitching a no-hitter. I give up a lot of hits."[335]

When Abbott arrived at Yankee Stadium the next day, reporters from as far off as Philadelphia and Boston surrounded his locker to talk about the previous day's no-no. He knew that their questions would be centered on the one-handed pitcher making his way—a story line he never cared for. "The stories could say what they wanted, but two-handed guys and one-handed guys don't throw no-hitters. Pitchers throw them," he wrote in his autobiography.[336]

A look back further into baseball's history finds that Abbott wasn't even the first one-handed pitcher to throw a no-hitter. The Cleveland Blues' Hugh Daily, who lost his left hand in an accident with a loaded musket, threw a no-hitter against the Philadelphia Quakers on September 13, 1883.

Three years after Abbott's unexpected gem, Yankee Stadium played host to another redemption no-no. Dwight "Doc" Gooden had seemed destined for Hall of Fame honors when he sped onto the New York sports scene back in 1984. The Mets' right-hander from Tampa, Florida, earned Na-

Although Dwight "Doc" Gooden was a rookie sensation with the New York Mets, he got his no-hitter as a Yankee in 1996. *(Photo from National Baseball Hall of Fame and Museum)*

tional League Rookie of the Year honors by posting a 17-9 record with a 2.60 ERA and a league-leading 276 strikeouts, and no sophomore slump awaited on the horizon. The next year, Gooden become the youngest 20-game winner in major-league history, his 24-4 record, 1.53 ERA, and 268 strikeouts earning him the Cy Young Award. But even as the strike-out ace helped the Mets capture the ball club's second World Series title in 1986, trouble was brewing beneath the surface.

Gooden was a no-show on Broadway as teammates soaked in adula-tion during the city's ticker-tape parade. He was in Long Island, nursing a brutal hangover after a night of vodka shots and cocaine lines, Gooden wrote in his 2013 book, *Doc: A Memoir.* He failed his first league drug test during spring training in 1987, and his battle with addiction contin-ued as he wound up missing the end of the 1994 season and sitting out all of 1995 on failed prohibited-substance tests.

Gooden, who's been clean and sober since 2011, said he was always ripe for addiction. "My whole life, whenever I had something I liked, I wanted more of it—way more of it, even if having more was a terrible idea," he wrote in his memoir.[337]

The Mets eventually parted ways with Gooden, prompting the fast-ball ace to embark on a 1996 comeback with the crosstown New York Yankees. Gooden struggled early, but injuries to the Yanks' starters thrust him into the rotation, and "Doctor K" got the ball for a May 14, 1996, contest against the Seattle Mariners.

That evening, with much of his mind back home in Tampa as his father prepared to undergo double-bypass surgery, Gooden dominated the Mariners lineup, scattering four walks and four strikeouts through eight innings while holding Seattle to zero hits.

He appeared to be running out of steam in the ninth frame as he walked Alex Rodriguez and Edgar Martínez and then threw a wild pitch to allow runners to reach second and third. But he recovered to strike out Jay Buhner and then got Paul Sorrento to pop out to short to com-plete the no-no. Teammates carried the 31-year-old hero off the Yankee Stadium field to the cheers of more than 20,000 fans.

In stark contrast to the 1986 World Series celebration, Gooden boarded the first morning flight to Tampa and arrived in time to give his dad the game ball before surgery. "Thinking of where I was a year and a half ago, I never even thought I would pitch again," Gooden told a reporter. "And then to throw a no-hitter I wouldn't have thought it was possible in my wildest dreams."[338]

LARGEST AND SMALLEST NO-NO RUN DIFFERENTIALS

Pud Galvin, shown in this Old Judge Cigarettes baseball card, threw the most lopsided no-hitter, an 18-0 win by the Buffalo Bisons over the Detroit Wolverines in 1884. *(Baseball card photo from the Benjamin K. Edwards Collection, Prints & Photographs Division, Library of Congress, LC-DIG-bbc-0355f)*

After running some numbers on the no-hitters thrown through the 2015 season, it appears that the average score of a no-hitter is 4.5 to 0.1. I've never seen run totals expressed in a box score using decimal places, so perhaps we should consider the median score instead of the average—a 4-0 victory for the no-no pitcher's team.

Of the 294 no-hitters through 2015, 53 games were won by one run, 41 were won by two runs, 30 were won by three runs, 39 were won by four runs, 32 were won by five runs, and 40 were won by six runs. Here are the no-hitters with the largest and smallest run differentials. Oddly, both games took place in 1884.

18—LARGEST RUN DIFFERENTIAL

Pud Galvin
Buffalo Bisons (NL)
Monday, August 4, 1884
Buffalo Bisons 18, Detroit Wolverines 0
Recreation Park (Detroit)
His second of two no-hitters.

0—SMALLEST RUN DIFFERENTIAL

Sam Kimber
Brooklyn Atlantics (AA)
Saturday, October 4, 1884
Brooklyn Atlantics 0, Toledo Blue Stockings 0 (10 inn.)
Washington Park (Brooklyn)
Game called for darkness.

It's highly unlikely that Brooklyn Robins manager Wilbert Robinson had
that kid keeping a pitch count or he wouldn't have let Leon Cadore
throw 26 innings. *(Photo from Bain News Service Collection, Prints &
Photographs Division, Library of Congress, LC-DIG-ggbain-31065)*

CHAPTER 31

WHAT PITCH COUNT?

Once I've started counting it's really hard to stop. Hey!
Faster, faster. It is so exciting!
I could count forever, count until I drop. Ha!

—COUNT VON COUNT, *Sesame Street*

Major-league baseball was more than a half-century away from tracking pitch counts in 1920, and it's unlikely that Brooklyn Robins manager Wilbert Robinson and Boston Braves skipper George Stallings scribbled any of their own clipboard markings during a May 1 matchup between the National League clubs.

Pitchers in that day were paid to pitch, and nary a manager sweated overworking his star hurler's golden arm. The contemporary piecemeal pitching roles of closer, long reliever, and setup man had yet to be established, and no left-handed specialist sat in the bullpen awaiting his one-batter call-in.

Robins starter Leon Cadore and Braves starter Joe Oeschger were expected to go the distance if they could continue retiring batters, but no one expected "the distance" that day to equate to 26 innings. Both managers would have likely tapped their weary pitchers to take the mound for a 27th frame had darkness not overtaken Braves Field to ensure a 1-1 final score.

No one knows for sure how many pitches Cadore and Oeschger

tossed that day, but a pitch-count formula developed by sabermetrics expert Tom "Tangotiger" Tango estimates that each of their tallies topped 300. That's about three times what's expected of a typical modern-day starting pitcher.

No-hitters often represent the cream of the crop of pitching performances, but not all no-nos result in low pitch counts. A flurry of walks, patient batters drawing first strikes, and pesky hitters repeatedly fouling off good pitches can accelerate the ticker quickly.

The Arizona Diamondbacks' Edwin Jackson needed 149 pitches to no-hit the Tampa Bay Rays on June 25, 2010, a mark unequaled for no-hitters thrown by a single pitcher since statisticians began tallying official pitch counts in 1988. (Note that six Astros pitchers used a combined 151 pitches to no-hit the Yankees in 2003.)

Jackson's night at Tropicana Field did not start smoothly. The German-born pitcher, who grew up in Columbus, Georgia, walked two batters and threw a wild pitch in the first inning, walked two in the second inning, and walked three in the third. He settled down by the fourth inning and nursed a 1-0 lead into the ninth, but the early damage put Jackson at 134 pitches.

The 26-year-old right-hander told Diamondbacks manager A. J. Hinch that it would take a hit to get him off the mound. He continued attacking the strike zone in the ninth and figured that whatever would happen would happen, he told a reporter.[339] Jackson issued one more base on balls before completing the no-no by retiring Jason Bartlett on a groundout on pitch No. 149. "I didn't even pay attention to the pitch count toward the end, because I didn't want it on my mind," he said in the postgame television interview. "I just wanted to keep throwing."[340]

THE SAN FRANCISCO GIANTS' Tim Lincecum pushed his stamina to the limit on July 13, 2013, while notching his first career no-hitter against the San Diego Padres. The 5-foot-11, 170-pound righty, nicknamed "the Freak" for his unconventional pitching mechanics, hit the pitch-count century mark by the sixth inning.

Giants pitching coach Dave Righetti had thrown his own no-hitter with the New York Yankees in 1983, so he knew what was at stake. Righetti told sportswriter Bernie Wilson that Lincecum wanted the no-no and was in his zone to get it. "The only way he was staying in was if he didn't give up a hit," the coach said.[341]

Lincecum didn't give up a hit, and his 148-pitch-count no-no sits just a single throw short of Jackson's record.

SEVERAL OF THE NO-HITTERS thrown prior to 1988 likely exceed the 149-pitch mark, but the lack of official counts kept them out of the record books.

The Cincinnati Reds' Jim Maloney set the bar for labored no-hitters in the summer of 1965, tossing two 10-inning no-hitters, though the record books credit just one of those as official.

On June 14, 1965, the right-hander held the Mets hitless through 10 innings but had little support from his offense. The Reds strung together a leadoff single, a sacrifice bunt, and a groundout in the bottom of the 10th to advance a runner to third, but Tommy Harper grounded out to send the still scoreless contest to the 11th frame.

Mets right fielder Johnny Lewis, who had struck out in his first three plate appearances, stepped into the box and launched a low fastball over Crosley Field's center-field wall, giving New York a 1-0 lead. The Reds couldn't muster a run in the bottom half of the 11th, and Maloney took the loss in a game in which he struck out 18 of the 35 batters he faced.

He quipped to sportswriter Gary Kale after the game that his arm "was tired only from tipping my hat to the many ovations."[342]

No official count exists, but Tango's pitch-count estimator based on plate appearances, strikeouts, and bases on balls offers an educated guess for such legacy games. Let's do the math:

$$(3.3 \times PA) + (1.5 \times SO) + (2.2 \times BB)$$
$$(3.3 \times 35) + (1.5 \times 18) + (2.2 \times 1)$$
$$115.5 + 27 + 2.2$$

About 145 pitches

If the formula's estimate is accurate, Maloney's 10-inning workload falls just shy of the nine-inning no-no counts from Jackson and Lincecum.

But Maloney blew away those modern hurlers about two months later while tossing his first official career no-hitter. The August 19, 1965, matchup between the Reds and the Cubs during a doubleheader opener at Wrigley Field comes complete with a pitch count, thanks to the intrepid on-air work of WGN television's Jack Brickhouse.

The unprecedented number: 187 pitches.

The Cubs and Reds were locked in a 0-0 tie in the top of the 10th when Reds shortstop Leo Cárdenas blasted a home run into the left-field foul-pole screen to give Cincinnati a 1-0 lead. Up next was a rejuvenated Maloney, who pounced on the first pitch for a chopper toward second and nearly beat out the throw. He returned to the dugout for a brief rest before taking the mound for the bottom of the 10th.

Maloney, showing signs of fatigue after throwing 173 pitches, opened with a walk and then pushed the count to 3-1 on Billy Williams before getting him to fly out to left. With the righty's pitch count now at 186, Ernie Banks jumped on the first pitch and poked a routine grounder to shortstop, which Cárdenas turned into a game-ending 6-4-3 double play.

Maloney finally had his no-hit victory, striking out 12 Cubs while issuing 10 walks and hitting one batsman. He told WGN's Lou Boudreau and Lloyd Pettit in a postgame interview that his fastball tends to sink and tail when he loses a little edge, and that extra movement proved effective in the final three innings. "I wasn't real sharp as I was against the Mets, but I think this is the biggest game of my career right here," Maloney said.[343]

. . .

AN ELEVATED NO-HITTER pitch count may have contributed to arm troubles suffered by one of the most dominant left-handed pitchers of this millennium. New York Mets fans rejoiced on June 1, 2012, when Johan Santana threw that club's first no-hitter in its 51-year history, but the feat came at a great cost.

Santana was making just his 11th start after returning from surgery to repair a left-shoulder tear that had sidelined him for the entire previous season. Mets Manager Terry Collins had been limiting Santana to 100 to 115 pitches per game, but Santana didn't want to give up the ball in the midst of a no-no. Collins acquiesced.

It took Santana 134 pitches to make Mets history, and the club's $137.5 million ace was never the same. He made just 10 more starts that season before again landing on the DL. Santana sat out the 2013 and 2014 seasons, and his quest to return to the majors continues to be stymied by injuries.

Collins, speaking to *New York Daily News* sportswriter Kristie Ackert on the one-year anniversary of Santana's historic accomplishment, said, "It wasn't necessarily the no-hitter that caused the injury, but I know it didn't help."[344]

NO-HITTERS BY PITCH COUNT

It took Edwin Jackson 149 pitches to throw his 2010 no-hitter
for the Arizona Diamondbacks. *(Photo by Dirk Lammers)*

Baseball statisticians didn't begin tallying official pitch counts until
1988, so there have most likely been no-hitters thrown with more than
149 pitches and fewer than 83 pitches. But, limiting this list to official no-hit pitch counts for single pitchers, here are the Top 3 lists for
no-hitters thrown using the most and the fewest pitches since 1988.

MOST PITCHES IN A NO-NO

1st—149 pitches
Edwin Jackson
Arizona Diamondbacks (NL) / Friday, June 25, 2010 / Arizona
    Diamondbacks 1, Tampa Bay Rays 0
Tropicana Field (St. Petersburg)

2nd—148 pitches
Tim Lincecum
San Francisco Giants (NL) / Saturday, July 13, 2013 / San Francisco
    Giants 9, San Diego Padres 0
Petco Park (San Diego)
His first of two no-hitters

3rd—138 pitches
Randy Johnson
Seattle Mariners (AL) / Saturday, June 2, 1990 / Seattle Mariners 2,
    Detroit Tigers 0
Kingdome (Seattle)
His first of two no-hitters
Note: A tandem of six Houston Astros pitchers threw a combined
151 pitches while no-hitting the New York Yankees on June 11,
2003.

FEWEST PITCHES IN A NO-NO

1st—83 pitches
Darryl Kile
Houston Astros (NL) / Wednesday, September 8, 1993 / Houston
    Astros 7, New York Mets 1
Astrodome (Houston)

2nd—88 pitches
David Cone
New York Yankees (AL) / Sunday, July 18, 1999 / New York Yankees
    6, Montreal Expos 0
Yankee Stadium (New York)
Perfect game

3rd (tie)—96 pitches
Dennis Martínez
Montreal Expos (NL) / Sunday, July 28, 1991 / Montreal Expos 2,
    Los Angeles Dodgers 0
Dodger Stadium (Los Angeles)
Perfect game

3rd (tie)—96 pitches
Philip Humber
Chicago White Sox (AL) / Saturday, April 21, 2012 / Chicago
    White Sox 4, Seattle Mariners 0
Safeco Field (Seattle)
Perfect game

Henderson Álvarez threw nine no-hit innings for the Florida Marlins on the final day of the 2013 baseball season, but it took a walk-off wild pitch in the bottom of the ninth to get him the win. *(Photo by KeithAllisonPhoto.com)*

CHAPTER 32

THE WILD WORLD OF WALK-OFF NO-NOS

I don't know that, in your life, you can envision a no-hitter ending like that.

—Miami Marlins manager Mike Redmond
to the *Miami Herald*

The walk-off win provides one of baseball's most thrilling outbursts, launching a couple dozen tense teammates out of the dugout into a frenzied mosh pit of elation. The celebration commences as the winning run crosses home plate, but its location and person of honor can vary.

For a walk-off base hit, the party wanders to the location of the guy who knocked in the winning run. For a walk-off home run, players form a half-circle around home plate and prepare to mob their hero as he crosses the plate.

September 29, 2013, marked the first time that walk-off festivities centered on the person waiting in the on-deck circle.

It was the final day of the 2013 baseball season, and the Miami Marlins' Henderson Álvarez no-hit the Detroit Tigers through nine innings. The Marlins couldn't score a run through eight, but things were looking up in the bottom of the ninth.

Tigers reliever Luke Putkonen got the first out, then gave up back-to-

back singles to Giancarlo Stanton and Justin Ruggiano. Adeiny Hecha-
varria stepped to the plate, and Putkonen threw a wild pitch that let
Ruggiano take second and Stanton grab third. Putkonen got Hechavar-
ria to ground out to shortstop but then walked Chris Coghlan to load
the bases for pinch hitter Greg Dobbs.

There was no way Álvarez would bat, as there were two outs and no
room on the bases. It seemed that either the game would end in victory,
with Dobbs being crowned the hero, or Álvarez would return to the
mound to pitch the top of the 10th in a still scoreless game.

Álvarez in this moment dutifully swung the donuted bat in the on-
deck circle, portraying the role of potential hitter as he silently offered a
prayer. "I thought to myself, 'God, give me this inning, a hit or whatever, to win and get the no-hitter," Álvarez told the *Miami Herald*.[345]

Putkonen tossed a low inside breaking ball that grazed the dirt and
skirted past catcher Brayan Peña. Stanton darted home with the winning
run, and the game was over. Álvarez tossed aside his batting helmet before a school of Marlins mobbed him behind home plate. "It's a no-hitter, Henderson Álvarez. Miami wins it," declared *Fox Sports Florida*
television announcer Tommy Hutton. "One of the strangest finishes
you'll ever see results in the fifth no-hitter in Marlin history."[346]

A Marlins ticket stub from Henderson Álvarez's walk-off no-no
that ended the 2013 season *(Photo by Dirk Lammers)*

The term "walk-off" hadn't yet been coined when baseball fans witnessed the first walk-off no-hitter just after the end of World War II.

Toronto-born Dick Fowler was less than a month removed from his discharge from the Canadian Army on September 9, 1945, and he got the start for the Philadelphia Athletics in the second game of a doubleheader against the St. Louis Browns. The 24-year-old right-hander threw nine innings of no-hit ball but had to return to the Athletics' dugout to watch as his teammates sought to break a 0-0 tie in the bottom of the ninth inning.

Right fielder Hal Peck, who had been unable to get a hit off the Browns' Ox Miller earlier in the game, led off the inning with a triple. Second baseman Irv Hall singled Peck home with a base hit up the middle to share hero honors with Fowler.

The pitcher said it was a wonderful feeling when Peck crossed the plate. "You don't think—you just sort of get a thrill all over," Fowler told a reporter after the game.[347]

JUST 2,215 FANS were on hand to witness the next walk-off no-no thrown seven years after Fowler's masterpiece, and the faithful who came out to Detroit's Briggs Stadium on May 15, 1952, were treated to a stellar pitchers' duel.

The Washington Senators' Bob Porterfield carried a no-hitter into the sixth inning and entered the bottom of the ninth having given up just three hits and a couple of walks. But the Tigers' Virgil Trucks outshone Porterfield, throwing nine innings of no-hit ball while issuing just a single base on balls. Detroit second baseman Jerry Priddy committed three errors, but none of the blunders led to a Senators run.

The contest was deadlocked at zero in the bottom of the ninth inning when Detroit's George Kell led off with a groundout. Pat Mullin foreshadowed the ending by driving a deep fly ball to right field, but Jackie Jensen snagged the ball five feet short of the wall.

Vic Wertz, who had tagged Porterfield for a double in the seventh inning but was left on base, drove Porterfield's knee-high inside fastball into the right-field stands just shy of the foul pole.

The celebration began before Wertz officially crossed home plate with the winning run. "As Wertz rounded the base Tiger teammates started backslapping Trucks, who hadn't won a game this season and gave up 13 hits in his last trip," wrote sportswriter Harry Stapler.[348]

IT WOULD BE a half-century before fans would see their next walk-off no-no, and the Pittsburgh Pirates' Francisco Córdova would have to share his celebration with both the hero hitter and a fellow member of his pitching staff.

Córdova was pitching a gem on July 12, 1997, delighting the more than 44,000 fans who packed Three Rivers Stadium for fireworks night and a Jackie Robinson tribute. Córdova used his sinkerball to hold the Houston Astros to zero runs on zero hits through nine innings.

Astros starter Chris Holt scattered five hits, but he and closer Billy Wagner kept the game scoreless as it headed into the 10th inning.

Córdova's tank was empty after throwing 121 pitches, and it was clear that manager Gene Lamont had to pull him. The normally upbeat Pirates bullpen crew sat nervously silent while waiting for the phone to ring, recalled pitcher Ricardo Rincón. "No one wanted to stand up," Rincón told the *Pittsburgh Tribune-Review*. "Everybody was so nervous. When they named me, I said to myself, 'Well, if this is what God wants ...'"[349] Rincón did his job, holding Houston hitless in the top of the 10th inning while maintaining the shutout.

Astros reliever John Hudek took the ball for the bottom of the 10th inning and put a couple of runners on base via walks while getting the first two outs. Lamont sent Mark Smith to the plate to pinch hit for Rincón, and Smith blasted an 0-1 fastball over the left field wall. "It's a home run. It's a no-hitter," called KDKA radio announcer Lanny Frattare. "You've got it all!"[350]

POSTSCRIPT:
RECORDS WERE MADE
TO BE BROKEN

From the moment I began writing this book early in the 2014 season, baseball has reminded me that its history is ever changing.

The Los Angeles Dodgers' Josh Beckett and Clayton Kershaw threw spring no-nos within a month's span to add to the franchise's already record-setting total, currently at 25. A week later, the San Francisco Giants' Tim Lincecum became just the second pitcher in major-league history to no-hit the same team twice (the San Diego Padres).

September brought a combined no-no by a Philadelphia Phillies tandem and baseball's second straight season-ending no-no, this one by the Washington Nationals' Jordan Zimmermann.

Even as the manuscript was seemingly being finalized in 2015, the San Francisco Giants' Chris Heston no-hit the Mets for no-hitter No. 288, and the Washington Nationals' Max Scherzer notched No. 289. Cole Hamels threw No. 290 just before the July trade deadline, making the Cubs a no no victim for the first time since 1965.

August brought three more no-nos: The Mariners' Hisashi Iwakuma threw No. 291 on August 12, breaking a 12-game National League streak; the Astros' Mike Fiers tossed No. 292 nine days later; and the

Cubs' Jake Arrieta threw No. 293 nine days after Fiers's gem. And then Scherzer notched his second of the year, No. 294, on the penultimate day of the 2015 season.

Who knows what the rest of the decade will bring. Perhaps the aggressive no-no pace of recent years will continue, and the majors will reach the 300 mark. Or maybe the Padres franchise will finally get its elusive no-hitter. I invite you to visit NoNoHitters.com to keep up with the latest news on everything related to no-hitters.

—Dirk Lammers

ACKNOWLEDGMENTS

Two thoughts come to mind as I finish the edit on this book, which has been in the works for nearly two years: It has been way more complex than I envisioned and way more fun than I imagined.

Such a venture would not have been possible without the love, support, and continual encouragement from my wonderful wife, Angela, who believed in me from Day 1 and never wavered. I am forever thankful for the person you are and the leap of faith you took.

Both my mom and my dad have passed on, but I see a great deal of both of them in this book.

My dad, Donald, took me to my first Mets game at Shea (Jerry Koosman's four-hit shutout of the Cubs in '75), and together we survived the painful late '70s and early '80s before finally getting to toast a world championship in '86. My favorite shared moment was celebrating the Mets' 19-inning 16-13 rain-delayed win over the Braves on July 4, 1985, which ended at 4 a.m. the next day. We watched every out of the marathon—the first nine innings on the main TV before retiring to our own rooms for extras—and met up in the kitchen for late-night snacks after the 13th and 18th frames.

My mom, Betty, was an amazing writer, and I am blessed to have inherited even a portion of her incredible wit, inquisitiveness, and eye for detail. She took great pride in every poem, magazine story or newspaper article she was able to get published—no small task considering she was busy raising six kids. My mom was a voracious reader, and I would have loved to be able to get a copy of this book into her hands.

I am grateful for my amazing sons, Michael and Alex, who joined me on some crazy baseball road trips that included a day game at Wrigley Field immediately followed by a night game at Shea. We even stopped off at the *Field of Dreams* movie site and played some pickup ball—a memory I will cherish forever.

I couldn't have asked for a better book foreword, and I greatly appreciate former Major League Baseball Commissioner Fay Vincent for taking the time to pen such wonderful words of praise and encouragement. The sport was lucky to have such a man at its helm.

I was fortunate for this project to team up with a great editor, Carl Lennertz, who not only offered invaluable suggestions to improve the manuscript but also shared my desire to incorporate a liberal dose of pop-culture references. Thanks, also, to literary agent Helen Zimmermann, who paired me with Carl and found a great home for *Baseball's No-Hit Wonders* at Unbridled Books. Publishers Fred Ramey and Greg Michaelson are avid baseball fans, and I am thankful that they saw enough promise in this idea to welcome it into their wonderful collection of titles.

Many people and organizations contributed images for this book, and they include photographers Keith Allison, E. M. During, and Bare Antolos, artist Dick Perez, the Topps Company, Hunt Auctions, Andy Sandler's All Sports Collectibles Auctions, and Robert Edward Auctions. John Horne with the National Baseball Hall of Fame was extremely helpful in finding additional images.

Thanks, too, to the many baseball players, managers, broadcasters, and fans who granted interviews, including Don Larsen, Clay Buchholz, Jim Bunning, Matt Garza, Steve Busby, Milt Pappas, Andy Hawkins, Bob Uecker, Ken Johnson, Jeff Torborg, Bill Schroeder, Robert Ford, and Linda Ruth Tosetti. I am also quite fortunate to have so many people continuing to contribute promotional blurbs to help this book reach a wide audience.

I'd also like to give a shout out to a couple of great websites that help make research and fact checking so easy, Retrosheet (www.retrosheet. org) and Baseball-Reference.com. It's hard to imagine tackling a topic of this magnitude without those tremendous tools.

Baseball's No-Hit Wonders has been a team effort, and I'm grateful to have such a great group of partners joining me on the field.

BASEBALL'S NO-HITTERS

1
George Washington Bradley
St. Louis Brown Stockings (NL)
Saturday, July 15, 1876
St. Louis Brown Stockings 2,
    Hartford Dark Blues 0
Sportsman's Park (St. Louis)

2
Lee Richmond
Worcester Ruby Legs (NL)
Saturday, June 12, 1880
Worcester Ruby Legs 1, Cleveland
    Blues 0
Worcester Driving Park Grounds
    (Worcester)
Perfect game

3
John Montgomery Ward
Providence Grays (NL)
Thursday, June 17, 1880
Providence Grays 5, Buffalo Bisons 0
Messer Street Grounds (Providence)
Perfect game

4
Larry Corcoran
Chicago White Stockings (NL)
Thursday, August 19, 1880
Chicago White Stockings 6, Boston
    Red Caps 0
Lakefront Park (Chicago)
His first of three no-hitters

5
Pud Galvin
Buffalo Bisons (NL)
Friday, August 20, 1880
Buffalo Bisons 1, Worcester Ruby
    Legs 0
Riverside Park (Buffalo)
His first of two no-hitters

6
Tony Mullane
Louisville Eclipse (AA)
Monday, September 11, 1882
Louisville Eclipse 2, Cincinnati Red
    Stockings 0
Bank Street Grounds (Cincinnati)

7

Guy Hecker
Louisville Eclipse (AA)
Tuesday, September 19, 1882
Louisville Eclipse 3, Pittsburgh
    Alleghenys 1
Exposition Park (Pittsburgh)

8

Larry Corcoran
Chicago White Stockings (NL)
Wednesday, September 20, 1882
Chicago White Stockings 5,
    Worcester Ruby Legs 0
Lake Front Park (Chicago)
His second of three no-hitters

9

Charles "Old Hoss" Radbourn
Providence Grays (NL)
Wednesday, July 25, 1883
Providence Grays 8, Cleveland
    Blues 0
Kennard Street Park (Cleveland)

10

Hugh Daily
Cleveland Blues (NL)
Thursday, September 13, 1883
Cleveland Blues 1, Philadelphia
    Quakers 0
Recreation Park (Philadelphia)

11

Al Atkinson
Philadelphia Athletics (AA)
Saturday, May 24, 1884
Philadelphia Athletics 10, Pittsburgh
    Alleghenys 1
Recreation Park (Philadelphia)
His first of two no-hitters

12

Ed Morris
Columbus Buckeyes (AA)
Thursday, May 29, 1884
Columbus Buckeyes 5, Pittsburgh
    Alleghenys 0
Recreation Park (Pittsburgh)

13

Frank Mountain
Columbus Buckeyes (AA)
Thursday, June 5, 1884
Columbus Buckeyes 12, Washington
    Nationals 0
Capitol Grounds (Washington, D.C.)

14

Larry Corcoran
Chicago White Stockings (NL)
Friday, June 27, 1884
Chicago White Stockings 6,
    Providence Grays 0
Lakefront Park (Chicago)
His third of three no-hitters

15
Pud Galvin
Buffalo Bisons (NL)
Monday, August 4, 1884
Buffalo Bisons 18, Detroit
  Wolverines 0
Recreation Park (Detroit)
His second of two no-hitters

16
Dick Burns
Cincinnati Outlaw Reds (UA)
Tuesday, August 26, 1884
Cincinnati Outlaw Reds 3, Kansas
  City Unions 1
Association Park (Kansas City)

17
Ed Cushman
Milwaukee Brewers (UA)
Sunday, September 28, 1884
Milwaukee Brewers 5, Washington
  Nationals 0
Wright Street Grounds (Milwaukee)

18
Sam Kimber
Brooklyn Atlantics (AA)
Saturday, October 4, 1884
Brooklyn Atlantics 0, Toledo Blue
  Stockings 0 (10 inn.)
Washington Park (Brooklyn)
Game called for darkness

19
John Clarkson
Chicago White Stockings (NL)
Monday, July 27, 1885
Chicago White Stockings 4,
  Providence Grays 0
Messer Street Grounds (Providence)

20
Charlie Ferguson
Philadelphia Quakers (NL)
Saturday, August 29, 1885
Philadelphia Quakers 1, Providence
  Grays 0
Recreation Park (Philadelphia)

21
Al Atkinson
Philadelphia Athletics (AA)
Saturday, May 1, 1886
Philadelphia Athletics 3, New York
  Metropolitans 2
Jefferson Street Grounds (Philadelphia)
His second of two no-hitters

22
Adonis Terry
Brooklyn Grays (AA)
Saturday, July 24, 1886
Brooklyn Grays 1, St. Louis Browns 0
Washington Park (Brooklyn)
His first of two no-hitters

23
Matt Kilroy
Baltimore Orioles (AA)
Wednesday, October 6, 1886
Baltimore Orioles 6, Pittsburgh
    Alleghenys 0
Recreation Park (Pittsburgh)

24
Adonis Terry
Brooklyn Bridegrooms (AA)
Sunday, May 27, 1888
Brooklyn Bridegrooms 4, Louisville
    Colonels 0
Ridgewood Park (Brooklyn)
His second of two no-hitters

25
Henry Porter
Kansas City Cowboys (AA)
Wednesday, June 6, 1888
Kansas City Cowboys 4, Baltimore
    Orioles 0
Oriole Park (Baltimore)

26
Ed Seward
Philadelphia Athletics (AA)
Thursday, July 26, 1888
Philadelphia Athletics 12, Cincinnati
    Red Stockings 2
Jefferson Street Grounds
    (Philadelphia)

27
Gus Weyhing
Philadelphia Athletics (AA)
Tuesday, July 31, 1888
Philadelphia Athletics 4, Kansas City
    Cowboys 0
Jefferson Street Grounds (Philadelphia)

28
Ledell "Cannonball" Titcomb
Rochester Broncos (AA)
Monday, September 15, 1890
Rochester Broncos 7, Syracuse Stars 0
Culver Field (Rochester)

29
Tom Lovett
Brooklyn Grooms (NL)
Monday, June 22, 1891
Brooklyn Grooms 4, New York
    Giants 0
Eastern Park (Brooklyn)

30
Amos Rusie
New York Giants (NL)
Friday, July 31, 1891
New York Giants 6, Brooklyn
    Grooms 0
Polo Grounds (New York)

31
Ted Breitenstein
St. Louis Browns (AA)
Sunday, October 4, 1891 (first game
    of doubleheader)
St. Louis Browns 8, Louisville
    Colonels 0
Sportsman's Park (St. Louis)
His first of two no-hitters

32
Jack Stivetts
Boston Beaneaters (NL)
Saturday, August 6, 1892
Boston Beaneaters 11, Brooklyn
    Grooms 0
Eastern Park (Brooklyn)

33
Ben Sanders
Louisville Colonels (NL)
Monday, August 22, 1892
Louisville Colonels 6, Baltimore
    Orioles 2
Eclipse Park (Louisville)

34
Charles "Bumpus" Jones
Cincinnati Reds (NL)
Saturday, October 15, 1892
Cincinnati Reds 7, Pittsburgh
    Pirates 1
League Park (Cincinnati)

35
Bill Hawke
Baltimore Orioles (NL)
Wednesday, August 16, 1893
Baltimore Orioles 5, Washington
    Senators 0
Boundary Field (Washington)

36
Cy Young
Cleveland Spiders (NL)
Saturday, September 18, 1897 (first
    game of doubleheader)
Cleveland Spiders 6, Cincinnati
    Reds 0
League Park (Cleveland)
His first of three no-hitters

37
Ted Breitenstein
Cincinnati Reds (NL)
Friday, April 22, 1898
Cincinnati Reds 11, Pittsburgh
    Pirates 0
League Park (Cincinnati)
His second of two no-hitters

38
Jim Jay Hughes
Baltimore Orioles (NL)
Friday, April 22, 1898
Baltimore Orioles 8, Boston
    Beaneaters 0
Union Park (Baltimore)

39
Frank "Red" Donahue
Philadelphia Phillies (NL)
Friday, July 8, 1898
Philadelphia Phillies 5, Boston
    Beaneaters 0
National League Park
    (Philadelphia)

40
Walter Thornton
Chicago Orphans (NL)
Sunday, August 21, 1898 (second
    game of doubleheader)
Chicago Orphans 2, Brooklyn
    Bridegrooms 0
West Side Park (Chicago)

41
Charles "Deacon" Phillippe
Louisville Colonels (NL)
Thursday, May 25, 1899
Louisville Colonels 7, New York
    Giants 0
Eclipse Park (Louisville)

42
Vic Willis
Boston Beaneaters (NL)
Monday, August 7, 1899
Boston Beaneaters 7, Washington
    Senators 1
Huntington Avenue Grounds
    (Boston)

43
Frank "Noodles" Hahn
Cincinnati Reds (NL)
Thursday, July 12, 1900
Cincinnati Reds 4, Philadelphia
    Phillies 0
League Park (Cincinnati)

44
Christy Mathewson
New York Giants (NL)
Monday, July 15, 1901
New York Giants 5, St. Louis
    Cardinals 0
Robison Field (St. Louis)
His first of two no-hitters

45
James "Nixey" Callahan
Chicago White Sox (AL)
Saturday, September 20, 1902 (first
    game of doubleheader)
Chicago White Sox 3, Detroit Tigers 0
South Side Park (Chicago)

46
Chick Fraser
Philadelphia Phillies (NL)
Friday, September 18, 1903 (second
    game of doubleheader)
Philadelphia Phillies 10, Chicago
    Cubs 0
West Side Park (Chicago)

47
Cy Young
Boston Americans (AL)
Thursday, May 5, 1904
Boston Americans 3, Philadelphia
   Athletics 0
Huntington Avenue Grounds
   (Boston)
*Perfect game, his second of three
   no-hitters*

48
Jesse Tannehill
Boston Americans (AL)
Wednesday, August 17, 1904
Boston Americans 6, Chicago White
   Sox 0
South Side Park (Chicago)

49
Christy Mathewson
New York Giants (NL)
Tuesday, June 13, 1905
New York Giants 1, Chicago Cubs 0
West Side Park (Chicago)
His second of two no-hitters

50
Weldon Henley
Philadelphia Athletics (AL)
Saturday, July 22, 1905 (first game
   of doubleheader)
Philadelphia Athletics 6, St. Louis
   Browns 0
Robison Field (St. Louis)

51
Frank Smith
Chicago White Sox (AL)
Wednesday, September 6, 1905
   (second game of doubleheader)
Chicago White Sox 15, Detroit
   Tigers 0
Bennett Park (Detroit)
His first of two no-hitters

52
Bill Dinneen
Boston Americans (AL)
Wednesday, September 27, 1905 (first
   game of doubleheader)
Boston Americans 2, Chicago White
   Sox 0
Huntington Avenue Grounds (Boston)

53
Johnny Lush
Philadelphia Phillies (NL)
Tuesday, May 1, 1906
Philadelphia Phillies 6, Brooklyn
   Superbas 0
Washington Park (Brooklyn)

54
Mal Eason
Brooklyn Superbas (NL)
Friday, July 20, 1906
Brooklyn Superbas 2, St. Louis
   Cardinals 0
Robison Field (St. Louis)

55
Frank "Big Jeff" Pfeffer
Boston Doves (NL)
Wednesday, May 8, 1907
Boston Doves 6, Cincinnati Reds 0
Huntington Avenue Grounds
    (Boston)

56
Nick Maddox
Pittsburgh Pirates (NL)
Friday, September 20, 1907
Pittsburgh Pirates 2, Brooklyn
    Superbas 1
Exposition Park (Pittsburgh)

57
Cy Young
Boston Red Sox (AL)
Tuesday, June 30, 1908
Boston Red Sox 8, New York
    Highlanders 0
Hilltop Park (New York)
His third of three no-hitters

58
George "Hooks" Wiltse
New York Giants (NL)
Saturday, July 4, 1908 (first game
    of doubleheader)
New York Giants 1, Philadelphia
    Phillies 0 (10 inn.)
Polo Grounds (New York)

59
George Napoleon "Nap" Rucker
Brooklyn Superbas (NL)
Saturday, September 5, 1908 (second
    game of doubleheader)
Brooklyn Superbas 6, Boston Doves 0
Washington Park (Brooklyn)

60
Bob "Dusty" Rhoads
Cleveland Naps (AL)
Friday, September 18, 1908
Cleveland Naps 2, Boston Red Sox 1
League Park (Cleveland)

61
Frank Smith
Chicago White Sox (AL)
Sunday, September 20, 1908
Chicago White Sox 1, Philadelphia
    Athletics 0
South Side Park (Chicago)
His second of two no-hitters

62
Addie Joss
Cleveland Naps (AL)
Friday, October 2, 1908
Cleveland Naps 1, Chicago White
    Sox 0
League Park (Cleveland)
Perfect game, his first of two no-hitters

63
Addie Joss
Cleveland Naps (AL)
Wednesday, April 20, 1910
Cleveland Naps 1, Chicago White
    Sox 0
South Side Park (Chicago)
His second of two no-hitters

64
Charles "Chief" Bender
Philadelphia Athletics (AL)
Thursday, May 12, 1910
Philadelphia Athletics 4, Cleveland
    Naps 0
Shibe Park (Philadelphia)

65
"Smokey" Joe Wood
Boston Red Sox (AL)
Saturday, July 29, 1911 (first game
    of doubleheader)
Boston Red Sox 5, St. Louis
    Browns 0
Huntington Avenue Grounds
    (Boston)

66
Ed Walsh
Chicago White Sox (AL)
Sunday, August 27, 1911
Chicago White Sox 5, Boston Red
    Sox 0
Comiskey Park (Chicago)

67
George Mullin
Detroit Tigers (AL)
Thursday, July 4, 1912 (second game
    of doubleheader)
Detroit Tigers 7, St. Louis Browns 0
Navin Field (Detroit)

68
Earl Hamilton
St. Louis Browns (AL)
Friday, August 30, 1912
St. Louis Browns 5, Detroit Tigers 1
Navin Field (Detroit)

69
Jeff Tesreau
New York Giants (NL)
Friday, September 6, 1912 (first game
    of doubleheader)
New York Giants 3, Philadelphia
    Phillies 0
National League Park (Philadelphia)

70
Joe Benz
Chicago White Sox (AL)
Sunday, May 31, 1914
Chicago White Sox 6, Cleveland
    Naps 1
Comiskey Park (Chicago)

71

George Davis
Boston Braves (NL)
Wednesday, September 9, 1914
    (second game of doubleheader)
Boston Braves 7, Philadelphia
    Phillies 0
Fenway Park (Boston)

72

Ed Lafitte
Brooklyn Tip-Tops (FL)
Saturday, September 19, 1914 (first
    game of doubleheader)
Brooklyn Tip-Tops 6, Kansas City
    Packers 2
Washington Park (Brooklyn)

73

Richard "Rube" Marquard
New York Giants (NL)
Thursday, April 15, 1915
New York Giants 2, Brooklyn
    Robins 0
Polo Grounds (New York)

74

Frank Allen
Pittsburgh Rebels (FL)
Saturday, April 24, 1915
Pittsburgh Rebels 2, St. Louis
    Terriers 0
Handlan's Park (St. Louis)

75

Claude Hendrix
Chicago Chi-Feds/Whales (FL)
Saturday, May 15, 1915
Chicago Chi-Feds/Whales 10,
    Pittsburgh Rebels 0
Exposition Park (Pittsburgh)

76

Miles "Alex" Main
Kansas City Packers (FL)
Monday, August 16, 1915
Kansas City Packers 5, Buffalo
    Buffeds/Blues 0
International Fair Association Grounds
    (Buffalo)

77

Jimmy Lavender
Chicago Cubs (NL)
Tuesday, August 31, 1915 (first game
    of doubleheader)
Chicago Cubs 2, New York Giants 0
Polo Grounds (New York)

78

Dave Davenport
St. Louis Terriers (FL)
Tuesday, September 7, 1915 (first
    game of doubleheader)
St. Louis Terriers 3, Chicago Chi-Feds/
    Whales 0
Handlan's Park (St. Louis)

79
Tom Hughes
Boston Braves (NL)
Friday, June 16, 1916
Boston Braves 2, Pittsburgh
 Pirates 0
Braves Field (Boston)

80
George "Rube" Foster
Boston Red Sox (AL)
Wednesday, June 21, 1916
Boston Red Sox 2, New York
 Yankees 0
Fenway Park (Boston)

81
Joe Bush
Philadelphia Athletics (AL)
Saturday, August 26, 1916
Philadelphia Athletics 5, Cleveland
 Indians 0
Shibe Park (Philadelphia)

82
Hubert "Dutch" Leonard
Boston Red Sox (AL)
Wednesday, August 30, 1916
Boston Red Sox 4, St. Louis
 Browns 0
Fenway Park (Boston)
His first of two no-hitters

83
Eddie Cicotte
Chicago White Sox (AL)
Saturday, April 14, 1917
Chicago White Sox 11, St. Louis
 Browns 0
Sportsman's Park (St. Louis)

84
George Mogridge
New York Yankees (AL)
Tuesday, April 24, 1917
New York Yankees 2, Boston Red
 Sox 1
Fenway Park (Boston)

85
Fred Toney
Cincinnati Reds (NL)
Wednesday, May 2, 1917
Cincinnati Reds 1, Chicago Cubs 0
 (10 inn.)
Weeghman Park (Chicago)

86
Ernie Koob
St. Louis Browns (AL)
Saturday, May 5, 1917
St. Louis Browns 1, Chicago White
 Sox 0
Sportsman's Park (St. Louis)

87
Bob Groom
St. Louis Browns (AL)
Sunday, May 6, 1917 (second game
of doubleheader)
St. Louis Browns 3, Chicago White
Sox 0
Sportsman's Park (St. Louis)

88
Babe Ruth (0 inn.), **Ernie Shore**
(9 inn.)
Boston Red Sox (AL)
Saturday, June 23, 1917 (first game
of doubleheader)
Boston Red Sox 4, Washington
Senators 0
Fenway Park (Boston)

89
Hubert "Dutch" Leonard
Boston Red Sox (AL)
Monday, June 3, 1918
Boston Red Sox 5, Detroit Tigers 0
Navin Field (Detroit)
His second of two no-hitters

90
Horace "Hod" Eller
Cincinnati Reds (NL)
Sunday, May 11, 1919
Cincinnati Reds 6, St. Louis
Cardinals 0
Redland Field (Cincinnati)

91
Ray Caldwell
Cleveland Indians (AL)
Wednesday, September 10, 1919 (first
game of doubleheader)
Cleveland Indians 3, New York
Yankees 0
Polo Grounds (New York)

92
Walter Johnson
Washington Senators (AL)
Thursday, July 1, 1920
Washington Senators 1, Boston Red
Sox 0
Fenway Park (Boston)

93
Charlie Robertson
Chicago White Sox (AL)
Sunday, April 30, 1922
Chicago White Sox 2, Detroit Tigers 0
Navin Field (Detroit)
Perfect game

94
Jesse Barnes
New York Giants (NL)
Sunday, May 7, 1922
New York Giants 6, Philadelphia
Phillies 0
Polo Grounds (New York)

95
"Sad" Sam Jones
New York Yankees (AL)
Tuesday, September 4, 1923
New York Yankees 2, Philadelphia
    Athletics 0
Shibe Park (Philadelphia)

96
Howard Ehmke
Boston Red Sox (AL)
Friday, September 7, 1923
Boston Red Sox 4, Philadelphia
    Athletics 0
Shibe Park (Philadelphia)

97
Jesse Haines
St. Louis Cardinals (NL)
Thursday, July 17, 1924
St. Louis Cardinals 5, Boston
    Braves 0
Sportsman's Park (St. Louis)

98
Charles "Dazzy" Vance
Brooklyn Robins (NL)
Sunday, September 13, 1925 (first
    game of doubleheader)
Brooklyn Robins 10, Philadelphia
    Phillies 1
Ebbets Field (Brooklyn)

99
Ted Lyons
Chicago White Sox (AL)
Saturday, August 21, 1926
Chicago White Sox 6, Boston Red
    Sox 0
Fenway Park (Boston)

100
Carl Hubbell
New York Giants (NL)
Wednesday, May 8, 1929
New York Giants 11, Pittsburgh
    Pirates 0
Polo Grounds (New York)

101
Wes Ferrell
Cleveland Indians (AL)
Wednesday, April 29, 1931
Cleveland Indians 9, St. Louis
    Browns 0
League Park (Cleveland)

102
Bobby Burke
Washington Senators (AL)
Saturday, August 8, 1931
Washington Senators 5, Boston Red
    Sox 0
Griffith Stadium (Washington, D.C.)

103
Paul Dean
St. Louis Cardinals (NL)
Friday, September 21, 1934 (second
    game of doubleheader)
St. Louis Cardinals 3, Brooklyn
    Dodgers 0
Ebbets Field (Brooklyn)

104
Vern Kennedy
Chicago White Sox (AL)
Saturday, August 31, 1935
Chicago White Sox 5, Cleveland
    Indians 0
Comiskey Park (Chicago)

105
Bill Dietrich
Chicago White Sox (AL)
Tuesday, June 1, 1937
Chicago White Sox 8, St. Louis
    Browns 0
Comiskey Park (Chicago)

106
Johnny Vander Meer
Cincinnati Reds (NL)
Saturday, June 11, 1938
Cincinnati Reds 3, Boston Bees 0
Crosley Field (Cincinnati)
His first of two no-hitters

107
Johnny Vander Meer
Cincinnati Reds (NL)
Wednesday, June 15, 1938
Cincinnati Reds 6, Brooklyn
    Dodgers 0
Ebbets Field (Brooklyn)
His second of two no-hitters

108
Monte Pearson
New York Yankees (AL)
Saturday, August 27, 1938 (second
    game of doubleheader)
New York Yankees 13, Cleveland
    Indians 0
Yankee Stadium (New York)

109
Bob Feller
Cleveland Indians (AL)
Tuesday, April 16, 1940
Cleveland Indians 1, Chicago White
    Sox 0
Comiskey Park (Chicago)
His first of three no-hitters

110
James "Tex" Carleton
Brooklyn Dodgers (NL)
Tuesday, April 30, 1940
Brooklyn Dodgers 3, Cincinnati
    Reds 0
Crosley Field (Cincinnati)

111
Lon Warneke
St. Louis Cardinals (NL)
Saturday, August 30, 1941
St. Louis Cardinals 2, Cincinnati
    Reds 0
Crosley Field (Cincinnati)

112
Jim Tobin
Boston Braves (NL)
Thursday, April 27, 1944
Boston Braves 2, Brooklyn Dodgers 0
Braves Field (Boston)

113
Clyde Shoun
Cincinnati Reds (NL)
Monday, May 15, 1944
Cincinnati Reds 1, Boston Braves 0
Crosley Field (Cincinnati)

114
Dick Fowler
Philadelphia Athletics (AL)
Sunday, September 9, 1945 (second
    game of doubleheader)
Philadelphia Athletics 1, St. Louis
    Browns 0
Shibe Park (Philadelphia)

115
Ed Head
Brooklyn Dodgers (NL)
Tuesday, April 23, 1946
Brooklyn Dodgers 5, Boston Braves 0
Ebbets Field (Brooklyn)

116
Bob Feller
Cleveland Indians (AL)
Tuesday, April 30, 1946
Cleveland Indians 1, New York
    Yankees 0
Yankee Stadium (New York)
His second of three no-hitters

117
Ewell Blackwell
Cincinnati Reds (NL)
Wednesday, June 18, 1947
Cincinnati Reds 6, Boston Braves 0
Crosley Field (Cincinnati)

118
Don Black
Cleveland Indians (AL)
Thursday, July 10, 1947 (first game of
    doubleheader)
Cleveland Indians 3, Philadelphia
    Athletics 0
Cleveland Stadium (Cleveland)

119
Bill McCahan
Philadelphia Athletics (AL)
Wednesday, September 3, 1947
Philadelphia Athletics 3, Washington
    Senators 0
Shibe Park (Philadelphia)

120

Bob Lemon

Cleveland Indians (AL)

Wednesday, June 30, 1948

Cleveland Indians 2, Detroit Tigers 0

Briggs Stadium (Detroit)

121

Rex Barney

Brooklyn Dodgers (NL)

Thursday, September 9, 1948

Brooklyn Dodgers 2, New York
   Giants 0

Polo Grounds (New York)

122

Vern Bickford

Boston Braves (NL)

Friday, August 11, 1950

Boston Braves 7, Brooklyn Dodgers 0

Braves Field (Boston)

123

Cliff Chambers

Pittsburgh Pirates (NL)

Sunday, May 6, 1951 (second game
   of doubleheader)

Pittsburgh Pirates 3, Boston Braves 0

Braves Field (Boston)

124

Bob Feller

Cleveland Indians (AL)

Sunday, July 1, 1951 (first game of
   doubleheader)

Cleveland Indians 2, Detroit Tigers 1

Cleveland Stadium (Cleveland)

His third of three no-hitters

125

Allie Reynolds

New York Yankees (AL)

Thursday, July 12, 1951

New York Yankees 1, Cleveland
   Indians 0

Cleveland Stadium (Cleveland)

His first of two no-hitters

126

Allie Reynolds

New York Yankees (AL)

Friday, September 28, 1951 (first game
   of doubleheader)

New York Yankees 8, Boston Red
   Sox 0

Yankee Stadium (New York)

His second of two no-hitters

127

Virgil Trucks

Detroit Tigers (AL)

Thursday, May 15, 1952

Detroit Tigers 1, Washington
   Senators 0

Briggs Stadium (Detroit)

His first of two no-hitters

128

Carl Erskine

Brooklyn Dodgers (NL)

Thursday, June 19, 1952

Brooklyn Dodgers 5, Chicago Cubs 0

Ebbets Field (Brooklyn)

His first of two no-hitters

129
Virgil Trucks
Detroit Tigers (AL)
Monday, August 25, 1952
Detroit Tigers 1, New York Yankees 0
Yankee Stadium (New York)
His second of two no-hitters

130
Alva "Bobo" Holloman
St. Louis Browns (AL)
Wednesday, May 6, 1953
St. Louis Browns 6, Philadelphia
    Athletics 0
Busch Stadium (St. Louis)

131
Jim Wilson
Milwaukee Braves (NL)
Sunday, June 12, 1954
Milwaukee Braves 2, Philadelphia
    Phillies 0
Milwaukee County Stadium
    (Milwaukee)

132
"Toothpick" Sam Jones
Chicago Cubs (NL)
Thursday, May 12, 1955
Chicago Cubs 4, Pittsburgh Pirates 0
Wrigley Field (Chicago)

133
Carl Erskine
Brooklyn Dodgers (NL)
Saturday, May 12, 1956
Brooklyn Dodgers 3, New York
    Giants 0
Ebbets Field (Brooklyn)
His second of two no-hitters

134
Mel Parnell
Boston Red Sox (AL)
Saturday, July 14, 1956
Boston Red Sox 4, Chicago White
    Sox 0
Fenway Park (Boston)

135
Sal Maglie
Brooklyn Dodgers (NL)
Tuesday, September 25, 1956
Brooklyn Dodgers 5, Philadelphia
    Phillies 0
Ebbets Field (Brooklyn)

136
Don Larsen
New York Yankees (World Series
    Game 5)
Monday, October 8, 1956
New York Yankees 2, Brooklyn
    Dodgers 0
Yankee Stadium (New York)
Perfect game

137
Bob Keegan
Chicago White Sox (AL)
Tuesday, August 20, 1957 (second
    game of doubleheader)
Chicago White Sox 6, Washington
    Senators 0
Comiskey Park (Chicago)

138
Jim Bunning
Detroit Tigers (AL)
Sunday, July 20, 1958 (first game
    of doubleheader)
Detroit Tigers 3, Boston Red
    Sox 0
Fenway Park (Boston)
His first of two no-hitters

139
Hoyt Wilhelm
Baltimore Orioles (AL)
Saturday, September 20, 1958
Baltimore Orioles 1, New York
    Yankees 0
Memorial Stadium (Baltimore)

140
Don Cardwell
Chicago Cubs (NL)
Sunday, May 15, 1960 (second
    game of doubleheader)
Chicago Cubs 4, St. Louis
    Cardinals 0
Wrigley Field (Chicago)

141
Lew Burdette
Milwaukee Braves (NL)
Thursday, August 18, 1960
Milwaukee Braves 1, Philadelphia
    Phillies 0
Milwaukee County Stadium
    (Milwaukee)

142
Warren Spahn
Milwaukee Braves (NL)
Friday, September 16, 1960
Milwaukee Braves 4, Philadelphia
    Phillies 0
Milwaukee County Stadium
    (Milwaukee)
His first of two no-hitters

143
Warren Spahn
Milwaukee Braves (NL)
Friday, April 28, 1961
Milwaukee Braves 1, San Francisco
    Giants 0
Milwaukee County Stadium
    (Milwaukee)
His second of two no-hitters

144
Bo Belinsky
Los Angeles Angels (AL)
Saturday, May 5, 1962
Los Angeles Angels 2, Baltimore
    Orioles 0
Dodger Stadium (Los Angeles)

145
Earl Wilson
Boston Red Sox (AL)
Tuesday, June 26, 1962
Boston Red Sox 2, Los Angeles
    Angels 0
Fenway Park (Boston)

146
Sandy Koufax
Los Angeles Dodgers (NL)
Saturday, June 30, 1962
Los Angeles Dodgers 5, New York
    Mets 0
Dodger Stadium (Los Angeles)
His first of four no-hitters

147
Bill Monbouquette
Boston Red Sox (AL)
Wednesday, August 1, 1962
Boston Red Sox 1, Chicago White
    Sox 0
Comiskey Park (Chicago)

148
Jack Kralick
Minnesota Twins (AL)
Sunday, August 26, 1962
Minnesota Twins 1, Kansas City
    Athletics 0
Metropolitan Stadium
    (Minneapolis)

149
Sandy Koufax
Los Angeles Dodgers (NL)
Saturday, May 11, 1963
Los Angeles Dodgers 8, San Francisco
    Giants 0
Dodger Stadium (Los Angeles)
His second of four no-hitters

150
Don Nottebart
Houston Colt .45s (NL)
Friday, May 17, 1963
Houston Colt .45s 4, Philadelphia
    Phillies 1
Colt Stadium (Houston)

151
Juan Marichal
San Francisco Giants (NL)
Saturday, June 15, 1963
San Francisco Giants 1, Houston
    Colt .45s 0
Candlestick Park (San Francisco)

152
Ken Johnson
Houston Colt .45s (NL)
Thursday, April 23, 1964
Houston Colt .45s 0, Cincinnati Reds
    1 (a Colts loss)
Colt Stadium (Houston)

153
Sandy Koufax
Los Angeles Dodgers (NL)
Thursday, June 4, 1964
Los Angeles Dodgers 3, Philadelphia
    Phillies 0
Connie Mack Stadium (Philadelphia)
His third of four no-hitters

154
Jim Bunning
Philadelphia Phillies (NL)
Sunday, June 21, 1964 (first game of
    doubleheader)
Philadelphia Phillies 6, New York
    Mets 0
Shea Stadium (Flushing)
Perfect game, his second of two no-hitters

155
Jim Maloney
Cincinnati Reds (NL)
Thursday, August 19, 1965 (first
    game of doubleheader)
Cincinnati Reds 1, Chicago Cubs 0
    (10 inn.)
Wrigley Field (Chicago)
His first of two no-hitters

156
Sandy Koufax
Los Angeles Dodgers (NL)
Thursday, September 9, 1965
Los Angeles Dodgers 1, Chicago
    Cubs 0
Dodger Stadium (Los Angeles)
Perfect game, his fourth of four no-hitters

157
Dave Morehead
Boston Red Sox (AL)
Thursday, September 16, 1965
Boston Red Sox 2, Cleveland
    Indians 0
Fenway Park (Boston)

158
Sonny Siebert
Cleveland Indians (AL)
Friday, June 10, 1966
Cleveland Indians 2, Washington
    Senators 0
Cleveland Stadium (Cleveland)

159
Steve Barber (8 2/3 inn.), **Stu Miller**
    (1/3 inn.)
Baltimore Orioles (AL)
Sunday, April 30, 1967 (first game
    of doubleheader)
Baltimore Orioles 1, Detroit Tigers 2
    (an Orioles loss)
Memorial Stadium (Baltimore)

160
Don Wilson
Houston Astros (NL)
Sunday, June 18, 1967
Houston Astros 2, Atlanta
    Braves 0
Astrodome (Houston)
His first of two no-hitters

161
Dean Chance
Minnesota Twins (AL)
Friday, August 25, 1967 (second
  game of doubleheader)
Minnesota Twins 2, Cleveland
  Indians 1
Cleveland Stadium (Cleveland)

162
Joel "Joe" Horlen
Chicago White Sox (AL)
Sunday, September 10, 1967 (first
  game of doubleheader)
Chicago White Sox 6, Detroit
  Tigers 0
Comiskey Park (Chicago)

163
Tom Phoebus
Baltimore Orioles (AL)
Saturday, April 27, 1968
Baltimore Orioles 6, Boston Red
  Sox 0
Memorial Stadium (Baltimore)

164
Jim "Catfish" Hunter
Oakland Athletics (AL)
Wednesday, May 8, 1968
Oakland Athletics 4, Minnesota
  Twins 0
Oakland–Alameda County Coliseum
  (Oakland)
Perfect game

165
George Culver
Cincinnati Reds (NL)
Monday, July 29, 1968 (second game
  of doubleheader)
Cincinnati Reds 6, Philadelphia
  Phillies 1
Connie Mack Stadium (Philadelphia)

166
Gaylord Perry
San Francisco Giants (NL)
Tuesday, September 17, 1968
San Francisco Giants 1, St. Louis
  Cardinals 0
Candlestick Park (San Francisco)

167
Ray Washburn
St. Louis Cardinals (NL)
Wednesday, September 18, 1968
St. Louis Cardinals 2, San Francisco
  Giants 0
Candlestick Park (San Francisco)

168
Bill Stoneman
Montreal Expos (NL)
Thursday, April 17, 1969
Montreal Expos 7, Philadelphia
  Phillies 0
Connie Mack Stadium (Philadelphia)
His first of two no-hitters

169
Jim Maloney
Cincinnati Reds (NL)
Wednesday, April 30, 1969
Cincinnati Reds 10, Houston
    Astros 0
Crosley Field (Cincinnati)
His second of two no-hitters

170
Don Wilson
Houston Astros (NL)
Thursday, May 1, 1969
Houston Astros 4, Cincinnati
    Reds 0
Crosley Field (Cincinnati)
His second of two no-hitters

171
Jim Palmer
Baltimore Orioles (AL)
Wednesday, August 13, 1969
Baltimore Orioles 8, Oakland
    Athletics 0
Memorial Stadium (Baltimore)

172
Ken Holtzman
Chicago Cubs (NL)
Tuesday, August 19, 1969
Chicago Cubs 3, Atlanta Braves 0
Wrigley Field (Chicago)
His first of two no-hitters

173
Bob Moose
Pittsburgh Pirates (NL)
Saturday, September 20, 1969
Pittsburgh Pirates 4, New York
    Mets 0
Shea Stadium (New York)

174
Dock Ellis
Pittsburgh Pirates (NL)
Friday, June 12, 1970 (first game of
    doubleheader)
Pittsburgh Pirates 2, San Diego
    Padres 0
San Diego Stadium (San Diego)

175
Clyde Wright
California Angels (AL)
Friday, July 3, 1970
California Angels 4, Oakland
    Athletics 0
Anaheim Stadium (Anaheim)

176
Bill Singer
Los Angeles Dodgers (NL)
Monday, July 20, 1970
Los Angeles Dodgers 5, Philadelphia
    Phillies 0
Dodger Stadium (Los Angeles)

177
Vida Blue
Oakland Athletics (AL)
Monday, September 21, 1970
Oakland Athletics 6, Minnesota
    Twins 0
Oakland–Alameda County Coliseum
    (Oakland)

178
Ken Holtzman
Chicago Cubs (NL)
Thursday, June 3, 1971
Chicago Cubs 1, Cincinnati Reds 0
Riverfront Stadium (Cincinnati)
His second of two no-hitters

179
Rick Wise
Philadelphia Phillies (NL)
Wednesday, June 23, 1971
Philadelphia Phillies 4, Cincinnati
    Reds 0
Riverfront Stadium (Cincinnati)

180
Bob Gibson
St. Louis Cardinals (NL)
Saturday, August 14, 1971
St. Louis Cardinals 11, Pittsburgh
    Pirates 0
Three Rivers Stadium (Pittsburgh)

181
Burt Hooton
Chicago Cubs (NL)
Sunday, April 16, 1972
Chicago Cubs 4, Philadelphia
    Phillies 0
Wrigley Field (Chicago)

182
Milt Pappas
Chicago Cubs (NL)
Saturday, September 2, 1972
Chicago Cubs 8, San Diego Padres 0
Wrigley Field (Chicago)

183
Bill Stoneman
Montreal Expos (NL)
Monday, October 2, 1972 (first game
    of doubleheader)
Montreal Expos 7, New York Mets 0
Parc Jarry (Montreal)
His second of two no-hitters

184
Steve Busby
Kansas City Royals (AL)
Friday, April 27, 1973
Kansas City Royals 3, Detroit
    Tigers 0
Tiger Stadium (Detroit)
His first of two no-hitters

185
Nolan Ryan
California Angels (AL)
Tuesday, May 15, 1973
California Angels 3, Kansas City
    Royals 0
Royals Stadium (Kansas City)
His first of seven no-hitters

186
Nolan Ryan
California Angels (AL)
Sunday, July 15, 1973
California Angels 6, Detroit
    Tigers 0
Tiger Stadium (Detroit)
His second of seven no-hitters

187
Jim Bibby
Texas Rangers (AL)
Monday, July 30, 1973
Texas Rangers 6, Oakland
    Athletics 0
Oakland–Alameda County
    Coliseum (Oakland)

188
Phil Niekro
Atlanta Braves (NL)
Sunday, August 5, 1973
Atlanta Braves 9, San Diego Padres 0
Atlanta–Fulton County Stadium
    (Atlanta)

189
Steve Busby
Kansas City Royals (AL)
Wednesday, June 19, 1974
Kansas City Royals 2, Milwaukee
    Brewers 0
Milwaukee County Stadium
    (Milwaukee)
His second of two no-hitters

190
Dick Bosman
Cleveland Indians (AL)
Friday, July 19, 1974
Cleveland Indians 4, Oakland
    Athletics 0
Cleveland Stadium (Cleveland)

191
Nolan Ryan
California Angels (AL)
Saturday, September 28, 1974
California Angels 4, Minnesota
    Twins 0
Anaheim Stadium (Anaheim)
His third of seven no-hitters

192
Nolan Ryan
California Angels (AL)
Sunday, June 1, 1975
California Angels 1, Baltimore
    Orioles 0
Anaheim Stadium (Anaheim)
His fourth of seven no-hitters

193
Ed Halicki
San Francisco Giants (NL)
Sunday, August 24, 1975 (second
    game of doubleheader)
San Francisco Giants 6, New York
    Mets 0
Candlestick Park (San Francisco)

194
Vida Blue (5 inn.), **Glenn Abbott**
    (1 inn.), **Paul Lindblad** (1 inn.),
    Rollie Fingers (2 inn.)
Oakland Athletics (AL)
Sunday, September 28, 1975
Oakland Athletics 5, California
    Angels 0
Oakland–Alameda County
    Coliseum (Oakland)

195
Larry Dierker
Houston Astros (NL)
Friday, July 9, 1976
Houston Astros 6, Montreal Expos 0
Astrodome (Houston)

196
John "Blue Moon" Odom (5 inn.),
    Francisco Barrios (4 inn.)
Chicago White Sox (AL)
Wednesday, July 28, 1976
Chicago White Sox 2, Oakland
    Athletics 1
Oakland–Alameda County Coliseum
    (Oakland)

197
John Candelaria
Pittsburgh Pirates (NL)
Monday, August 9, 1976
Pittsburgh Pirates 2, Los Angeles
    Dodgers 0
Three Rivers Stadium (Pittsburgh)

198
John Montefusco
San Francisco Giants (NL)
Wednesday, September 29, 1976
San Francisco Giants 9, Atlanta
    Braves 0
Atlanta–Fulton County Stadium
    (Atlanta)

199
Jim Colborn
Kansas City Royals (AL)
Saturday, May 14, 1977
Kansas City Royals 6, Texas Rangers 0
Royals Stadium (Kansas City)

200
Dennis Eckersley
Cleveland Indians (AL)
Monday, May 30, 1977
Cleveland Indians 1, California
    Angels 0
Cleveland Stadium (Cleveland)

201
Bert Blyleven
Texas Rangers (AL)
Thursday, September 22, 1977
Texas Rangers 6, California
    Angels 0
Anaheim Stadium (Anaheim)

202
Bob Forsch
St. Louis Cardinals (NL)
Sunday, April 16, 1978
St. Louis Cardinals 5, Philadelphia
    Phillies 0
Busch Stadium (St. Louis)
His first of two no-hitters

203
Tom Seaver
Cincinnati Reds (NL)
Friday, June 16, 1978
Cincinnati Reds 4, St. Louis
    Cardinals 0
Riverfront Stadium (Cincinnati)

204
Ken Forsch
Houston Astros (NL)
Saturday, April 7, 1979
Houston Astros 6, Atlanta
    Braves 0
Astrodome (Houston)

205
Jerry Reuss
Los Angeles Dodgers (NL)
Friday, June 27, 1980
Los Angeles Dodgers 8, San Francisco
    Giants 0
Candlestick Park (San Francisco)

206
Charlie Lea
Montreal Expos (NL)
Sunday, May 10, 1981 (second game
    of doubleheader)
Montreal Expos 4, San Francisco
    Giants 0
Olympic Stadium (Montreal)

207
Len Barker
Cleveland Indians (AL)
Friday, May 15, 1981
Cleveland Indians 3, Toronto Blue
    Jays 0
Cleveland Stadium (Cleveland)
Perfect game

208
Nolan Ryan
Houston Astros (NL)
Saturday, September 26, 1981
Houston Astros 5, Los Angeles
    Dodgers 0
Astrodome (Houston)
His fifth of seven no-hitters

209
Dave Righetti
New York Yankees (AL)
Monday, July 4, 1983
New York Yankees 4, Boston Red
    Sox 0
Yankee Stadium (New York)

210
Bob Forsch
St. Louis Cardinals (NL)
Monday, September 26, 1983
St. Louis Cardinals 3, Montreal
    Expos 0
Busch Stadium (St. Louis)
His second of two no-hitters

211
Mike Warren
Oakland Athletics (AL)
Thursday, September 29, 1983
Oakland Athletics 3, Chicago
    White Sox 0
Oakland–Alameda County
    Coliseum (Oakland)

212
Jack Morris
Detroit Tigers (AL)
Saturday, April 7, 1984
Detroit Tigers 4, Chicago White
    Sox 0
Comiskey Park (Chicago)

213
Mike Witt
California Angels (AL)
Sunday, September 30, 1984
California Angels 1, Texas Rangers 0
Arlington Stadium (Texas)
Perfect game

214
Joe Cowley
Chicago White Sox (AL)
Friday, September 19, 1986
Chicago White Sox 7, California
    Angels 1
Anaheim Stadium (Anaheim)

215
Mike Scott
Houston Astros (NL)
Thursday, September 25, 1986
Houston Astros 2, San Francisco
    Giants 0
Astrodome (Houston)

216
Juan Nieves
Milwaukee Brewers (AL)
Wednesday, April 15, 1987
Milwaukee Brewers 7, Baltimore
    Orioles 0
Memorial Stadium (Baltimore)

217
Tom Browning
Cincinnati Reds (NL)
Friday, September 16, 1988
Cincinnati Reds 1, Los Angeles
    Dodgers 0
Riverfront Stadium (Cincinnati)
Perfect game

218
Mark Langston (7 inn.), **Mike Witt**
    (2 inn.)
California Angels (AL)
Wednesday, April 11, 1990
California Angels 1, Seattle
    Mariners 0
Anaheim Stadium (Anaheim)

219
Randy Johnson
Seattle Mariners (AL)
Saturday, June 2, 1990
Seattle Mariners 2, Detroit Tigers 0
Kingdome (Seattle)
His first of two no-hitters

220
Nolan Ryan
Texas Rangers (AL)
Monday, June 11, 1990
Texas Rangers 5, Oakland
    Athletics 0
Oakland–Alameda County
    Coliseum (Oakland)
His sixth of seven no-hitters

221
Dave Stewart
Oakland Athletics (AL)
Friday, June 29, 1990
Oakland Athletics 5, Toronto Blue
    Jays 0
SkyDome (Toronto)

222
Fernando Valenzuela
Los Angeles Dodgers (NL)
Friday, June 29, 1990
Los Angeles Dodgers 6, St. Louis
    Cardinals 0
Dodger Stadium (Los Angeles)

223
Terry Mulholland
Philadelphia Phillies (NL)
Wednesday, August 15, 1990
Philadelphia Phillies 6, San Francisco
    Giants 0
Veterans Stadium (Philadelphia)

224
Dave Stieb
Toronto Blue Jays (AL)
Sunday, September 2, 1990
Toronto Blue Jays 3, Cleveland
    Indians 0
Cleveland Stadium (Cleveland)

225
Nolan Ryan
Texas Rangers (AL)
Wednesday, May 1, 1991
Texas Rangers 3, Toronto Blue
    Jays 0
Arlington Stadium (Texas)
His seventh of seven no-hitters

226
Tommy Greene
Philadelphia Phillies (NL)
Thursday, May 23, 1991
Philadelphia Phillies 2, Montreal
    Expos 0
Olympic Stadium (Montreal)

227
Bob Milacki (6 inn.), **Mike
    Flanagan** (1 inn.), **Mark
    Williamson** (1 inn.),
    Gregg Olson (1 inn.)
Baltimore Orioles (AL)
Saturday, July 13, 1991
Baltimore Orioles 2, Oakland
    Athletics 0
Oakland–Alameda County
    Coliseum (Oakland)

228
Dennis Martínez
Montreal Expos (NL)
Sunday, July 28, 1991
Montreal Expos 2, Los Angeles
    Dodgers 0
Dodger Stadium (Los Angeles)
Perfect game

229
Wilson Álvarez
Chicago White Sox (AL)
Sunday, August 11, 1991
Chicago White Sox 7, Baltimore
    Orioles 0
Memorial Stadium (Baltimore)

230
Bret Saberhagen
Kansas City Royals (AL)
Monday, August 26, 1991
Kansas City Royals 7, Chicago
    White Sox 0
Royals Stadium (Kansas City)

231
Kent Mercker (6 inn.), **Mark
    Wohlers** (2 inn.), **Alejandro
    Peña** (1 inn.)
Atlanta Braves (NL)
Wednesday, September 11, 1991
Atlanta Braves 1, San Diego
    Padres 0
Atlanta–Fulton County Stadium
    (Atlanta)

232
Kevin Gross
Los Angeles Dodgers (NL)
Monday, August 17, 1992
Los Angeles Dodgers 2, San Francisco
    Giants 0
Dodger Stadium (Los Angeles)

233
Chris Bosio
Seattle Mariners (AL)
Thursday, April 22, 1993
Seattle Mariners 7, Boston Red
    Sox 0
Kingdome (Seattle)

234
Jim Abbott
New York Yankees (AL)
Saturday, September 4, 1993
New York Yankees 4, Cleveland
    Indians 0
Yankee Stadium (New York)

235
Darryl Kile
Houston Astros (NL)
Wednesday, September 8, 1993
Houston Astros 7, New York
    Mets 1
Astrodome (Houston)

236
Kent Mercker
Atlanta Braves (NL)
Friday, April 8, 1994
Atlanta Braves 6, Los Angeles
    Dodgers 0
Dodger Stadium (Los Angeles)

237
Scott Erickson
Minnesota Twins (AL)
Wednesday, April 27, 1994
Minnesota Twins 6, Milwaukee
    Brewers 0
Hubert H. Humphrey Metrodome
    (Minneapolis)

238
Kenny Rogers
Texas Rangers (AL)
Thursday, July 28, 1994
Texas Rangers 4, California Angels 0
The Ballpark at Arlington (Texas)
Perfect game

239
Ramón Martínez
Los Angeles Dodgers (NL)
Friday, July 14, 1995
Los Angeles Dodgers 7, Florida
    Marlins 0
Dodger Stadium (Los Angeles)

240
Al Leiter
Florida Marlins (NL)
Saturday, May 11, 1996
Florida Marlins 11, Colorado
    Rockies 0
Joe Robbie Stadium (Miami)

241
Dwight "Doc" Gooden
New York Yankees (AL)
Tuesday, May 14, 1996
New York Yankees 2, Seattle
    Mariners 0
Yankee Stadium (New York)

242
Hideo Nomo
Los Angeles Dodgers (NL)
Tuesday, September 17, 1996
Los Angeles Dodgers 9, Colorado
    Rockies 0
Coors Field (Denver)
His first of two no-hitters

243
Kevin Brown
Florida Marlins (NL)
Tuesday, June 10, 1997
Florida Marlins 9, San Francisco
    Giants 0
Candlestick Park (San Francisco)

244
Francisco Cordova (9 inn.), **Ricardo
    Rincon** (1 inn.)
Pittsburgh Pirates (NL)
Saturday, July 12, 1997
Pittsburgh Pirates 3, Houston
    Astros 0 (10 inn.)
Three Rivers Stadium (Pittsburgh)

245
David Wells
New York Yankees (AL)
Sunday, May 17, 1998
New York Yankees 4, Minnesota
    Twins 0
Yankee Stadium (New York)
Perfect game

246
José Jiménez
St. Louis Cardinals (NL)
Friday, June 25, 1999
St. Louis Cardinals 1, Arizona
    Diamondbacks 0
Bank One Ballpark (Phoenix)

247
David Cone
New York Yankees (AL)
Sunday, July 18, 1999
New York Yankees 6, Montreal
    Expos 0
Yankee Stadium (New York)
Perfect game

248
Eric Milton
Minnesota Twins (AL)
Saturday, September 11, 1999
Minnesota Twins 7, Anaheim Angels 0
Hubert H. Humphrey Metrodome
    (Minneapolis)

249
Hideo Nomo
Boston Red Sox (AL)
Wednesday, April 4, 2001
Boston Red Sox 3, Baltimore
    Orioles 0
Oriole Park at Camden Yards
    (Baltimore)
His second of two no-hitters

250
A. J. Burnett
Florida Marlins (NL)
Saturday, May 12, 2001
Florida Marlins 3, San Diego
    Padres 0
Qualcomm Stadium (San Diego)

251
Bud Smith
St. Louis Cardinals (NL)
Monday, September 3, 2001
St. Louis Cardinals 4, San Diego
    Padres 0
Qualcomm Stadium (San Diego)

252
Derek Lowe
Boston Red Sox (AL)
Saturday, April 27, 2002
Boston Red Sox 10, Tampa Bay
    Devil Rays 0
Fenway Park (Boston)

253
Kevin Millwood
Philadelphia Phillies (NL)
Sunday, April 27, 2003
Philadelphia Phillies 1, San Francisco
    Giants 0
Veterans Stadium (Philadelphia)

254
Roy Oswalt (1 inn.), **Peter Munro** (2
    2/3 inn.), **Kirk Saarloos** (1 1/3
    inn.), **Brad Lidge** (2 inn.), **Octavio
    Dotel** (1 inn.), **Billy Wagner** (1
    inn.)
Houston Astros (NL)
Wednesday, June 11, 2003
Houston Astros 8, New York
    Yankees 0
Yankee Stadium (New York)

255
Randy Johnson
Arizona Diamondbacks (NL)
Tuesday, May 18, 2004
Arizona Diamondbacks 2, Atlanta
    Braves 0
Turner Field (Atlanta)
Perfect game, his second of two no-hitters

256
Aníbal Sánchez
Florida Marlins (NL)
Wednesday, September 6, 2006
Florida Marlins 2, Arizona
    Diamondbacks 0
Pro Player Stadium (Miami)

257
Mark Buehrle
Chicago White Sox (AL)
Wednesday, April 18, 2007
Chicago White Sox 6, Texas
    Rangers 0
U.S. Cellular Field (Chicago)
His first of two no-hitters

258
Justin Verlander
Detroit Tigers (AL)
Tuesday, June 12, 2007
Detroit Tigers 4, Milwaukee
    Brewers 0
Comerica Park (Detroit)
His first of two no-hitters

259
Clay Buchholz
Boston Red Sox (AL)
Saturday, September 1, 2007
Boston Red Sox 10, Baltimore
    Orioles 0
Fenway Park (Boston)

260
Jon Lester
Boston Red Sox (AL)
Monday, May 19, 2008
Boston Red Sox 7, Kansas City
    Royals 0
Fenway Park (Boston)

261
Carlos Zambrano
Chicago Cubs (NL)
Sunday, September 14, 2008
Chicago Cubs 5, Houston Astros 0
Miller Park (Milwaukee)—Astros
    were the home team in a neutral-
    site game relocated due to
    Hurricane Ike

262
Jonathan Sánchez
San Francisco Giants (NL)
Friday, July 10, 2009
San Francisco Giants 8, San Diego
    Padres 0
AT&T Park (San Francisco)

263
Mark Buehrle
Chicago White Sox (AL)
Thursday, July 23, 2009
Chicago White Sox 5, Tampa Bay
    Rays 0
U.S. Cellular Field (Chicago)
Perfect game, his second of two no-hitters

264
Ubaldo Jiménez
Colorado Rockies (NL)
Saturday, April 17, 2010
Colorado Rockies 4, Atlanta Braves 0
Turner Field (Atlanta)

265
Dallas Braden
Oakland Athletics (AL)
Sunday, May 9, 2010
Oakland Athletics 4, Tampa Bay
    Rays 0
Oakland–Alameda County Coliseum
    (Oakland)
Perfect game

266
Roy Halladay
Philadelphia Phillies (NL)
Saturday, May 29, 2010
Philadelphia Phillies 1, Florida
    Marlins 0
Sun Life Stadium (Miami)
Perfect game, his first of two no-hitters

267
Edwin Jackson
Arizona Diamondbacks (NL)
Friday, June 25, 2010
Arizona Diamondbacks 1, Tampa
    Bay Rays 0
Tropicana Field (St. Petersburg)

268
Matt Garza
Tampa Bay Rays (AL)
Monday, July 26, 2010
Tampa Bay Rays 5, Detroit Tigers 0
Tropicana Field (St. Petersburg)

269
Roy Halladay
Philadelphia Phillies (NLDS Game 1)
Wednesday, October 6, 2010
Philadelphia Phillies 4, Cincinnati
    Reds 0
Citizens Bank Park (Philadelphia)
His second of two no-hitters

270
Francisco Liriano
Minnesota Twins (AL)
Tuesday, May 3, 2011
Minnesota Twins 1, Chicago White
    Sox 0
U.S. Cellular Field (Chicago)

271
Justin Verlander
Detroit Tigers (AL)
Saturday, May 7, 2011
Detroit Tigers 9, Toronto Blue Jays 0
Rogers Centre (Toronto)
His second of two no-hitters

272
Ervin Santana
Los Angeles Angels (AL)
Wednesday, July 27, 2011
Los Angeles Angels 3, Cleveland
    Indians 1
Jacobs Field (Cleveland)

273
Philip Humber
Chicago White Sox (AL)
Saturday, April 21, 2012
Chicago White Sox 4, Seattle
    Mariners 0
Safeco Field (Seattle)
Perfect game

274
Jered Weaver
Los Angeles Angels (AL)
Wednesday, May 2, 2012
Los Angeles Angels 9, Minnesota
    Twins 0
Angel Stadium of Anaheim (Anaheim)

275
Johan Santana
New York Mets (NL)
Friday, June 1, 2012
New York Mets 8, St. Louis
    Cardinals 0
Citi Field (Flushing)

276
Kevin Millwood (6 inn.), **Charlie**
    Furbush (2/3 inn.), **Stephen Pryor**
    (1/3 inn.), **Lucas Luetge** (1/3
    inn.), **Brandon League** (2/3 inn.),
    Tom Wilhelmsen (1 inn.)
Seattle Mariners (AL)
Friday, June 8, 2012
Seattle Mariners 1, Los Angeles
    Dodgers 0
Safeco Field (Seattle)

277
Matt Cain
San Francisco Giants (NL)
Wednesday, June 13, 2012
San Francisco Giants 10, Houston
    Astros 0
AT&T Park (San Francisco)
Perfect game

278
Félix Hernández
Seattle Mariners (AL)
Wednesday, August 15, 2012
Seattle Mariners 1, Tampa Bay
    Rays 0
Safeco Field (Seattle)
Perfect game

279
Homer Bailey
Cincinnati Reds (NL)
Friday, September 28, 2012
Cincinnati Reds 1, Pittsburgh
    Pirates 0
PNC Park (Pittsburgh)
His first of two no-hitters

280
Homer Bailey
Cincinnati Reds (NL)
Tuesday, July 2, 2013
Cincinnati Reds 3, San Francisco
    Giants 0
Great American Ball Park (Cincinnati)
His second of two no-hitters

281
Tim Lincecum
San Francisco Giants (NL)
Saturday, July 13, 2013
San Francisco Giants 9, San Diego
     Padres 0
Petco Park (San Diego)
His first of two no-hitters

282
Henderson Álvarez
Miami Marlins (NL)
Sunday, September 29, 2013
Miami Marlins 1, Detroit Tigers 0
Marlins Park (Miami)

283
Josh Beckett
Los Angeles Dodgers (NL)
Sunday, May 25, 2014
Los Angeles Dodgers 6, Philadelphia
     Phillies 0
Citizens Bank Park (Philadelphia)

284
Clayton Kershaw
Los Angeles Dodgers (NL)
Wednesday, June 18, 2014
Los Angeles Dodgers 8, Colorado
     Rockies 0
Dodger Stadium (Los Angeles)

285
Tim Lincecum
San Francisco Giants (NL)
Wednesday, June 25, 2014
San Francisco Giants 4, San Diego
     Padres 0
AT&T Park (San Francisco)
His second of two no-hitters

286
Cole Hamels (6 inn.), **Jake Diekman**
     (1 inn.), **Ken Giles** (1 inn.),
     Jonathan Papelbon (1 inn.)
Philadelphia Phillies (NL)
Monday, September 1, 2014
Philadelphia Phillies 7, Atlanta
     Braves 0
Turner Field (Atlanta)

287
Jordan Zimmermann
Washington Nationals (NL)
Sunday, September 28, 2014
Washington Nationals 1, Miami
     Marlins 0
Nationals Park (Washington, D.C.)

288
Chris Heston
San Francisco Giants (NL)
Tuesday, June 9, 2015
San Francisco Giants 5, New York
     Mets 0
Citi Field (New York)

289
Max Scherzer
Washington Nationals (NL)
Saturday, June 20, 2015
Washington Nationals 6, Pittsburgh
    Pirates 0
Nationals Park (Washington, D.C.)
First of two no-hitters

290
Cole Hamels
Philadelphia Phillies (NL)
Saturday, July 25, 2015
Philadelphia Phillies 5, Chicago
    Cubs 0
Wrigley Field (Chicago)

291
Hisashi Iwakuma
Seattle Mariners (AL)
Wednesday, August 12, 2015
Seattle Mariners 3, Baltimore
    Orioles 0
Safeco Field (Seattle)

292
Mike Fiers
Houston Astros (AL)
Friday, August 21, 2015
Houston Astros 3, Los Angeles
    Dodgers 0
Minute Maid Park (Houston)

293
Jake Arrieta
Chicago Cubs (NL)
Sunday, August 30, 2015
Chicago Cubs 2, Los Angeles
    Dodgers 0
Dodger Stadium (Los Angeles)

294
Max Scherzer
Washington Nationals (NL)
Saturday, October 3, 2015 (second
    game of doubleheader)
Washington Nationals 2, New York
    Mets 0
Citi Field (New York)
*His second of two no-hitters, both
    thrown in same season*

BASEBALL'S PERFECT GAMES

1. **Lee Richmond** / Worcester Ruby Legs (NL) @ Worcester Driving Park Grounds (Worcester)
   Saturday, June 12, 1880 / Worcester Ruby Legs 1, Cleveland Blues 0
2. **John Montgomery Ward** / Providence Grays (NL) @ Messer Street Grounds (Providence)
   Thursday, June 17, 1880 / Providence Grays 5, Buffalo Bisons 0
3. **Cy Young** / Boston Americans (AL) @ Huntington Avenue Grounds (Boston)
   Thursday, May 5, 1904 / Boston Americans 3, Philadelphia Athletics 0
4. **Addie Joss** / Cleveland Naps (AL) @ League Park (Cleveland)
   Friday, October 2, 1908 / Cleveland Naps 1, Chicago White Sox 0
5. **Charlie Robertson** / Chicago White Sox (AL) @ Navin Field (Detroit)
   Sunday, April 30, 1922 / Chicago White Sox 2, Detroit Tigers 0
6. **Don Larsen** / New York Yankees (AL in World Series Game 5) @ Yankee Stadium
   Monday, October 8, 1956 / New York Yankees 2, Brooklyn Dodgers 0
7. **Jim Bunning** / Philadelphia Phillies (NL) @ Shea Stadium
   Sunday, June 21, 1964 (first game of doubleheader) / Philadelphia Phillies 6, New York Mets 0
8. **Sandy Koufax** / Los Angeles Dodgers (NL) @ Dodger Stadium
   Thursday, September 9, 1965/ Los Angeles Dodgers 1, Chicago Cubs 0

9. **Jim "Catfish" Hunter** / Oakland Athletics (AL) @ Oakland–Alameda County Coliseum
Wednesday, May 8, 1968 / Oakland Athletics 4, Minnesota Twins 0

10. **Len Barker** / Cleveland Indians (AL) @ Cleveland Stadium (Cleveland)
Friday, May 15, 1981 / Cleveland Indians 3, Toronto Blue Jays 0

11. **Mike Witt** / California Angels (AL) @ Arlington Stadium (Texas)
Sunday, September 30, 1984 / California Angels 1, Texas Rangers 0

12. **Tom Browning** / Cincinnati Reds (NL) @ Riverfront Stadium (Cincinnati)
Friday, September 16, 1988 / Cincinnati Reds 1, Los Angeles Dodgers 0

13. **Dennis Martínez** / Montreal Expos (NL) @ Dodger Stadium
Sunday, July 28, 1991 / Montreal Expos 2, Los Angeles Dodgers 0

14. **Kenny Rogers** / Texas Rangers (AL) @ The Ballpark at Arlington (Texas)
Thursday, July 28, 1994 / Texas Rangers 4, California Angels 0

15. **David Wells** / New York Yankees (AL) @ Yankee Stadium
Sunday, May 17, 1998 / New York Yankees 4, Minnesota Twins 0

16. **David Cone** / New York Yankees (AL) @ Yankee Stadium
Sunday, July 18, 1999 / New York Yankees 6, Montreal Expos

17. **Randy Johnson** / Arizona Diamondbacks (NL) @ Turner Field (Atlanta)
Tuesday, May 18, 2004 / Arizona Diamondbacks 2, Atlanta Braves 0

18. **Mark Buehrle** / Chicago White Sox (AL) @ U.S. Cellular Field (Chicago)
Thursday, July 23, 2009 / Chicago White Sox 5, Tampa Bay Rays 0

19. **Dallas Braden** / Oakland Athletics (AL) @ Oakland–Alameda County Coliseum (Oakland)
Sunday, May 9, 2010 / Oakland Athletics 4, Tampa Bay Rays 0

20. **Roy Halladay** / Philadelphia Phillies (NL) @ Sun Life Stadium (Miami)
Saturday, May 29, 2010 / Philadelphia Phillies 1, Florida Marlins 0

21. **Philip Humber** / Chicago White Sox (AL) @ Safeco Field (Seattle)
Saturday, April 21, 2012 / Chicago White Sox 4, Seattle Mariners 0

22. **Matt Cain** / San Francisco Giants (NL) @ AT&T Park (San Francisco)
Wednesday, June 13, 2012 / San Francisco Giants 10, Houston Astros 0

23. **Félix Hernández** / Seattle Mariners (AL) @ Safeco Field (Seattle)
Wednesday, August 15, 2012 / Seattle Mariners 1, Tampa Bay Rays 0

NO-HITTERS THROWN
BY A FRANCHISE

At the start of the 2010 season, four major-league franchises were awaiting their first no-hitter: the New York Mets, the San Diego Padres, the Colorado Rockies, and the Tampa Bay Rays.

The Rockies and Rays exited the no no-no club in 2010, and the Mets followed in 2012 to break a 50-year, 8,019-game streak. That left the circa-1969 Padres as the sole member of the no no-no club.

Here is the ranking of franchises' no hitters, with each club's other historical team names in parentheses.

25   **Los Angeles Dodgers** (Brooklyn Atlantics/Brooklyn Grays/Brooklyn Bridegrooms/
Brooklyn Grooms/Brooklyn Superbas/Brooklyn Trolley Dodgers/
Brooklyn Robins/Brooklyn Dodgers)

18   **Boston Red Sox** (Boston Americans)

18   **Chicago White Sox** (Chicago White Stockings)

17   **San Francisco Giants** (New York Gothams/New York Giants)

16   **Cincinnati Reds** (Cincinnati Red Stockings/Cincinnati Redlegs)

14   **Cleveland Indians** (Cleveland Bluebirds/Cleveland Naps)

14   **Atlanta Braves** (Boston Red Caps/Boston Beaneaters/Boston Doves/
Boston Rustlers/Boston Bees/Boston Braves/Milwaukee Braves)

14   **Chicago Cubs** (Chicago White Stockings/Chicago Colts/Chicago Orphans)

13   Philadelphia Phillies (Philadelphia Quakers)

11   Oakland Athletics (Philadelphia Athletics/Kansas City Athletics)

11   New York Yankees (New York Highlanders/Baltimore Orioles)

11   Houston Astros (Houston Colt .45s)

10   Los Angeles Angels (California Angels/Anaheim Angels)

10   St. Louis Cardinals (St. Louis Browns/St. Louis Perfectos)

9   Baltimore Orioles (Milwaukee Brewers/St. Louis Browns)

7   Minnesota Twins (Washington Senators)

7   Detroit Tigers

7   Washington Nationals (Montreal Expos)

6   Pittsburgh Pirates (Pittsburgh Alleghenys)

5   Texas Rangers (Washington Senators)

5   Miami Marlins (Florida Marlins)

5   Seattle Mariners

4   Kansas City Royals

2   Arizona Diamondbacks

1   Milwaukee Brewers (Seattle Pilots)

1   Toronto Blue Jays

1   Colorado Rockies

1   Tampa Bay Rays (Tampa Bay Devil Rays)

1   New York Mets

0   San Diego Padres

DEFUNCT FRANCHISES

4   Philadelphia Athletics (AA)

4   Louisville Eclipse/Colonels (NL, AA)

3   Baltimore Orioles (AA, NL)

2   St. Louis Browns/Brown Stockings (NL, AA)

2   Buffalo Bisons (NL)

2   Columbus Buckeyes (AA)

2   Providence Grays (NL)

1   Cleveland Blues (NL); Cincinnati Outlaw Reds (UA); Chicago Chi-Feds/Whales (FL—Federal League); Milwaukee Brewers (UA); Kansas City Packers (FL); Pittsburgh Rebels (FL); Cleveland Spiders (AA, NL); Worcester Ruby Legs (NL); Brooklyn Tip-Tops (FL); St. Louis Terriers (FL); Kansas City Cowboys (AA); Rochester Broncos (AA)

NO-HITTERS THROWN
AGAINST A FRANCHISE

No baseball team likes to head to the locker room after getting no-hit, but every major-league franchise has fallen victim to an opposing pitcher's prowess at least twice. The Chicago Cubs held back the no-no from September 1965 through July 2015 (although my guess is that fans would gladly trade that streak for a more elusive world championship).

Here is the ranking of no-hitters thrown against the major-league franchises, with each club's other historical team names in parentheses.

19	**Philadelphia Phillies** (Philadelphia Quakers)
19	**Los Angeles Dodgers** (Brooklyn Atlantics/Brooklyn Grays/Brooklyn Bridegrooms/Brooklyn Grooms/Brooklyn Superbas/Brooklyn Trolley Dodgers/Brooklyn Robins/Brooklyn Dodgers)
17	**Atlanta Braves** (Boston Red Caps/Boston Beaneaters/Boston Doves/Boston Rustlers/Boston Bees/Boston Braves/Milwaukee Braves)
16	**San Francisco Giants** (New York Gothams/New York Giants)
15	**Baltimore Orioles** (Milwaukee Brewers/St. Louis Browns)
14	**Detroit Tigers**
14	**Oakland Athletics** (Philadelphia Athletics/Kansas City Athletics)
13	**Chicago White Sox** (Chicago White Stockings)
12	**Pittsburgh Pirates** (Pittsburgh Alleghenys)
11	**Cleveland Indians** (Cleveland Bluebirds/Cleveland Naps)

11	**Boston Red Sox** (Boston Americans)
11	**Cincinnati Reds** (Cincinnati Red Stockings/Cincinnati Redlegs)
9	**Minnesota Twins** (Washington Senators)
9	**San Diego Padres**
9	**St. Louis Cardinals** (St. Louis Browns/St. Louis Perfectos)
8	**New York Mets**
7	**New York Yankees** (New York Highlanders/Baltimore Orioles)
7	**Los Angeles Angels** (California Angels/Anaheim Angels)
7	**Chicago Cubs** (Chicago White Stockings/Chicago Colts/Chicago Orphans)
5	**Houston Astros** (Houston Colt .45s)
5	**Tampa Bay Rays** (Tampa Bay Devil Rays)
4	**Washington Nationals** (Montreal Expos)
4	**Texas Rangers** (Washington Senators)
4	**Toronto Blue Jays**
3	**Milwaukee Brewers** (Seattle Pilots)
3	**Seattle Mariners**
3	**Colorado Rockies**
3	**Miami Marlins** (Florida Marlins)
2	**Arizona Diamondbacks**
2	**Kansas City Royals**

DEFUNCT FRANCHISES

3	**Providence Grays** (NL)
2	**Washington Nationals** (AA, UA)
2	**Worcester Ruby Legs** (NL)
2	**Baltimore Orioles** (AA, NL)
2	**Washington Statesmen/Senators** (AA, NL)
2	**Louisville Eclipse/Colonels** (NL, AA)
2	**Cleveland Blues** (AA)
1	**Kansas City Packers** (FL), **Buffalo Buffeds/Blues** (FL), **Buffalo Bisons** (NL), **Kansas City Unions** (UA), **St. Louis Terriers** (FL), **Syracuse Stars** (AA), **Pittsburgh Rebels** (FL), **New York Metropolitans** (AA), **Chicago Chi-Feds/Whales** (FL), **Kansas City Cowboys** (AA), **Hartford Dark Blues** (NL), **Detroit Wolverines** (NL), **Toledo Blue Stockings** (AA)

CURRENT FRANCHISES'
FIRST NO-HITTERS

AMERICAN LEAGUE

Baltimore Orioles *(franchise's earlier names: Milwaukee Brewers/St. Louis Browns)*
Earl Hamilton
Friday, August 30, 1912
St. Louis Browns 5, Detroit Tigers 1
Navin Field (Detroit)
First no-hitter after move to Baltimore was Hoyt Wilhelm on Saturday, September 20, 1958.

Boston Red Sox *(franchise's earlier name: Boston Americans)*
Cy Young
Thursday, May 5, 1904
Boston Americans 3, Philadelphia Athletics 0 (perfect game)
Huntington Avenue Grounds (Boston)

Chicago White Sox *(franchise's earlier name: Chicago White Stockings)*
Jimmy "Nixey" Callahan
Saturday, September 20, 1902 (first game of doubleheader)
Chicago White Sox 3, Detroit Tigers 0
South Side Park (Chicago)

Cleveland Indians *(franchise's earlier names: Cleveland Bluebirds/Cleveland Naps)*
Bob "Dusty" Rhoads
Friday, September 18, 1908
Cleveland Naps 2, Boston Red Sox 1
League Park (Cleveland)

Detroit Tigers
George Mullin
Thursday, July 4, 1912 (second game of doubleheader)
Detroit Tigers 7, St. Louis Browns 0
Navin Field (Detroit)

Houston Astros *(franchise's earlier name: Houston Colt .45s)*
Don Nottebart
Friday, May 17, 1963
Houston Colt .45s 4, Philadelphia Phillies 1
Colt Stadium (Houston)
Nottebart's no-hitter occurred when the franchise was a National League team.

Kansas City Royals
Steve Busby
Friday, April 27, 1973
Kansas City Royals 2, Detroit Tigers 0
Tiger Stadium, Detroit

Los Angeles Angels *(franchise's earlier names: California Angels/Anaheim Angels)*
Bo Belinsky
Saturday, May 5, 1962
Los Angeles Angels 2, Baltimore Orioles 0
Dodger Stadium (Los Angeles)

Minnesota Twins *(franchise's earlier name: Washington Senators I)*
Walter Johnson
Thursday, July 1, 1920
Washington Senators 1, Boston Red Sox 0
Fenway Park (Boston)

First no-hitter after the move to Minnesota was by Jack Kralick on Sunday, August 26, 1962.

New York Yankees *(franchise's earlier names: New York Highlanders/Baltimore Orioles)*
George Mogridge
Tuesday, April 24, 1917
New York Yankees 2, Boston Red Sox 1
Fenway Park (Boston)

Oakland Athletics *(franchise's earlier names: Kansas City Athletics/Philadelphia Athletics)*
Weldon Henley
Saturday, July 22, 1905 (first game of doubleheader)
Philadelphia Athletics 6, St. Louis Browns 0
Sportsman's Park (St. Louis)
No no-hitters as Kansas City Athletics; first no-hitter after move to Oakland was by Jim "Catfish" Hunter, a perfect game on Wednesday, May 8, 1968.

Seattle Mariners
Randy Johnson
Saturday, June 2, 1990
Seattle Mariners 2, Detroit Tigers 0
Kingdome (Seattle)
Johnson also threw the Arizona Diamondbacks' first no-hitter.

Tampa Bay Rays *(franchise's earlier name: Tampa Bay Devil Rays)*
Matt Garza
Monday, July 26, 2010
Tampa Bay Rays 5, Detroit Tigers 0
Tropicana Field (St. Petersburg)

Texas Rangers *(franchise's earlier name: Washington Senators II)*
Jim Bibby
Monday, July 30, 1973

Texas Rangers 6, Oakland Athletics 0
Oakland–Alameda County Coliseum (Oakland)

Toronto Blue Jays
Dave Stieb
Sunday, September 2, 1990
Toronto Blue Jays 3, Cleveland Indians 0
Cleveland Stadium (Cleveland)

NATIONAL LEAGUE
Arizona Diamondbacks
Randy Johnson
Tuesday, May 18, 2004
Arizona Diamondbacks 2, Atlanta Braves 0 (perfect game)
Turner Field (Atlanta)
Johnson also threw the Seattle Mariners' first no-hitter.

Atlanta Braves *(franchise's earlier names: Boston Red Caps/Boston Beaneaters/Boston*
    Doves/Boston Rustlers/Boston Bees/Boston Braves/Milwaukee Braves)
Jack Stivetts
Saturday, August 6, 1892
Boston Beaneaters 11, Brooklyn Grooms 0
Eastern Park (Brooklyn)
First no-hitter after move to Milwaukee was by Jim Wilson on Sunday, June 12,
    1954; first no-hitter after move to Atlanta was by Phil Niekro on Sunday,
    August 5, 1973

Chicago Cubs *(franchise's earlier names: Chicago White Stockings/Chicago Colts/*
    Chicago Orphans)
Larry Corcoran
Thursday, August 19, 1880
Chicago White Stockings 6, Boston Red Caps 0
Lakefront Park (Chicago)

Cincinnati Reds *(franchise's earlier name: Cincinnati Red Stockings/team was called*
    the Cincinnati Redlegs 1954–1959)

Charles "Bumpus" Jones
Saturday, October 15, 1892
Cincinnati Reds 8, Pittsburgh Pirates 1
League Park I (Cincinnati)

Colorado Rockies
Ubaldo Jiménez
Saturday, April 17, 2010
Colorado Rockies 4, Atlanta Braves 0
Turner Field (Atlanta)

Los Angeles Dodgers *(franchise's earlier names: Brooklyn Atlantics/Brooklyn Grays/*
    Brooklyn Bridegrooms/Brooklyn Grooms/Brooklyn Superbas/Brooklyn Trolley
    Dodgers/Brooklyn Robins/Brooklyn Dodgers)
Sam Kimber
Saturday, October 4, 1884
Brooklyn Atlantics 0, Toledo Blue Stockings 0 (10 inn.)
    Washington Park (Brooklyn)
Kimber's no-hitter was when the franchise was an American Association team; first
    no-hitter after move to Los Angeles was by Sandy Koufax on Saturday, June 30,
    1962.

Miami Marlins *(franchise's earlier name: Florida Marlins)*
Al Leiter
Saturday, May 11, 1996
Florida Marlins 11, Colorado Rockies 0
Joe Robbie Stadium (Miami)

Milwaukee Brewers *(franchise's earlier name: Seattle Pilots)*
Juan Nieves
Wednesday, April 15, 1987
Milwaukee Brewers 7, Baltimore Orioles 0
Memorial Stadium (Baltimore)
Nieves's no-hitter was when the franchise was an American League team.

New York Mets
Johan Santana
Friday, June 1, 2012
New York Mets 8, St. Louis Cardinals 0
Citi Field (New York)
Santana's no-hitter ended the franchise's 50-year, 8,019-game drought.

Philadelphia Phillies *(franchise's earlier name: Philadelphia Quakers)*
Charles Ferguson
Saturday, August 29, 1885
Philadelphia Phillies 1, Providence Grays 0
Recreation Park (Philadelphia)

Pittsburgh Pirates *(franchise's earlier name: Pittsburgh Alleghenys)*
Nick Maddox
Friday, September 20, 1907
Pittsburgh Pirates 2, Brooklyn Superbas 1
Exposition Park (Pittsburgh)

San Diego Padres
The Padres, a 1969 expansion team, are still awaiting the club's first no-hitter.

San Francisco Giants *(franchise's earlier names: New York Gothams/New York Giants)*
Amos Rusie
Friday, July 31, 1891
New York Giants 6, Brooklyn Grooms 0
Polo Grounds (New York)
First no-hitter after move to San Francisco was by Juan Marichal on Saturday, June 15, 1963.

St. Louis Cardinals *(franchise's earlier names: St. Louis Browns/St. Louis Perfectos)*
Ted Breitenstein
Sunday, October 4, 1891
St. Louis Browns 8, Louisville Cardinals 0
Sportsman's Park (St. Louis)

Washington Nationals *(franchise's earlier name: Montreal Expos)*
Bill Stoneman
Thursday, April 17, 1969
Montreal Expos 7, Philadelphia Phillies 0
Connie Mack Stadium (Philadelphia)
Expos got the first no-hitter in the franchise's ninth game; first no-hitter after move to
Washington was by Jordan Zimmermann on Sunday, September 28, 2014.

NO-HITTERS BY BALLPARK (CURRENT STADIUMS)

Of Major League Baseball's 30 current ballparks, Boston's Fenway Park has hosted the most no-hitters. The first no-no at Fenway was actually thrown not by a member of the Red Sox but by the Boston Braves' George Davis.

Oddly, baseball's second-oldest park, Wrigley Field, doesn't take second place. That honor goes to Dodger Stadium, which opened 50 years after Fenway.

Here is the list of the number of no-hitters thrown at *current* ballparks with stadiums' previous names noted as well, if it is the same structure.

NO-HITTERS	BALLPARK
14	Fenway Park (Boston)
12	Dodger Stadium (Los Angeles)
9	O.co Coliseum (Oakland) / Previous names: Oakland–Alameda County Coliseum, Network Associates Coliseum, McAfee Coliseum, Overstock.com Coliseum
8	Wrigley Field (Chicago) / Previous name: Weeghman Park
7	Angel Stadium of Anaheim (Anaheim) / Previous name: Anaheim Stadium
4	Safeco Field (Seattle)
3	AT&T Park (San Francisco)

3	Kauffman Stadium (Kansas City) / Previous name: Royals Stadium
3	Turner Field (Atlanta)
3	U.S. Cellular Field (Chicago) / Previous name: Comiskey Park II
3	Citi Field (New York)
2	Citizens Bank Park (Philadelphia)
2	Rogers Centre (Toronto) / Previous name: SkyDome
2	Tropicana Field (St. Petersburg)
2	Nationals Park (Washington, D.C.)
1	Oriole Park at Camden Yards Baltimore
1	Chase Field (Phoenix) / Previous name: Bank One Ballpark
1	Comerica Park (Detroit)
1	Coors Field (Denver)
1	Globe Life Park in Arlington (Texas) / Previous name: The Ballpark at Arlington
1	Great American Ball Park (Cincinnati)
1	Progressive Field (Cleveland) / Previous name: Jacobs Field
1	Marlins Park (Miami)
1	Miller Park (Milwaukee)
1	Petco Park (San Diego)
1	PNC Park (Pittsburgh)
1	Minute Maid Park (Houston)
0	Target Field (Minneapolis)
0	Yankee Stadium II (New York)
0	Busch Stadium II (St. Louis)

NO-HITTERS BY BALLPARK
(FORMER STADIUMS)

Of the many ballparks that no longer exist or no longer serve as home to a major-league franchise, the original Yankee Stadium (1923–2008) has hosted the most no-hitters with 11.

In sharp contrast to the success at the House That Ruth Built, the Pittsburgh Pirates' longtime home of Forbes Field (1909–1971) failed to host a single no-no.

Here is the list of former major-league ballparks that have hosted at least one no-hitter during their histories (stadiums' other names in parentheses).

NO-HITTERS	BALLPARK
11	Yankee Stadium I (New York)
9	Cleveland Stadium (Cleveland)
9	Comiskey Park I (Chicago)
9	Connie Mack Stadium (Philadelphia) / Previous name: Shibe Park
8	Crosley Field (Cincinnati) / Previous name: Redland Field
8	Polo Grounds (New York)
8	Tiger Stadium (Detroit) / Previous names: Briggs Stadium, Navin Field

7	Ebbets Field (Brooklyn)
6	Astrodome (Houston)
6	Candlestick Park (San Francisco)
6	Memorial Stadium (Baltimore)
5	Busch Stadium I (St. Louis) / Previous name: Sportsman's Park
5	Huntington Avenue Grounds (Boston)
5	Milwaukee County Stadium (Milwaukee)
4	Braves Field (Boston)
4	League Park (Cleveland)
4	Riverfront Stadium (Cincinnati)
4	South Side Park III (Chicago)
3	Atlanta–Fulton County Stadium (Atlanta)
3	Jefferson Street Grounds (Philadelphia)
3	Qualcomm Stadium (San Diego) / Previous names: Jack Murphy Stadium, San Diego Stadium
3	Recreation Park (Philadelphia)
3	Robison Field (St. Louis)
3	Joe Robbie Stadium (Miami) / Previous names: Sun Life Stadium, Pro Player Stadium
3	Three Rivers Stadium (Pittsburgh)
3	West Side Park II (Chicago)
2	Arlington Stadium (Texas); Busch Stadium II (St. Louis); Colt Stadium (Houston); Eastern Park (Brooklyn); Handlan's Park (St. Louis); Hubert H. Humphrey Metrodome (Minneapolis); Kingdome (Seattle); Lakefront Park II (Chicago); Messer Street Grounds (Providence); National League Park (Philadelphia) / Previous name: Baker Bowl; Olympic Stadium (Montreal); League Park (Cincinnati) / Previous name: Palace of the Fans; Recreation Park (Pittsburgh); Shea Stadium (New York); Sportsman's Park I (St. Louis); Veterans Stadium (Philadelphia); Washington Park I (Brooklyn); Washington Park II (Brooklyn)

1   Association Park (Kansas City); Bank Street Grounds
(Cincinnati); Bennett Park (Detroit); Boundary Field
(Washington, D.C.); Capitol Grounds (Washington,
D.C.); Culver Field (Rochester); Eclipse Park I
(Louisville); Eclipse Park II (Louisville); Exposition Park I
(Pittsburgh); Exposition Park II (Pittsburgh); Exposition
Park III (Pittsburgh); Griffith Stadium (Washington,
D.C.); Hilltop Park (New York); International Fair
Association Grounds (Buffalo); Kennard Street Park
(Cleveland); Lakefront Park I (Chicago); League Park I
(Cincinnati); Metropolitan Stadium (Minneapolis);
Oriole Park I (Baltimore); Parc Jarry (Montreal);
Recreation Park (Detroit); Ridgewood Park (Brooklyn);
Riverside Park (Buffalo); Union Park (Baltimore);
Washington Park III (Brooklyn); Worcester Driving Park
Grounds (Worcester); Wright Street Grounds
(Milwaukee)

0   Forbes Field (Pittsburgh)

ROOKIES WHO HAVE THROWN NO-HITTERS

Lee Richmond
Worcester Ruby Legs (NL) / Saturday, June 12, 1880 / Worcester Ruby Legs 1,
   Cleveland Blues 0 / Worcester Driving Park Grounds (Worcester)
Perfect game

Larry Corcoran
Chicago White Stockings (NL) / Thursday, August 19, 1880 / Chicago White
   Stockings 6, Boston Red Caps 0 / Lakefront Park (Chicago)
His first of three no-hitters

Tony Mullane
Louisville Eclipse (AA) / Monday, September 11, 1882 / Louisville Eclipse 2,
   Cincinnati Red Stockings 0 / Bank Street Grounds (Cincinnati)

Guy Hecker
Louisville Eclipse (AA) / Tuesday, September 19, 1882 / Louisville Eclipse 3,
   Pittsburgh Alleghenys 1 / Exposition Park (Pittsburgh)

Al Atkinson
Philadelphia Athletics (AA) / Saturday, May 24, 1884 / Philadelphia Athletics 10,
   Pittsburgh Alleghenys 1 / Recreation Park (Philadelphia)
His first of two no-hitters

Ed Morris
Columbus Buckeyes (AA) / Thursday, May 29, 1884 / Columbus Buckeyes 5,
    Pittsburgh Alleghenys 0 / Recreation Park (Pittsburgh)

Sam Kimber
Brooklyn Atlantics (AA) / Saturday, October 4, 1884 / Brooklyn Atlantics 0,
    Toledo Blue Stockings 0 (10 inn.) / Washington Park (Brooklyn)
Game called for darkness

Matt Kilroy
Baltimore Orioles (AA) / Wednesday, October 6, 1886 / Baltimore Orioles 6,
    Pittsburgh Alleghenys 0 / Recreation Park (Pittsburgh)

Ted Breitenstein
St. Louis Browns (AA) / Sunday, October 4, 1891 (first game of doubleheader) /
    St. Louis Browns 8, Louisville Colonels 0 / Sportsman's Park (St. Louis)
*Breitenstein throws a no-hitter in his first major-league start—his first of two no-
    hitters.*

Charles "Bumpus" Jones
Cincinnati Reds (NL) / Saturday, October 15, 1892 / Cincinnati Reds 7,
    Pittsburgh Pirates 1 / League Park (Cincinnati)
Jones throws a no-hitter in his first major league appearance.

Jim Jay Hughes
Baltimore Orioles (NL) / Friday, April 22, 1898 / Baltimore Orioles 8, Boston
    Beaneaters 0 / Union Park (Baltimore)

Charles "Deacon" Phillippe
Louisville Colonels (NL) / Thursday, May 25, 1899 / Louisville Colonels 7, New
    York Giants 0 / Eclipse Park (Louisville)

Christy Mathewson
New York Giants (NL) / Monday, July 15, 1901 / New York Giants 5, St. Louis
    Cardinals 0 / Robison Field (St. Louis)
His first of two no-hitters

Jeff Tesreau

New York Giants (NL) / Friday, September 6, 1912 (first game of doubleheader) / New York Giants 3, Philadelphia Phillies 0 / National League Park (Philadelphia)

Charlie Robertson

Chicago White Sox (AL) / Sunday, April 30, 1922/ Chicago White Sox 2, Detroit Tigers 0 / Navin Field (Detroit)
Perfect game

Paul Dean

St. Louis Cardinals (NL) / Friday, September 21, 1934 (second game of doubleheader) / St. Louis Cardinals 3, Brooklyn Dodgers 0/ Ebbets Field (Brooklyn)

Vern Kennedy

Chicago White Sox (AL) / Saturday, August 31, 1935 / Chicago White Sox 5, Cleveland Indians 0 / Comiskey Park (Chicago)

Bill McCahan

Philadelphia Athletics (AL) / Wednesday, September 3, 1947 / Philadelphia Athletics 3, Washington Senators 0 / Shibe Park (Philadelphia)

Alva "Bobo" Holloman

St. Louis Browns (AL) / Wednesday, May 6, 1953 / St. Louis Browns 6, Philadelphia Athletics 0 / Busch Stadium (St. Louis)
Holloman throws a no-hitter in his first major-league start.

Sam "Toothpick" Jones

Chicago Cubs (NL) / Thursday, May 12, 1955 / Chicago Cubs 4, Pittsburgh Pirates 0 / Wrigley Field (Chicago)

Bo Belinsky

Los Angeles Angels (AL) / Saturday, May 5, 1962 / Los Angeles Angels 2, Baltimore Orioles 0 / Dodger Stadium (Los Angeles)

Don Wilson

Houston Astros (NL) / Sunday, June 18, 1967 / Houston Astros 2, Atlanta
    Braves 0 / Astrodome (Houston)
His first of two no-hitters

Vida Blue

Oakland Athletics (AL) / Monday, September 21, 1970 / Oakland Athletics 6,
    Minnesota Twins 0 / Oakland–Alameda County Coliseum (Oakland)

Burt Hooton

Chicago Cubs (NL) / Sunday, April 16, 1972 / Chicago Cubs 4, Philadelphia
    Phillies 0 / Wrigley Field (Chicago)

Steve Busby

Kansas City Royals (AL) / Friday, April 27, 1973 / Kansas City Royals 3, Detroit
    Tigers 0 / Tiger Stadium (Detroit)
His first of two no-hitters

Jim Bibby

Texas Rangers (AL) / Monday, July 30, 1973 / Texas Rangers 6, Oakland
    Athletics 0 / Oakland–Alameda County Coliseum (Oakland)

Mike Warren

Oakland Athletics (AL) / Thursday, September 29, 1983 / Oakland Athletics 3,
    Chicago White Sox 0 / Oakland–Alameda County Coliseum (Oakland)

Wilson Álvarez

Chicago White Sox (AL) / Sunday, August 11, 1991 / Chicago White Sox 7,
    Baltimore Orioles 0 / Memorial Stadium (Baltimore)
Álvarez throws a no-hitter in his second major-league start.

José Jiménez

St. Louis Cardinals (NL) / Friday, June 25, 1999 / St. Louis Cardinals 1, Arizona
    Diamondbacks 0 / Bank One Ballpark (Phoenix)

Bud Smith
St. Louis Cardinals (NL) / Monday, September 3, 2001 / St. Louis Cardinals 4,
   San Diego Padres 0 / Qualcomm Stadium (San Diego)

Aníbal Sánchez
Florida Marlins (NL) / Wednesday, September 6, 2006 / Florida Marlins 2,
   Arizona Diamondbacks 0 / Pro Player Stadium (Miami)

Clay Buchholz
Boston Red Sox (AL) / Saturday, September 1, 2007 / Boston Red Sox 10,
   Baltimore Orioles 0 / Fenway Park (Boston)
Buchholz throws a no-hitter in his second major-league start.

Chris Heston
San Francisco Giants (NL) / Tuesday, June 9, 2015 / San Francisco Giants 5,
   New York Mets 0 / Citi Field (New York)

UNOFFICIAL NO-HITTERS
OF LESS THAN 9 INNINGS

When baseball's committee for statistical accuracy established the first official definition of a no hitter in 1991, it declared: "A no-hitter is a game in which a pitcher
or pitchers complete a game of nine innings or more without allowing a hit."

That knocked from the record books these 36 previously credited no-nos shortened due to rain, darkness, or other factors. The decision also preempted a five-inning rain-shortened no-no thrown by Devern Hansack in 2006.

Here's the list of unofficial mini-no-nos.

Larry McKeon
Indianapolis Hoosiers (AA) / Tuesday, May 6, 1884 / Indianapolis Hoosiers 0,
    Cincinnati Red Stockings 0 (6 inn.) / League Park (Cincinnati)
Game called for rain

Charlie Geggus
Washington Nationals (UA) / Thursday, August 21, 1884 / Washington
    Nationals 12, Wilmington Quicksteps 1 (8 inn.) / Capitol Grounds
    (Washington, D.C.)
Game called by mutal consent

Charlie "Pretzels" Getzien

Detroit Wolverines (NL) / Wednesday, October 1, 1884 / Detroit Wolverines 1,
    Philadelphia Phillies 0 (6 inn.) / Recreation Park (Detroit)
Game called for rain

Charlie Sweeney (2 inn.), **Henry Boyle** (3 inn.)

St. Louis Maroons (UA) / Sunday, October 5, 1884 / St. Louis Maroons 0, St.
    Paul Whitecaps 1 (5 inn.) / Union Grounds (St. Louis)
Game called for rain

Fred "Dupee" Shaw

Providence Grays (NL) / Wednesday, October 7, 1885 (first game of
    doubleheader) / Providence Grays 4, Buffalo Bisons 0 (5 inn.) / Olympic Park
    (Buffalo)
Teams planned a doubleheader, with each game five innings long.

George Van Haltren

Chicago White Stockings (NL) / Thursday, June 21, 1888 / Chicago White
    Stockings 1, Pittsburgh Alleghenys 0 (6 inn.)
West Side Park (Chicago)
Game called for rain

Ed Crane

New York Giants (NL) / Thursday, September 27, 1888 / New York Giants 3,
    Washington Nationals 0 (7 inn.) / Polo Grounds (New York)
Game called for darkness

Matt Kilroy

Baltimore Orioles (AA) / Saturday, July 29, 1889 (second game of doubleheader)
    / Baltimore Orioles 0, St. Louis Browns 0 (7 inn.) / Oriole Park (Baltimore)
Game called for darkness

George Nicol

St. Louis Browns (AA) / Tuesday, September 23, 1890 / St. Louis Browns 21,
    Philadelphia Athletics 2 (7 inn.) / Sportsman's Park (St. Louis)
Game called for darkness

Hank Gastright

Columbus Solons (AA) / Sunday, October 12, 1890 / Columbus Solons 6,
Toledo Maumees 0 (8 inn.) / Recreation Park (Columbus)
Game called for darkness

Jack Stivetts

Boston Braves (NL) / Saturday, October 15, 1892 (second game of doubleheader)
/ Boston Braves 4, Washington Senators 0 (5 inn.) / Boundary Field
(Washington, D.C.)
Game called by mutual consent

Elton "Ice Box" Chamberlain

Cincinnati Reds (NL) / Saturday, September 23, 1893 (second game of
doubleheader) / Cincinnati Reds 6, Boston Beaneaters 0 (7 inn.) / League
Park (Cincinnati)
Game called for darkness

Ed Stein

Brooklyn Grooms (NL) / Saturday, June 2, 1894 / Brooklyn Grooms 1, Chicago
White Stockings 0 (6 inn.) / Eastern Park (Brooklyn)
Game called for rain

Red Ames

New York Giants (NL) / Monday, September 14, 1903 (second game of
doubleheader) / New York Giants 5, St. Louis Cardinals 0 (5 inn.) / Robison
Field (St. Louis)
Game called for darkness

Rube Waddell

Philadelphia Athletics (AL) / Tuesday, August 15, 1905 / Philadelphia Athletics 2,
St. Louis Browns 0 (5 inn.) / Columbia Park (Philadelphia)
Game called for rain

Jake Weimer
Cincinnati Reds (NL) / Friday, August 24, 1906 (second game of double-
    header) / Cincinnati Reds 1, Brooklyn Superbas 0 (7 inn.) / League Park
    (Cincinnati)
Nightcap planned as seven-inning game

Jim Dygert (3 inn.), **Rube Waddell** (2 inn.)
Philadelphia Athletics (AL) / Wednesday, August 29, 1906 / Philadelphia
    Athletics 4, Chicago White Sox 3 (5 inn.) / Columbia Park (Philadelphia)
Game called for rain

Grant "Stoney" McGlynn
St. Louis Cardinals (NL) / Monday, September 24, 1906 (second game of
    doubleheader) / St. Louis Cardinals 1, Brooklyn Superbas 1 (7 inn.) /
    Washington Park (Brooklyn)
Game called for darkness

Al "Lefty" Leifield
Pittsburgh Pirates (NL) / Wednesday, September 26, 1906 (second game of
    doubleheader) / Pittsburgh Pirates 8, Philadelphia Phillies 0 (6 inn.)/
    National League Park (Philadelphia)
Game called for darkness

Ed Walsh
Chicago White Sox (AL) / Sunday, May 26, 1907/ Chicago White Sox 8, New
    York Highlanders 1 (5 inn.) / South Side Park (Chicago)
Game called for rain

Ed Karger
St. Louis Cardinals (NL)
Sunday, August 11, 1907 (second game of doubleheader) / St. Louis Cardinals 4,
    Boston Doves 0 (7 inn., perfect game) / Robison Field (St. Louis)
Nightcap planned as a seven-inning game

Howie Camnitz

Pittsburgh Pirates (NL) / Friday, August 23, 1907 (second game of doubleheader)
/ Pittsburgh Pirates 1, New York Giants 0 (5 inn.) / Polo Grounds (New
York)
Game called for darkness

Harry "Rube" Vickers

Philadelphia Athletics (AL) / Saturday, October 5, 1907 (second game of
doubleheader) / Philadelphia Athletics 4, Washington Senators 0 (5 inn.,
perfect game) / National Park (Washington)
Game called for darkness

Johnny Lush

Philadelphia Athletics (AL) / Thursday, August 6, 1908 / St. Louis Cardinals 2,
Brooklyn Superbas 0 (6 inn.) / Washington Park (Brooklyn)
Game called for rain

Len "King" Cole

Chicago Cubs (NL) / Sunday, July 31, 1910 (second game of doubleheader) /
Chicago Cubs 4, St. Louis Cardinals 0 (7 inn.) / Robison Field (St. Louis)
Managers agreed to call the game at 5 p.m. Central so teams could catch their trains.

Jay Carl Cashion

Washington Senators (AL) / Tuesday, August 20, 1912 (second game of
doubleheader) / Washington Senators 2, Cleveland Naps 0 (6 inn.) / Griffith
Stadium (Washington)
Game called at end of sixth inning to allow Cleveland team to catch a train

Walter Johnson

Washington Senators (AL) / Monday, August 25, 1924 (first game of
doubleheader) / Washington Senators 2, St. Louis Browns 0 (7 inn.) / Griffith
Stadium (Washington)
Game called for rain; second game of doubleheader canceled

Fred Frankhouse
Brooklyn Dodgers (NL) / Friday, August 27, 1937 (first game of doubleheader) /
   Brooklyn Dodgers 5, Cincinnati Reds 0 (8 inn.) / Ebbets Field (Brooklyn)
*Opener called due to rain after seven and two-thirds innings; second game of
   doubleheader canceled*

Johnny Whitehead
St. Louis Browns (AL) / Monday, August 5, 1940 (second game of double-
   header) / St. Louis Browns 4, Detroit Tigers 0 (6 inn.) / Sportsman's Park
   (St. Louis)
Game called for rain

Jim Tobin
Boston Braves (NL) / Thursday, June 22, 1944 (second game of doubleheader) /
   Boston Braves 7, Philadelphia Phillies 0 (5 inn.) / Braves Field (Boston)
Game called for darkness

Mike McCormick
San Francisco Giants (NL) / Friday, June 12, 1959 / San Francisco Giants 3,
   Philadelphia Phillies 0 (5 inn.) / Connie Mack Stadium (Philadelphia)
*Game called for rain. McCormick allowed a single and then walked the bases loaded
   in the sixth inning, but because that inning was never completed, statistically the
   hit never happened.*

"Toothpick" Sam Jones
San Francisco Giants (NL) / Friday, September 26, 1959 / San Francisco Giants
   4, St. Louis Cardinals 0 (7 inn.) / Busch Stadium (St. Louis)
Game called for rain

Dean Chance
Minnesota Twins (AL) / Thursday, August 6, 1967 / Minnesota Twins 2, Boston
   Red Sox 0 (5 inn., perfect game) / Metropolitan Stadium (Minneapolis)
Game called for rain

David Palmer

Montreal Expos (NL) / Saturday, April 21, 1984 (second game of doubleheader) / Montreal Expos 4, St. Louis Cardinals 0 (5 inn., perfect game) / Busch Stadium (St. Louis)

Game called for rain

Pascual Pérez

Montreal Expos (NL) / Saturday, September 24, 1988 / Montreal Expos 1, Philadelphia Phillies 0 (5 inn.) / Veterans Stadium (Philadelphia)

Game called for rain

Mélido Pérez

Chicago White Sox (AL) / Thursday, July 12, 1990 / Chicago White Sox 8, New York Yankees 0 (6 inn.) / Yankee Stadium (New York)

Game called for rain

Devern Hansack

Boston Red Sox (AL) / Sunday, October 1, 2006 / Boston Red Sox 9, Baltimore Orioles 0 (5 inn.) / Fenway Park (Boston)

Game called for rain

TEAM NO-HITTERS BEFORE OTHERS WERE TOSSED

The no-hitter spotlight often pans around the majors, but sometimes it stays fixated on a particular team before letting another accomplish the feat. The Milwaukee Braves are the only team in the majors to throw three consecutive no-hitters—without another team chiming in (1960–1961)—while several others have notched two no-nos without being interrupted.

THREE NO-HITTERS BY THE SAME TEAM
BEFORE ANY OTHERS WERE THROWN

Milwaukee Braves—1960–1961

Lew Burdette: Thursday, August 18, 1960 / Braves 1, Philadelphia Phillies 0 / Milwaukee County Stadium

Warren Spahn: Friday, September 16, 1960 / Braves 4, Phillies 0 / Milwaukee County Stadium

Warren Spahn: Friday, April 28, 1961 / Braves 1, San Francisco Giants 0 / Milwaukee County Stadium

TWO NO-HITTERS BY THE SAME TEAM
BEFORE ANY OTHERS WERE THROWN

Louisville Eclipse (AA)—1882
Tony Mullane: Monday, September 11, 1882 / Eclipse 2, Cincinnati Red
    Stockings 0 / Bank Street Grounds (Cincinnati)
Guy Hecker: Tuesday, September 19, 1882 / Eclipse 3, Pittsburgh Alleghenys 1 /
    Exposition Park (Pittsburgh)

Columbus Buckeyes—1884
Ed Morris: Thursday, May 29, 1884 / Buckeyes 5, Pittsburgh Alleghenys 0 /
    Recreation Park (Pittsburgh)
Frank Mountain: Thursday, June 5, 1884 / Buckeyes 12, Washington Nationals
    0 / Capitol Grounds (Washington, D.C.)

Philadelphia Athletics—1888
Ed Seward: Thursday, July 26, 1888 / Athletics 12, Cincinnati Red Stockings 2 /
    Jefferson Street Grounds (Philadelphia)
Gus Weyhing: Tuesday, July 31, 1888 / Athletics 4, Kansas City Cowboys 0 /
    Jefferson Street Grounds

Boston Americans—1904
Cy Young: Thursday, May 5, 1904 / Americans 3, Philadelphia Athletics 0
    (perfect game) / Huntington Avenue Grounds (Boston)
Jesse Tannehill: Wednesday, August 17, 1904 / Americans 6, Chicago White Sox
    0 / South Side Park (Chicago)

Cleveland Naps—1908–1910
Addie Joss: Friday, October 2, 1908 / Naps 1, White Sox 0 (perfect game) /
    League Park (Cleveland)
Addie Joss: Wednesday, April 20, 1910 / Naps 1, White Sox 0 / South Side Park

St. Louis Browns—1917
Consecutive days, separated by first game of doubleheader
Ernie Koob: Saturday, May 5, 1917 / Browns 1, White Sox 0 / Sportsman's Park
    (St. Louis)

Bob Groom: Sunday, May 6, 1917 (second game of doubleheader) / Browns 3, White Sox 0 / Sportsman's Park

Boston Red Sox—1917

Babe Ruth (0 inn.), **Ernie Shore** (9 inn.): Saturday, June 23, 1917 (first game of doubleheader) / Red Sox 4, Washington Senators 0 / Fenway Park

Hubert "Dutch" Leonard: Monday, June 3, 1918 / Red Sox 5, Detroit Tigers 0 / Navin Field (Detroit)

Chicago White Sox—1935

Vern Kennedy: Saturday, August 31, 1935 / White Sox 5, Cleveland Indians 0 / Comiskey Park (Chicago)

Bill Dietrich: Tuesday, June 1, 1937 / White Sox 8, St. Louis Browns 0 / Comiskey Park (Chicago)

Cincinnati Reds—1938

Consecutive starts

Johnny Vander Meer: Saturday, June 11, 1938 / Reds 3, Boston Bees 0 / Crosley Field (Cincinnati)

Johnny Vander Meer: Wednesday, June 15, 1938 / Reds 6, Brooklyn Dodgers 0 / Ebbets Field (Brooklyn)

New York Yankees—1951

Allie Reynolds: Thursday, July 12, 1951 / Yankees 1, Indians 0 / Cleveland Stadium

Allie Reynolds: Friday, September 28, 1951 (first game of doubleheader) / Yankees 8, Red Sox 0 / Yankee Stadium

Chicago Cubs—1972

Burt Hooton: Sunday, April 16, 1972 / Chicago Cubs 4, Philadelphia Phillies 0 / Wrigley Field (Chicago)

Milt Pappas: Saturday, September 2, 1972 / Chicago Cubs 8, San Diego Padres 0 / Wrigley Field

California Angels—1973

Nolan Ryan: Tuesday, May 15, 1973 / Angels 3, Kansas City Royals 0 / Royals Stadium (Kansas City)

Nolan Ryan: Sunday, July 15, 1973 / Angels 6, Detroit Tigers 0 / Tiger Stadium (Detroit)

California Angels—1974–1975

Nolan Ryan: Saturday, September 28, 1974 / Angels 4, Minnesota Twins 0 / Anaheim Stadium

Nolan Ryan: Sunday, June 1, 1975 / Angels 1, Baltimore Orioles 0 / Anaheim Stadium

Boston Red Sox—2007–2008

Clay Buchholz: Saturday, September 1, 2007 / Red Sox 10, Baltimore Orioles 0 / Fenway Park

Jon Lester: Monday, May 19, 2008 / Red Sox 7, Royals 0 / Fenway Park

Cincinnati Reds—2012–2013

Homer Bailey: Friday, September 28, 2012 / Cincinnati Reds 1, Pittsburgh Pirates 0 / PNC Park (Pittsburgh)

Homer Bailey: Tuesday, July 2, 2013 / Reds 3, San Francisco Giants 0 / Great American Ball Park (Cincinnati)

Los Angeles Dodgers—2014

Josh Beckett: Sunday, May 25, 2014 / Dodgers 6, Philadelphia Phillies 0 / Citizens Bank Park (Philadelphia)

Clayton Kershaw: Wednesday, June 18, 2014 / Dodgers 8, Colorado Rockies 0 / Dodger Stadium

BIBLIOGRAPHY

Abbott, Jim, and Tim Brown. 2012. *Imperfect: An Improbable Life*. New York: Ballantine Books.

Ackert, Kristie. June 1, 2013. "Year after Johan Santana No-Hitter, Mets Manager Terry Collins Managing Emotions." *New York Daily News*.

Albom, Mitch. June 3, 2010. "Yo, Bud Selig, Blown Call Is a Perfect Call to Action." *Detroit Free Press*.

Anderson, Dave, New York Times. May 5, 1991. "For Ryan, Another Shot at Vander Meer." *Star-News*, 4C.

Antonen, Mel. July 13, 2012. "Despite Close Calls, Padres Only Members of the No No-Hitters Club." *Sports Illustrated*, http://www.si.com/more-sports/2012/06/13/padres-no-hitters.

The Associated Press. September 30, 1990. "A's Stewart No-Hits Blue Jays: 4th in Majors this Season; 3rd in June." *Standard-Speaker*, 13.

The Associated Press. September 5, 1993. "Abbott Hurls No-Hitter as New York Downs Cleveland." *The Times-News*, 1C.

The Associated Press. September 19, 1968. "Another No-Hitter: Washburn." *Des Moines Register*, 21–22.

The Associated Press. May 29, 1994. "At 15, Joe Nuxhall Was Majors' Youngest Player." *The Kokomo Tribune*, 17.

The Associated Press. August 15, 1964. "Belinsky Suspended for Striking Writer." *The Daily Telegram*, 8.

The Associated Press. May 18, 1953. "Bunt Robs Dodgers' Erskine of No-Hitter; Blanks Reds 10-0." *Milwaukee Sentinel*, 8.

The Associated Press. June 24, 1994. "Bunt Ruins Witt's No-Hitter: Gagne Ruled Safe at First on Controversial Call." *The Free Lance-Star*, 8.

The Associated Press. June 5, 1960. "Can't Hide No-Hitter from Fans—Erksine." *The Miami News*, 18.

The Associated Press. June 20, 1938. "Cincinnati Tops Boston Bees, 14-1: Losers Stop Johnny Vander Meer's Streak of Hitless Innings." *The Gazette and Daily*, 4.

The Associated Press. June 5, 1970. "Clarke Spoils Rooker's Bid." *The Montana Standard*, 14.

The Associated Press. September 21, 1986. "Cowley's No-Hitter Didn't Seem Like One." *The Telegraph*, C8.

The Associated Press. May 15, 1996. "Doc's Not Done: Gooden No-Hits Mariners 2-0." *The Daily Globe*, 8.

The Associated Press. December 6, 2012. "Don Larsen's 1956 World Series Perfect Game Uniform Sells for $756,000 at Auction." *New York Daily News*.

The Associated Press. May 17, 1951. "Duel Sends Old-Timers to Dusty Record Books." *The Milwaukee Journal*, 45.

The Associated Press. May 13, 1956. "Erskine Spins No-Hit, No-Run Game." *Kingsport Times-News*, 21.

The Associated Press. April 21, 1938. "Feller 'Robbed' by Scratch Hit: Billy Sullivan, Ex-Teammate, Beats Out Bunt to Prevent 'Perfect' Game." *The Norwalk Hour*, 15.

The Associated Press. April 17, 1940. "Feller's No-Hit Game Features Season's Start." *Gettysburg Times*, 3.

The Associated Press. September 27, 1983. "Forsch Collects Second No-Hitter." *Gadsden Times*, 6.

The Associated Press. September 10, 1945. "Fowler for Macks Pitches No-Hitter." *The Kane Republican*, 3.

The Associated Press. July 23, 1971. "Gomez Puts Win before No-Hitter: Kirby Lifted Three Outs from Fame." *Sarasota Herald-Tribune*, 2C.

The Associated Press. September 6, 1974. "Gomez Right Says Astros' Don Wilson." *The Victoria Advocate*, 5B.

The Associated Press. September 4, 1991. "Haddix No-Hitter Is Axed." *The Telegraph*, 47.

The Associated Press. May 7, 1953. "Holloman Hurls No-Hitter for Browns in Debut." *Sarasota Herald-Tribune*, 13.

The Associated Press. April 9, 1979. "Houston's Ken Forsch: Miserable Spring Leads to No-Hitter." *The Spokesman-Review*, 23.

The Associated Press. April 24, 1964. "'It Was My Fault, Not Nellie's,' Says Hurler." *The Daily Times-News*, 28.

The Associated Press. October 1, 1986. "Jackson Loses No-Hitter in Ninth, but Wins Game." *The Fort Scott Tribune*, 14.

The Associated Press. October 2, 1988. "Jays' Stieb Inflicted by Deja-Vu." *The News-Journal*, 4D.

The Associated Press. June 5, 1986. "Joe Niekro Just Misses No-Hitter at Age 41." *The Dispatch*, 8.

The Associated Press. August 11, 1976. "John Candalaria Throws No-Hitter." *The Spokesman-Review*, 21.

The Associated Press. May 19, 2004. "Johnson Perfect: Arizona Pitcher Retires All 27 Braves Batters." *The Index-Journal*, 9.

The Associated Press. August 27, 1962. "Kralick: 'Walking Alusik Better Than Hit.'" *The Winona Daily News*, 12.

The Associated Press. February 24, 2007. "Larsen, Berra Watch 1956 Perfect Game Broadcast." *Sun Journal*, C7.

The Associated Press. July 29, 1991. "Martinez Hurls Perfect Game." *Pharos-Tribune*, B1.

The Associated Press. July 30, 1991. "No-Hitter Epidemic." *The Telegraph*, 19.

The Associated Press. February 11, 1965. "No-Hitter Loss Haunts Johnson." *The Victoria Advocate*, 13A.

The Associated Press. September 22, 1934. "Paul Dean Yields No Hits, Dizzy Three as Deans Blank Brooklyn Twice." *The Gettysburg Times*, 3.

The Associated Press. September 3, 1972. "Pitches to Stahl Not Far Off—Pappas." *The Pantagraph*, 11.

The Associated Press. April 10, 1990. "Rangers' Ryan, A's off to Blazing Starts." *The Index Journal*, 7.

The Associated Press. April 10, 1959. "Rating Orioles Triple Play; Feller's No-Hitter Still Stands as the Best Opening Day Effort." *Ocala Star Banner*, 8.

The Associated Press. September 28, 1981. "Ryan Passes Koufax with 5th No-Hitter." *Ludington Daily News*, 11.

The Associated Press. September 25, 1988. "Stieb Loses a No-Hitter Once Again." *The San Bernadino County Sun*, C12.

The Associated Press. July 16, 1952. "Vander Meer Has No-Hitter Again after 14 Years." *Toledo Blade*, 24.

The Associated Press. June 16, 1938. "Vander Meer of Reds Pitches Second Successive No-Hit, No-Run Victory." *The Montreal Gazette*, 14.

The Associated Press. July 11, 1927. "Virgil Barnes Allows One Hit as Cardinals and Giants Split Double-Header." *The Bridgeport Telegram*, 14.

Bacon, James, The Associated Press. June 14, 1962. "Guys, Gals and Parties—Featuring Bo Belinsky." *Standard-Speaker*, 24.

Baldassaro, Lawrence. 2011. *Beyond DiMaggio: Italian Americans in Baseball*. Lincoln: University of Nebraska Press.

Barber, Red. May 23, 1971. "Moments in Sportscasting." *Family Weekly*, 4–5.

Barber, Red. 1982. *1947: When All Hell Broke Loose in Baseball*. Boston, Mass.: Da Capo Press.

"Base-ball: Detroit 14; Chicago 0." July 16, 1884. *Chicago Daily Tribune*, 7.

"Base-ball Gossip." October 16, 1892. *The Cincinnati Enquirer*, 6.

The Baseball Project. 2008. "Harvey Haddix." On *Volume 1: Frozen Ropes and Dying Quails*. Hillsborough, N.C.: Yep Roc Records.

Beck, Jason, MLB.com. June 3, 2010. "Galarraga Brings Lineup to Tearful Joyce: Umpire Displays Emotion in Meeting Day after Blown Call." MLB.com, http://mlb.mlb.com/news/article.jsp?ymd=20100603&content_id=10754978&vkey=news_mlb&fext=.jsp&c_id=mlb.

Beck, Jason, MLB.com. May 23, 2002. "Right-Hander Throws One-Hitter." Detroit Tigers, MLB.com, http://detroit.tigers.mlb.com/news/article.jsp?ymd=20020523&content_id=31195&vkey=news_det&fext=.jsp&c_id=det.

Beard, Gordon, The Associated Press. June 11, 1966. "Birds Bump Boston, 9-2: Bosox Spoiled Bunker's Bid for No-Hitter." *The Daily Mail (Hagerstown, Md.)*, 14.

Bena, Parker. 2013. *Inventing Baseball: The 100 Greatest Games of the Nineteenth Century*, edited by Bill Felber. Society for American Baseball Research.

Braucher, Bill, Central Press. April 25, 1938. "Tales in Tidbits." *New Castle News*, 12.

Brickhouse, Jack. September 2, 1972. "Memorable Moments in Chicago Sports." Media Burn Independent Video Archive, http://mediaburn.org/video/memorable-moments-in-chicago-sports.

Brinster, Dick, The Associated Press. June 12, 1990. "Nolan Ryan again Pitches No-Hitter." *Daily Sitka Sentinel*, 8.

The Brooklyn Daily Eagle. May 7, 1917. "Bob Groom's Remarkable Feat Another Big League Record." *The Brooklyn Daily Eagle*, 7.

The Brooklyn Daily Eagle. June 24, 1917. "Ernie Shore in Hall of Fame; Not a Senator Reaches First." *The Brooklyn Daily Eagle*, 28.

The Brooklyn Daily Eagle. October 5, 1884. "An Unprecedented Base Ball Contest at Washington Park." *The Brooklyn Daily Eagle*, 1.

Brodsky, Chuck, composer and performer. 2002. "Dock Ellis' No-No." On *The Baseball Ballads*. Decatur, Ga.: K. Bush.

Bryson, Mike, The Associated Press. April 18, 1969. "Expos' Bill Stoneman Hurls First No-Hitter." *The Corbin Times-Tribune*, 2.

Buchholz, Clay. May 20, 2015. D. Lammers interview with Clay Buchholz.

Bunning, Jim. May 1, 2015. D. Lammers interview with Jim Bunning.

Busby, Steve. May 20, 2015. D. Lammers interview with Steve Busby.

CTV. September 2, 1990. CTV postgame interview with Dave Stieb, https://www.youtube.com/watch?v=EO_pEfD99lQ.

Campanella, Roy. September 25, 1958. "The Way I See It." *Jet*, 56–57.

Carlisle, Jim, Scripps Howard News Service. June 19, 1996. "Mel Allen Remembered as among Best in His Business." *The Dallas Morning News*, 5B.

Carr, Kenneth, United Press International. April 24, 1964. "First Time in History—Ken Johnson Pitches a No-Hitter but Loses to Cincy Reds, 1 to 0." *Greensburg Daily News*, 2.

Chass, Murray. April 17, 1992. "On Baseball: What Is a No-Hitter? Matt Young Knows." *The New York Times*.

Chass, Murray, The Associated Press. April 24, 1964. "Colts' Johnson First Hurler to Drop 9-Inning No-Hitter." *Del Rio News Herald*, 4.

Chass, Murray, The Associated Press. May 1, 1967. "Steve Barber and Stu Miller Combine for No-Hitter and Lose Game." *The Day (New London, Conn.)*, 27.

The Chicago Daily Tribune. August 20, 1880. "Base-Ball: Chicago vs. Boston." *The Chicago Daily Tribune*, 8.

The Chicago Daily Tribune. September 21, 1882. "Brilliant Close to the Championship Season by the Chicagos at Home." *The Chicago Daily Tribune*, 8.

The Chicago Daily Tribune. October 5, 1891. "Louisville and St. Louis Play Twice, Each Club Winning Once." *The Chicago Daily Tribune*, 6.

The Chicago Daily Tribune. April 23, 1898. "Phenomenal Pitching Feats: Hughes

Shuts Out Boston and Breitenstein Shuts Out Pittsburg without a Hit." *The Chicago Daily Tribune*, 7.

The Cincinnati Enquirer. October 16, 1892. "Base-ball Gossip." *The Cincinnati Enquirer*, 6.

The Cincinnati Enquirer. October 16, 1882. "Not a Hit: Big Work of 'Bumpus Jones'; Pittsburgs Taken in by a Raw Recruit." *The Cincinnati Enquirer*, 6.

The Cincinnati Enquirer. September 19, 1897. "Not One Hit Off Young." *The Cincinnati Enquirer*, 2.

Cobbledick, Gordon. April 17, 1940. "Feller Hurls No-Hitter to Win, 1 to 0." *Cleveland Plain Dealer*, 1, 21.

Cobbledick, Gordon. April 14, 1940. "Plain Dealing: Feller Gives Credit to Mack, Keltner and Chapman; Says He Has Been in Better Form." *Cleveland Plain Dealer*, 21.

Couch, Dick, The Associated Press. July 3, 1970. "Clarke Breaks Up Third No-Hitter." *The Amarillo Globe-Times*, 8.

Courier-Journal. August 23, 1892. "Only One Hit: Sanders Pitches a Phenomenal Game Against Baltimore's Strong Batters," *Courier-Journal*, 6.

Crusinberry, James. May 3, 1917. "Cubs Hitless as Toney Wins in 10th, 1 to 0." *The Chicago Daily Tribune*, 13.

Donaghy, Jim, The Associated Press. April 29, 1992. "Houston Loses to New York as Cone Loses No-Hitter." *New Braunfels Herald-Zeitung*, 8.

Donaghy, Jim, The Associated Press. April 14, 1992. "Is Revised No-Hitter Rule a No-No?" *Eugene Register-Guard*, 2D.

Down, Fred, United Press International. July 16, 1973. "Will Nolan Ryan Get Another One?" *The Times Standard*, 10.

Durso, Joseph. December 10, 1970. "Mets Trade Ryan. No Kidding!" *The New York Times*.

Elber, Lynn, The Associated Press. June 23, 2009. "'Tonight' Sidekick Ed McMahon Dies in LA at 86." *San Diego Union-Tribune*.

Ellis, Dock. March 29, 2008. "An LSD No-No." Neille Illel and Donnell Alexander interview with Dock Ellis. *Weekend America*.

Elston, Gene. April 23, 1964. "Cincinnati Reds at Houston Colt .45s." *Colts Network*.

Emory, Tom, The Associated Press. July 19, 1972. "Padres' Steve Arlin Has Near No-Hitter until Manager 'Messes It Up' in Ninth," *The Daily Reporter*, B3.

Enberg, Dick, with Jim Perry. 2004. *Dick Enberg: Oh My!* Champaign, Ill.: Sports Publishing.

Feder, Sid. June 21, 1938. "Sports by Day." *The Times Recorder.*

Feder, Sid. June 16, 1938. "Vander Meer Hurls Another No-Hitter." *The Sarasota Herald-Tribune*, 7.

Feldman, Sam. July 12, 1962. "High & Inside by Jim McKone." *The San Bernardino County Sun*, 25.

Fleitz, David. 2004. Ghosts in the Gallery at Cooperstown: *Sixteen Forgotten Members of the Hall of Fame.* Jefferson, North Carolina: McFarland.

Ford, Rob. October 6, 2014. D. Lammers interview with Robert Ford.

Fox Sports Florida. September 29, 2013. "Detroit Tigers vs. Miami Marlins." MLB.com, http://mlb.mlb.com/news/article/mlb/marlins-right-hander-henderson-alvarez-tosses-no-hitter-against-detroit-tigers?ymd=20130929&content_id=62119746.

Fraley, Gerry. May 2, 1991. "Rangers' Nolan Ryan Throws His Seventh Career No-Hitter." *Dallas Morning News.*

Fullerton, Hugh S., Jr., The Associated Press. April 18, 1934. "187,000 Fans Hail Baseball Inaugural as Pitchers Star." *Alton Evening Telegraph*, 8.

Garno, Greg. September 4, 1993. "Ruiz ties MLB mark for catching no-hitters." MLB.com. http://m.mlb.com/news/article/138728956/carlos-ruiz-has-caught-four-no-hitters

Garza, Matt. June 24, 2015. D. Lammers interview with Matt Garza.

Gergen, Joe, United Press International. September 18, 1968. "Perry Hurls No-Hitter at Cards." *The Delta Democrat-Times*, 7.

Goldstein, Richard. November 27, 2001. "Bo Belinsky, 64, the Playboy Pitcher, Dies." *The New York Times.*

Goldstein, Richard. October 31, 1996. "Ewell Blackwell, Pitcher, 74; Noted for His Whip-Like Style." *The New York Times.*

Gooden, Dwight, and Ellis Henican. 2013. *Doc: A Memoir.* Boston, Mass.: Houghton Mifflin Harcourt.

Green, Bob, The Associated Press. March 21, 1962. "Sam's Illness Cripples Tigers." *Northwest Arkansas Times*, 13.

Gustkey, Earl. June 23, 2000. "He Was No Angel." *The Los Angeles Times.*

Hand, Jack, The Associated Press. May 1, 1946. "Bob Feller Unfolds No-Hitter." *The Evening Citizen*, 14.

The Harrisburg Telegraph. April 23, 1898. "Two Great Pitching Feats." *The Harrisburg Telegraph*, 2.

Hartford Beaten Once More by St. Louis. July 16, 1876. *Chicago Daily Tribune*, 3.

Hawkins, Andy. May 20, 2015. D. Lammers interview with Andy Hawkins.

Herschberg, Neil, United Press International. July 5, 1972. "Broken Bat Single in Ninth Costs Met Ace No-Hitter." *The Ludington Daily News*, 8.

Hilligan, Earl, The Associated Press. April 17, 1940. "Young Indians Star Turns in No Hit Victory." *The Lewiston Daily Sun*, 8.

The Inter Ocean. August 7, 1890. "National League: Anson's Loss and Gain." *The Inter Ocean*, 6.

Iott, Chris. July 31, 2011. "Views Differ on Eighth-Inning Bunt Attempt by Angels' Erick Aybar." MLive.com, http://www.mlive.com/tigers/index.ssf/2011/07/views_differ_on_eighth-inning.html.

Jackson, Edwin. June 25, 2010. Edwin Jackson talks to broadcasters about his no-hitter and receives a "gift" from his teammates. "Arizona Diamondbacks at Tampa Bay Rays." Fox Sports Arizona.

Johnson, Ken. May 15, 2014. D. Lammers interview with Ken Johnson.

Jones, David, ed. 2006. *Deadball Stars of the American League* . Washington, D.C.: Potomac Books.

Jones, Tom. July 27, 2010. "Tom Jones' 2 Cents: Don't Jinx the No-Hitter." *Tampa Bay Times*, http://www.tampabay.com/blogs/twocents/content/dont-jinx-no-hitter.

Joyce, Jim. June 3, 2010. "Ump Joyce on Controversial Call." MLB.com, http://m.mlb.com/video/v8632475.

The Kane Republican. September 8, 1923. "Another No Hit, No Run Game Played." *The Kane Republican*, 5.

KDKA. May 26, 1959. "Pittsburgh Pirates vs. Milwaukee Braves." KDKA, Milwaukee, Wis.

Kale, Gary, United Press International. June 15, 1965. "Reds' Maloney Loses 10-Inning No-Hitter." *The Daily Times*, 10.

Kaplan, Thomas. May 21, 2008. "Red Sox' No-Hitter Puts Varitek in Record Books." *The New York Times*.

Kershaw, Clayton. September 2, 2014. B. Olney interview, "Clayton Kershaw SportsCenter Conversation." *SportsCenter*, ESPN.

Koufax, Sandy. August 7, 1972. "Sanford Koufax—Induction Speech." National Baseball Hall of Fame and Museum, http://baseballhall.org/node/11133.

Koufax, Sandy. 1964. M. Glickman interview with Sandy Koufax, Sports Record Talking Baseball Card. Sports Champions Inc.

Langford, George C., United Press International. September 10, 1965. "Koufax Perfect Game Makes Four No-Hitters for Lefty." *Naugatuck Daily News*, 4.

Larsen, Don. September 30, 2014. D. Lammers interview with Don Larsen.

Larsen, Don, with Mike Shaw. 1996. *The Perfect Yankee*. Champaign, Ill.: Sports Publishing.

Leavy, Jane. 2002. *Sandy Koufax: A Lefty's Legacy.* New York: HarperCollins.

Lewiston Evening Journal. October 30, 1930. "Old Time Hurler Is Retired as Officer." *Lewiston Evening Journal*, 7.

Liska, Jerry, The Associated Press. May 13, 1955. "Sam Jones Hurls No-Hitter for Cubs; Gets Gold Toothpick." *Dixon Evening Telegraph*, 10.

Maher, Charles, The Associated Press. May 7, 1962. "Angels' Bo Belinsky Throws a No-Hitter." *Greeley Daily Tribune*, 8.

Maher, Charles, The Associated Press. July 2, 1962. "Dodgers Finally 'Harness' Koufax." *The San Bernardino County Sun*, 12.

Maher, Charles, The Associated Press. May 12, 1963. "Koufax Says Saturday No-Hitter Top Thrill." *Park City Daily News*, 9.

Maloney, Jim. June 14, 1965. L. B. Pettit interview with Jim Maloney. "Cincinnati Reds at Chicago Cubs." WGN Television, Chicago, Ill.

Marichal, Juan, with Lew Freedman. 2011. *Juan Marichal: My Journey from the Dominican Republic to Cooperstown.* Minneapolis, Minn.: MVP Books.

Martin, Edward F. June 24, 1917. "Ernie Shore Relieves Babe Ruth, Throws Perfect Game." *The Boston Globe*.

Maule, Tex. May 8, 1961. "The Masterpiece in Milwaukee: 'Everything Seemed Easy.'" *Sports Illustrated*, 24–27.

Mcalester, Kevin. June 16, 2005. "Balls Out: How to Throw a No-Hitter on Acid, and Other Lessons from the Career of Baseball Legend Dock Ellis." *The Dallas Observer*.

MLB.com. October 8, 1956. "BB Moments: Larsen Is Perfect." MLB.com video. http://m.mlb.com/video/topic/7759164/v3295361

MLB.com. July 4, 1983. "BB Moments: Righetti's No-Hitter." MLB.com, http://m.mlb.com/video/v3977857/bb-moments-7483-righettis-yankee-doodle-nono/?c_id=mlb.

MLB.com. August 21, 2012. "Fernando's Memorable No-Hitter." MLB.com, http://m.mlb.com/video/v24097343/fernando-valenzuelas-1990-nohitter.

MLB.com. June 2, 2010. "Missed Call Ends Galarraga's Perfect Bid." MLB.com, http://mlb.mlb.com/news/article.jsp?ymd=20100602&content_id=10727590.

MLB Network. September 3, 2010. "Milt Pappas' No-Hitter in 1972." *MLB Network Remembers* with Bob Costas, http://m.mlb.com/video/v11681195/mlb-network-remembers-pappas-nohitter.

Mockler, Stan. May 7, 1953. "Holloman of Browns First Rookie to Hurl No-Hitter. "*The Daily Republican.*

Moffi, Larry, and Jonathan Kronstadt. 1994. *Crossing the Line: Black Major Leaguers, 1947–1959.* Lincoln: University of Nebraska Press.

Moore, Robert T., The Associated Press. May 2, 1969. "Wilson Sets Down the Reds on No-Hit Shutout." *Beatrice Daily Sun*, 3.

Morning Tulsa Daily World. May 6, 1917. "No-Hit Honor Is Credited to Koob: Substitute Official Scorer Makes Favorable Decision on Questionable Blow." *Morning Tulsa Daily World*, 10.

Mueller, Lee, NEA. June 27, 1969. "Joe Borden, Author of First No-Hitter, Never Knew He Made Baseball History." *The Gadsden Times*, 14.

Mulligan, Brian. 2005. *The 1940 Cincinnati Reds: A World Championship and Baseball's Only In-Season Suicide.* Jefferson, N.C.: Mcfarland & Co.

Murphy, David. October 7, 2010. "Halladay Throws No-Hitter in Postseason Debut as Phils Beat Reds." *Philadelphia Inquirer.*

National Baseball Hall of Fame and Museum. "Cy Young." *National Hall of Fame and Museum.* http://baseballhall.org/hof/young-cy

New York Press. August 29, 1912. "Redding Pitches Hitless Game." *New York Press*, 7.The New York Times. June 1, 1908. "No Hits for Yankees off Veteran Young." *New York Times*, 5.

The New York Times. July 1, 1917. "Ruth Suspended One Week." *The New York Times*, 29.

The New York Times. October 6, 1906. "Wild Pitching Hurts Giants: H. Mathewson Gives 14 Bases on Balls and Boston Wins by 7 to 1." *The New York Times*, 7.

New-York Tribune. July 5, 1908. "Giants Win Two from the Quakers: Wiltse Pitches No-Hit 10-Inning Game." *New-York Tribune*, 10.

Newspaper Enterprise Association. May 17, 1947. "Where Are They? Pitchers Today Have Easy Life, Hippo Vaughn." *The Evening Independent*, 2.

Nidetz, Steve. August 26, 1985. "Jays' Stieb Keeps It All in Perspective." *The Chicago Tribune*, 1C.

Nissenson, Herschel, The Associated Press. September 18, 1968. "Gaylord Perry Hurls No-Hitter at Cards." *Cumberland Evening Times*, 37.

Olderman, Murray, United Press International. June 19, 1973. "Where Has All the Glamor Gone? The Last Fling for Bo Belinsky." *Mt. Vernon Register-News*, 14.

Overmyer, James E. 2014. *Black Ball and the Boardwalk: The Bacharach Giants of Atlantic City, 1916–1929*. New York: McFarland.

Owens, Brick. March 11, 1941. "Brick Owens Tells: Shore's Perfect Game Most Extraordinary Feat." *The Milwaukee Journal*, 6.

Page, Don. July 9, 1960. "Vin Scully Gets Nod on All-Star Game." *Los Angeles Times*.

Paige, Satchel. "Satchel Paige Quotes," *Satchel Paige: The Official Web Site*, accessed March 13, 2015, http://www.satchelpaige.com/quote2.html.

Paladino, Larry, The Associated Press. July 16, 1973. "Ryan Wanted Shutout, Got No-Hitter." *Reading Eagle*, 18.

Paschke, Jim. April 15, 1987. "MLB Classics: Juan Nieves's No-Hitter," https://www.youtube.com/watch?v=LJmjQaX5S68.

Pappas, Milt. April 30, 2015. D. Lammers interview with Milt Pappas.

The Philadelphia Times. April 23, 1898. "New York Lost the Third Game: Piatt Effective While Rusie Was Batted Hard." *The Philadelphia Times*, 8.

The Pittsburgh Courier. July 16, 1932. "New York Yanks Win Series from Crawfords." *The Pittsburgh Courier*, 15.

The Pittsburgh Press. June 24, 1917. "Pitcher Babe Ruth Punches Umpire Owens on Jaw: Separated by Players." *The Pittsburgh Press*, 18.

Portsmouth Daily Times. May 3, 1917. "Fred Toney Pitches No Hit Game; Reds Win, Score 1 to 0: Only One Hit Was Made in Ten Innings." *Portsmouth Daily Times*, 12.

Pucin, Diane. May 3, 2012. "Did Angels Announcers Make Right Call on Jered Weaver No-Hitter?" *Los Angeles Times*.

Rainey, Chris. "Bumpus Jones." Society for American Baseball Research Biography Project, accessed May 22, 2014, http://sabr.org/bioproj/person/c68a9ba1.

Recht, Mike, The Associated Press. May 1, 1969. "Maloney Takes No-No Calmly." *Port Angeles Evening News*, 23.

Reichler, Joe, The Associated Press. June 28, 1947. "Ewell Blackwell Misses Second Straight No-Hitter by 2 Putouts; 'Winningest' Pitcher in Majors." *Times Daily*.

Reichler, Joe, The Associated Press. May 27, 1959. "Greatest Pitching Feat in History Just Another Loss to Harvey Haddix." *Toledo Blade*, 1.

Richman, Milton, United Press International. September 5, 1962. "Belinky Frowns on Trade to A's." *Daily News-Texan*, 6.

Richman, Milton, United Press International. July 16, 1973. "Ryan's Mother Happy, Wants Perfect Game." *The Daily Herald*, 8.

Riley, Daniel. October 2011. "Vin Scully Remembers His Greatest Calls." *GQ*.

Riley, James. A. 2012. *Of Monarchs and Black Barons: Essays on Baseball's Negro Leagues.* Jefferson, N.C.: McFarland.

Rosenbloom, Steve. May 12, 2012. "All Stress, No Glory." *Chicago Tribune*.

Rubin, Mike, The Associated Press. June 2, 1974. "Ryan Hurls Fourth No-Hitter." *The Courier News*, 15.

Ruth, George Herman. 1928. *Babe Ruth's Own Book of Baseball.* New York: G. P. Putnam's Sons.

Ryan, Allan. August 5, 1989. "Oh So Close—Again! Stieb's Perfect Game Is Spoiled with Two Yankees out in Ninth." *The Toronto Star*, C1.

Ryan, Allan. September 3, 1990. "Stieb Pitches Jays' 1st No-Hitter: 'I Can Hardly Believe What I Did'. *The Toronto Star*, A1.

Ryan, Nolan. July 25, 1999. "Lynn Nolan Ryan—Induction Speech." National Baseball Hall of Fame and Museum, http://baseballhall.org/node/11303.

Sainsbury, Ed, United Press. May 13, 1955. "Jones' Sense of Security Got a Boost." *The Ottawa Journal*, 28.

San Francisco Chronicle. May 6, 1904. "Pitcher Young Breaks Record." *San Francisco Chronicle*, 10.

Sanborn, I. E. May 6, 1917. "Koob Tames Sox in One Hit Game, 1-0." *Chicago Sunday Tribune*, Part 2-1. http://archives.chicagotribune.com/1917/05/06/page/17/article/koob-tames-sox-in-one-hit-game-1-0

Santana, Johan. June 1, 2012. "Mets No Hitter: Johan Santana Pitches First No-Hit Game in Franchise History." *Huffington Post*, http://www.huffingtonpost.com/2012/06/01/johan-santana-no-hitter-mets-history-first-video_n_1564256.html.

Schechter, G. 2004. "Hooks Wiltse." Society for American Baseball Research Biography Project, http://sabr.org/bioproj/person/ce9bc9aa.

Schulman, Henry. August 29, 2014. "Petit sets record while pitching Giants to 4-1 win over Rockies." *San Francisco Chronicle*. http://www.sfgate.com/giants/article/Petit-sets-record-while-pitching-Giants-to-4-1-5719577.php

Scott, Vernon, United Press International. February 8, 1963. "The Hollywood Scene." *Eureka Humboldt Standard*, 4.

Scully, Vin. September 9, 2014. "Happy Anniversary to Koufax's Perfect Game" (video). MLBlogs Network, http://dodgers.mlblogs.com/2014/09/09/video-happy-anniversary-to-koufaxs-perfect-game.

Selig, Bud. June 3, 2010. "Major League Baseball Statement." MLB.com, http://mlb.mlb.com/news/press_releases/press_release.jsp?ymd=20100603&content_id=10760448&vkey=pr_mlb&fext=.jsp&c_id=mlb.

Sharp, Drew. August 2, 2011. "Tigers' Justin Verlander Wrong for 'Bush League' Blast on Erick Aybar." *Detroit Free Press*, http://www.freep.com/article/20110802/COL08/108020425/Drew-Sharp-Verlander-wrong-bush-league-blast.

Siwoff, Seymour. 2014. *The Elias Book of Baseball Records.* New York: Elias Sports Bureau.

Skipper, John C. 1997. *Umpires: Classic Baseball Stories from the Men Who Made the Calls.* Jefferson, N.C.: Mcfarland & Co.

Spencer, Clark. September 30, 2013. "Henderson Alvarez Closes Miami Marlins Season with No-Hitter; Marlins 1, Tigers 0." *The Miami Herald*.

SportsNet New York. June 1, 2012. "Santana Completes No-Hitter." MLB.com, http://m.mlb.com/video/v21938903/stlnym-santana-fans-freese-to-complete-nohitter.

Staats, Dewayne. September 4, 1993. "Abbott's No-Hitter." MLB.com, http://m.mlb.com/video/v2685734/9493-jim-abbotts-nohitter.

Stapler, Harry, The Associated Press. May 16, 1952. "Virgil Trucks Hurls No-Hitter as Tigers Nip Nats 1-0." *The Oneonta Star*, 12.

Starkey, Joe. July 8, 2007. "Cordova, Rincon No-Hitter Carved a Place in History." *Pittsburgh Tribune-Review*, http://triblive.com/x/pittsburghtrib/sports/pirates/s_516245.html#axzz39QtpUaK4.

Stellino, Vito, United Press International. June 13, 1970. "Ellis Fires No-Hitter." *The Times-News*, 7.

Stellino, Vito, United Press International. (1970, July 3). Single in ninth: Niekro no-hitter spoiled. *Boca Raton News*, 5.

Time. September 21, 1959. "Sport: The Tortured Arm." *Time*.

Torborg, Jeff. October 6, 2014. D. Lammers interview with Jeff Torborg.

Tosetti, Linda Ruth. May 19, 2014. D. Lammers interview with Linda Ruth Tosetti.

Uecker, Bob. June 24, 2015. D. Lammers interview with Bob Uecker.

United Press. July 2, 1951. "Bob Feller Pitches His 3rd No-Hitter: But Stengel Shuns Him as All-Star." *The Pittsburgh Press*, 18.

United Press. June 11, 1944. "Cards Swamp Reds, 18-0, as Boy Twirls." *The Brooklyn Daily Eagle*, 17.

United Press. July 2, 1951. "Cy Young Says Feller among Best." *The High Point Enterprise*, 12.

United Press. October 9, 1956. "Ninth Inning Still Hazy, Says Don Larsen of Perfect Game." *Reading Eagle*, 19.

United Press. July 10, 1936. "Some Feller! Sandlot Kid Has More Speed Than Johnson." *Xenia Daily Gazette* , 5.

United Press. June 12, 1938. "Vander Meer Hurls No-Hit, No-Run Game." *The Pittsburgh Press*, 15.

United Press International. June 30, 1990. "A's Dave Stewart No-Hits Blue Jays." *Tyrone Daily Herald*, 5.

United Press International. September 30, 1974. "Big Balaz Catch Saves No-Hitter." *El Paso Herald-Post*, 24.

United Press International. September 10, 1965. "Catcher Norm Sherry's Advice Started Koufax on Way to Top." *Naugatuck Daily News*, 4.

United Press International. July 22, 1971. "Gomez Booed for Controversial Move: Deprives Kirby of No-Hit Bid." *Progress Bulletin*, E3.

United Press International. August 6, 1973. "Niekro No-Hitter an Atlanta First." *Sarasota Journal*, 15.

United Press International. June 20, 1970. Seven Pitches End Bid for Second No-Hitter. *Traverse City Record-Eagle*, 12.

United Press International. June 17, 1978. "Seaver Done? No-Hitter Silences Critics." *The Deseret News*, A7.

Vander Meer, Johnny. August 27, 1938. "Two Games Don't Make a Pitcher." *Saturday Evening Post* , 10–11, 42–44.

Vaughn, Hippo. 1945. *My Greatest Day in Baseball: As Told to John P. Carmichael and Other Noted Sportswriters*, edited by H. Totten. Lincoln: University of Nebraska Press.

Veeck, Bill. 1962. *Veeck—as in Wreck: The Autobiography of Bill Veeck*. Chicago, Ill.: University of Chicago Press.

Vincent, Fay. October 6, 2014. D. Lammers interview with Fay Vincent.

WFAN. June 1, 2012. "St. Louis Cardinals vs. New York Mets." WFAN, New York.

The Washington Post. April 16, 1909. "Giants Fail to Score: Superbas Gain Shut-Out in Thirteen-Inning Struggle." *The Washington Post*, 8.

The Washington Post. July 1, 1909. "Pirates in New Home: Forbes Field Dedicated With Appropriate Ceremonies." *The Washington Post*, 8.

The Washington Post. June 24, 1917. "Shore in No-Hit Feat; Griffs Blanked Twice." *The Washington Post*, 7.

Wells, David, with Chris Kreske. 2004. *Perfect I'm Not: Boomer on Beer, Brawls, Backaches, and Baseball*. New York: It Books.

White, Paul, and Seth Livingstone. June 3, 2010. "Missed Call Leaves Detroit's Armando Galarraga One Out Shy of Perfect Game." *USA Today*.

Wild, Danny, and Jake Seiner. August 11, 2014. "Wings' Darnell, May Combine on No-Hitter." MiLB.com, http://www.milb.com/news/article.jsp?ymd= 20140811&content_id=89120466&fext=.jsp&vkey=news_milb.

Williams, Robin. December 6, 2009. "Weapons of Self Destruction." HBO, Washington, D.C.

Wilson, Bernie, The Associated Press. June 5, 1995. "Expos' Martinez Never Lost Control." *The Day*, 16.

Wilson, Bernie, The Associated Press. July 14, 2014. "Lincecum Still the Freak after 148 Pitch No Hitter."

Wilson, Bernie, The Associated Press. May 13, 2001. "Marlins' Burnett No-Hits Padres: Nine Walks Is Record for Nine-Inning No-No." *The Cincinnati Enquirer*.

Wilson, Bernie, The Associated Press. May 28, 2001. "Schilling Almost Perfect: Bunt in 8th for Hit Angers Arizona." *Bangor Daily News*, 34.

Winchell, Walter. June 18, 1962. "Interview with a Reporter." *The Pocono Record*, 4.

Wolf, Bob. June 6, 1990. "REMEMBER WHEN: His One Chance for Fame: No No-Hitter." *The Los Angeles Times*.

Wilks, Ed, The Associated Press. July 1, 1959. "Fluke Robs Sad Sam of No-Hitter; Blanks L.A." *The Achison Daily Globe*, 9.

Zinn, J. 2013. *Inventing Baseball: The 100 Greatest Games of the Nineteenth Century*, edited by B. Felber. Society for American Baseball Research.

NOTES

Introduction

[1] D. Lammers interview with Clay Buchholz, May 20, 2015.

[2] D. Lammers interview with Jim Bunning, May 1, 2015.

[3] Associated Press, "John Candalaria Throws No-Hitter," *Spokesman-Review*, August 11, 1976, 21.

[4] Dick Enberg with Jim Perry, *Dick Enberg: Oh My!* (Champaign, Ill.: Sports Publishing, 2004).

[5] D. Lammers interview with Bob Uecker, June 24, 2015.

[6] Ibid.

Chapter 1

[7] George Herman Ruth, *Babe Ruth's Own Book of Baseball* (New York: G. P. Putnam's Sons, 1928).

[8] Edward F. Martin, "Ernie Shore Relieves Babe Ruth, Throws Perfect Game," *Boston Globe*, June 24, 1917.

[9] D. Lammers interview with Linda Ruth Tosetti, May 19, 2014.

[10] Brick Owens, "Brick Owens Tells: Shore's Perfect Game Most Extraordinary Feat," *Milwaukee Journal*, March 11, 1941, 6.

[11] Martin, "Ernie Shore Relieves Babe Ruth."

[12] Ibid.

13 "Shore in No-Hit Feat; Griffs Blanked Twice," *Washington Post*, June 24, 1917, 7.

14 "Pitcher Babe Ruth Punches Umpire Owens on Jaw: Separated by Players," *Pittsburgh Press*, June 24, 1917, 18.

15 Owens, "Brick Owen Tells."

16 "Ernie Shore in Hall of Fame; Not a Senator Reaches First," *Brooklyn Daily Eagle*, June 24, 1917, 28.

17 "Ruth Suspended One Week, "*New York Times*, July 1, 1917, 29.

18 Owens, "Brick Owen Tells."

Chapter 2

19 "Sport: The Tortured Arm," *Time*, September 21, 1959.

20 Roy Campanella, "The Way I See It," *Jet*, September 25, 1958, 56–57.

21 Jerry Liska, "Sam Jones Hurls No-Hitter for Cubs; Gets Gold Toothpick," *Dixon Evening Telegraph*, May 13, 1955, 10.

22 Ed Sainsbury, "Jones' Sense of Security Got a Boost," *Ottawa Journal*, May 13, 1955, 28.

23 Liska, "Sam Jones Hurls No-Hitter for Cubs."

24 Ibid.

25 Ed Wilks, "Fluke Robs Sad Sam of No-Hitter; Blanks L.A.," *Achison Daily Globe*, July 1, 1959, 9.

26 "Sport."

27 Bob Green, "Sam's Illness Cripples Tigers," *Northwest Arkansas Times*, March 21, 1962, 13.

28 Campanella, "The Way I See It."

Chapter 3

29 Parker Bena, *Inventing Baseball: The 100 Greatest Games of the Nineteenth Century*, edited by Bill Felber (Society for American Baseball Research, 2013).

30 "Old Time Hurler Is Retired as Officer," *Lewiston Evening Journal*, October 30, 1930, 7.

31 J. Zinn, *Inventing Baseball: The 100 Greatest Games of the Nineteenth Century*, edited by B. Felber (Society for American Baseball Research, 2013).

32 Lee Mueller, NEA, "Joe Borden, Author of First No-Hitter, Never Knew He Made Baseball History," *Gadsden Times*, June 27, 1969, 14.

[33] Zinn, *Inventing Baseball.*

[34] Ibid.

[35] "Old Time Hurler Is Retired as Officer."

Chapter 4

[36] Chris Rainey, "Bumpus Jones," Society for American Baseball Research Baseball Biography Project, accessed May 22, 2014, http://sabr.org/bioproj/person/c68a9ba1

[37] "Base-ball Gossip," *Cincinnati Enquirer*, October 16, 1892, 6.

[38] Rainey, "Bumpus Jones."

[39] "Base-ball Gossip."

[40] "Not a Hit: Big Work of 'Bumpus Jones'; Pittsburgs Taken in by a Raw Recruit," *Cincinnati Enquirer*, October 16, 1882, 6.

[41] Ibid.

[42] Ibid.

[43] "Louisville and St. Louis Play Twice, Each Club Winning Once," *Chicago Daily Tribune*, October 5, 1891, 6.

[44] Stan Mockler, "Holloman of Browns First Rookie to Hurl No-Hitter," *Daily Republican*, May 7, 1953.

[45] Bill Veeck, *Veeck—as in Wreck: The Autobiography of Bill Veeck* (Chicago, Ill.: University of Chicago Press, 1962).S

[46] Rainey, "Bumpus Jones,"

Chapter 5

[47] D. Lammers interview with Don Larsen, September 30, 2013.

[48] Ibid.

[49] Ibid.

[50] Ibid.

[51] United Press, "Ninth Inning Still Hazy, Says Don Larsen of Perfect Game," *Reading Eagle*, October 9, 1956, 19.

[52] John C. Skipper, *Umpires: Classic Baseball Stories from the Men Who Made the Calls* (Jefferson, N.C.: Mcfarland & Co., 1997).

[53] Interview with Don Larsen.

[54] Don Larsen with Mike Shaw, *The Perfect Yankee* (Champaign, Ill.: Sports Publishing, 1996).

[55] Interview with Don Larsen.

[56] Ibid.

[57] Larsen with Shaw, *The Perfect Yankee.*

[58] Ibid.

[59] Interview with Don Larsen.

[60] David Murphy, "Halladay Throws No-Hitter in Postseason Debut as Phils Beat Reds," *Philadelphia Inquirer*, October 7, 2010.

[61] Associated Press, "Don Larsen's 1956 World Series Perfect Game Uniform Sells for $756,000 at Auction," *New York Daily News,* December 6, 2012.

DID YOU KNOW? MILWAUKEE NEEDS A HOME-BREWED NO-NO

[62] D. Lammers interview with Bill Schroeder, June 24, 2015.

Chapter 6

[63] Associated Press, "Duel Sends Old-Timers to Dusty Record Books," *Milwaukee Journal*, May 17, 1951, 45.

[64] "Fred Toney Pitches No Hit Game; Reds Win, Score 1 to 0: Only One Hit Was Made in Ten Innings," *Portsmouth Daily Times*, May 3, 1917, 12.

[65] James Crusinberry, "Cubs Hitless as Toney Wins in 10th, 1 to 0," *Chicago Daily Tribune*, May 3, 1917, 13.

[66] Ibid.

[67] Ibid.

[68] Ibid.

[69] Hippo Vaughn, *My Greatest Day in Baseball: As Told to John P. Carmichael and Other Noted Sportswriters*, edited by H. Totten (Lincoln: University of Nebraska Press, 1945).

[70] Crusinberry, "Cubs Hitless as Toney Wins in 10th, 1 to 0."

[71] Associated Press, "Duel Sends Old-Timers to Dusty Record Books."

[72] Newspaper Enterprise Association, "Where Are They?: Pitchers Today Have Easy Life, Hippo Vaughn," *Evening Independent*, May 17, 1947, 2.

DID YOU KNOW? UPON FURTHER REVIEW

[73] "Only One Hit: Sanders Pitches a Phenomenal Game Against Baltimore's Strong Batters," *Courier-Journal*, August 23, 1892, 6.

[74] "Not One Hit Off 'Cy' Young," *Cincinnati Enquirer*, September 19, 1897, 2.

[75] National Baseball Hall of Fame and Museum, "Cy Young," http://baseballhall. org/hof/young-cy.

[76] David Fleitz, *Ghosts in the Gallery at Cooperstown: Sixteen Forgotten Members of the Hall of Fame* (Jefferson, North Carolina: McFarland, 2004), 177.

[77] I.E. Sanborn, "Koob Tames Sox in One Hit Game, 1-0," *Chicago Sunday Tribune*. May 6, 1917, Part 2-1. http://archives.chicagotribune.com/1917/05/06/ page/17/article/koob-tames-sox-in-one-hit-game-1-0.

[78] "No-Hit Honor Is Credited to Koob: Substitute Official Scorer Makes Favorable Decision on Questionable Blow," *Morning Tulsa Daily World*, May 6, 1917, 10.

[79] "Another No Hit, No Run Game Played," *The Kane Republican*, September 8, 1923, 5.

[80] Ibid.

Chapter 7

[81] Gene Elston, "Cincinnati Reds at Houston Colt .45s," *Colts Network*, April 23, 1964.

[82] Ibid.

[83] D. Lammers interview with Ken Johnson, May 15, 2014.

[84] Associated Press, "It Was My Fault, Not Nellie's," Says Hurler," *Daily Times-News*, April 24, 1964, 28.

[85] Kenneth Carr, "First Time in History—Ken Johnson Pitches a No-Hitter but Loses to Cincy Reds, 1 to 0," *Greensburg Daily News*, April 24, 1964, 2.

[86] Ibid.

[87] Murray Chass, "Steve Barber and Stu Miller Combine for No-Hitter and Lose Game," *The Day* (New London, Conn.), May 1, 1967, 27.

[88] Ibid.

[89] "An Unprecedented Base Ball Contest at Washington Park," *Brooklyn Daily Eagle*, October 5, 1884, 1.

DID YOU KNOW? A CROWNING ACHIEVEMENT

[90] D. Lammers interview with Steve Busby, May 20, 2015.

[91] Ibid.

[92] Ibid.

[93] Ibid.

Chapter 8

[94] James E. Overmyer, *Black Ball and the Boardwalk: The Bacharach Giants of Atlantic City, 1916–1929* (New York: McFarland, 2014).

[95] "Redding Pitches Hitless Game," *New York Press*, August 29, 1912, 7.

[96] James A. Riley, *Of Monarchs and Black Barons: Essays on Baseball's Negro Leagues* (Jefferson, N.C.: McFarland, 2012).

[97] Ibid.

[98] "New York Yanks Win Series from Crawfords," *The Pittsburgh Courier*, July 16, 1932, 15.

Chapter 9

[99] Jim Donaghy, "Houston Loses to New York as Cone Loses No-Hitter," *New Braunfels Herald-Zeitung*, April 29, 1992, 8.

[100] D. Lammers Interview with Robert Ford, October 6, 2014.

[101] Donaghy, "Houston Loses to New York as Cone Loses No-Hitter."

[102] Interview with Robert Ford.

[103] Joseph Durso, "Mets Trade Ryan. No Kidding!" *New York Times*, December 10, 1970.

[104] Neil Herschberg, "Broken Bat Single in Ninth Costs Met Ace No-Hitter," *Ludington Daily News*, July 5, 1972, 8.

[105] "Seaver Done? No-Hitter Silences Critics," *Deseret News*, June 17, 1978, A7.

[106] Interview with Robert Ford.

[107] Ibid.

[108] SportsNet New York, "Santana Completes No-Hitter," June 1, 2012, http://m.mlb.com/video/v21938903/stlnym-santana-fans-freese-to-complete-nohitter

[109] Ibid.

[110] Johan Santana, "Mets No Hitter: Johan Santana Pitches First No-Hit Game In Franchise History," *Huffington Post*, June 1, 2012, http://www.huffingtonpost.com/2012/06/01/johan-santana-no-hitter-mets-history-first-video_n_1564256.html.

[111] Ibid.

DID YOU KNOW? NO-HITTER DROUGHTS BY TEAM, DAYS AND FIELD

[112] "Pirates in New Home: Forbes Field Dedicated With Appropriate Ceremonies." *Washington Post*, July 1, 1909, 8.

Chapter 10

[113] "Giants Fail to Score: Superbas Gain Shut-out in Thirteen-Inning Struggle," *Washington Post*, April 16, 1909, 8.

[114] Hugh S. Fullerton Jr., "187,000 Fans Hail Baseball Inaugural as Pitchers Star," *Alton Evening Telegraph*, April 18, 1934, 8.

[115] Gordon Cobbledick, "Feller Hurls No-Hitter to Win, 1 to 0," *Cleveland Plain Dealer*, April 17, 1940, 1, 21.

[116] Ibid.

[117] Earl Hilligan, "Young Indians Star Turns in No Hit Victory," *Lewiston Daily Sun*, April 17, 1940, 8.

[118] Gordon Cobbledick, "Plain Dealing: Feller Gives Credit to Mack, Keltner and Chapman; Says He Has Been in Better Form," *Cleveland Plain Dealer*, April 14, 1940, 21.

[119] Ibid.

[120] "Rangers' Ryan, A's off to Blazing Starts," *Index Journal*, April 10, 1990, 7.

Chapter 11

[121] Bernie Wilson, "Marlins' Burnett No-Hits Padres: Nine Walks Is Record for Nine-Inning No-No," *Cincinnati Enquirer*, May 13, 2001.

[122] Ibid.

[123] Associated Press, "Feller 'Robbed' by Scratch Hit: Billy Sullivan, Ex-Teammate, Beats Out Bunt to Prevent 'Perfect' Game," *Norwalk Hour*, April 21, 1938, 15.

[124] Associated Press, "Bunt Robs Dodgers' Erskine of No-Hitter; Blanks Reds 10-0," *Milwaukee Sentinel*, May 18, 1953, 8.

[125] Tex Maule, "The Masterpiece in Milwaukee: 'Everything Seemed Easy,'" *Sports Illustrated*, May 8, 1961, 24–27.

[126] Associated Press, "Jackson Loses No-Hitter in Ninth, but Wins Game," *Fort Scott Tribune*, October 1, 1986, 14.

[127] Ibid.

[128] Associated Press, "Bunt Ruins Witt's No-Hitter: Gagne Ruled Safe at First on Controversial Call," *Free Lance-Star*, June 24, 1994, 8.

[129] Ibid.

[130] Chris Iott, "Views Differ on Eighth-Inning Bunt Attempt by Angels' Erick Aybar," MLive.com, July 31, 2011, http://www.mlive.com/tigers/index.ssf/2011/07/views_differ_on_eighth-inning.html.

131 Drew Sharp, "Tigers' Justin Verlander Wrong for 'Bush League' Blast on Erick Aybar," *Detroit Free Press*, August 2, 2011, http://www.freep.com/article/20110802/COL08/108020425/Drew-Sharp-Verlander-wrong-bush-league-blast.

132 Ibid.

Chapter 12

133 Associated Press, "Cincinnati Tops Boston Bees, 14-1: Losers Stop Johnny Vander Meer's Streak of Hitless Innings," *Gazette and Daily*, June 20, 1938, 4.

134 United Press, "Vander Meer Hurls No-Hit, No-Run Game," *Pittsburgh Press*, June 12, 1938, 15.

135 Ibid.

136 Sid Feder, "Vander Meer Hurls Another No-Hitter," *Sarasota Herald-Tribune*, June 16, 1938, 7.

137 D. Lammers interview with Fay Vincent, October 6, 2014.

138 Johnny Vander Meer, "Two Games Don't Make a Pitcher," *Saturday Evening Post*, August 27, 1938, 10–11, 42–44.

139 Sid Feder, "Sports by Day," *Times Recorder*, June 21, 1938.

140 Feder, "Vander Meer Hurls Another No-Hitter."

141 Joe Reichler, "Ewell Blackwell Misses Second Straight No-Hitter by 2 Putouts; 'Winningest' Pitcher in Majors," *Times Daily*, June 28, 1947.

142 Richard Goldstein, "Ewell Blackwell, Pitcher, 74; Noted for His Whip-Like Style," *New York Times*, October 31, 1996.

143 Dave Anderson, "For Ryan, Another Shot at Vander Meer," *Star-News*, May 5, 1991, 4C.

144 Ibid.

DID YOU KNOW? A RAY OF LIGHT IN TAMPA
145 D. Lammers interview with Matt Garza, June 24, 2015.

146 Ibid.

147 Ibid.

148 Associated Press, "Johnson Perfect: Arizona Pitcher Retires All 27 Braves Batters," *Index-Journal*, May 19, 2004, 9.

Chapter 13

[149] D. Lammers interview with Milt Pappas, April 30, 2015.

[150] Ibid.

[151] Jack Brickhouse, "Memorable Moments in Chicago Sports," Media Burn Independent Video Archive, September 2, 1972, http://mediaburn.org/video/memorable-moments-in-chicago-sports.

[152] Ibid.

[153] Ibid.

[154] Interview with Milt Pappas.

[155] "Milt Pappas' No-Hitter in 1972," *MLB Network Remembers* with Bob Costas, September 3, 2010, http://m.mlb.com/video/v11681195/mlb-network- remembers-pappas-nohitter.

[156] Interview with Milt Pappas.

[157] "Giants Win Two from the Quakers: Wiltse Pitches No-Hit 10-Inning Game," *New-York Tribune*, July 5, 1908, 10.

[158] G. Schechter, "Hooks Wiltse," Society for American Baseball Research Baseball Biography Project, accessed May 1, 2015, http://sabr.org/bioproj/person/ce9bc9aa.

[159] Associated Press, "Pitches to Stahl Not Far off—Pappas," *Pantagraph*, September 3, 1972, 11.

[160] Interview with Milt Pappas.

[161] Interview with Milt Pappas.

[162] Interview with Milt Pappas.

DID YOU KNOW? OTHER STREAKS OF NOTE

[163] Henry Schulman, "Petit sets record while pitching Giants to 4-1 win over Rockies," *San Francisco Chronicle*, August 29, 2014. http://www.sfgate.com/giants/article/Petit-sets-record-while-pitching-Giants-to-4-1-5719577.php

Chapter 14

[164] Associated Press, "Houston's Ken Forsch: Miserable Spring Leads to No-Hitter," *Spokesman-Review*, April 9, 1979, 23.

[165] Associated Press, "Forsch Collects Second No-Hitter," *Gadsden Times*, September 27, 1983, 6.

[166] "Base-ball: Detroit 14; Chicago 0," *Chicago Daily Tribune*, July 16, 1884, 7.

167 "Wild Pitching Hurts Giants: H. Mathewson Gives 14 Bases on Balls and Boston Wins by 7 to 1," *New York Times*, October 6, 1906, 7.

168 Associated Press, "Virgil Barnes Allows One Hit as Cardinals and Giants Split Double-Header," *Bridgeport Telegram*, July 11, 1927, 14.

169 United Press International, "Niekro No-Hitter an Atlanta First," *Sarasota Journal*, August 6, 1973, 15.

170 Vito Stellino, "Ellis Fires No-Hitter," *Times-News*, June 13, 1970, 7.

171 Associated Press, "Joe Niekro Just Misses No-Hitter at Age 41," *Dispatch*, June 5, 1986, 8.

172 Associated Press, "Paul Dean Yields No Hits, Dizzy Three as Deans Blank Brooklyn Twice," *Gettysburg Times*, September 22, 1934, 3.

173 Ibid.

Chapter 15

174 "Pittsburgh Pirates vs. Milwaukee Braves," KDKA, Milwaukee, Wis., May 26, 1959.

175 Ibid.

176 Ibid.

177 Joe Reichler, "Greatest Pitching Feat in History Just Another Loss to Harvey Haddix," *Toledo Blade*, May 27, 1959, 1.

178 Ibid.

179 Associated Press, "Haddix No-Hitter Is Axed," *Telegraph*, September 4, 1991, 47.

Chapter 16

180 United Press International, "Seven Pitches End Bid for Second No-Hitter," *Traverse City Record-Eagle*, June 20, 1970, 12.

Chapter 17

181 Jason Beck, "Galarraga Brings Lineup to Tearful Joyce: Umpire Displays Emotion in Meeting Day after Blown Call," Detroit Tigers, MLB.com, June 3, 2010, http://mlb.mlb.com/news/article.jsp?ymd=20100603&content_id=10754978&vkey=news_mlb&fext=.jsp&c_id=mlb.

[182] Jim Joyce, "Ump Joyce on Controversial Call," MLB.com, June 3, 2010, http://m.mlb.com/video/v8632475.

[183] Paul White and Seth Livingstone, "Missed Call Leaves Detroit's Armando Galarraga One Out Shy of Perfect Game," *USA Today*, June 3, 2010.

[184] D. Lammers interview with Milt Pappas, April 30, 2015.

[185] Bud Selig, "Major League Baseball Statement," MLB.com, June 3, 2010, http://mlb.mlb.com/news/press_releases/press_release.jsp?ymd=20100603&-content_id=10760448&vkey=pr_mlb&fext=.jsp&c_id=mlb.

[186] Mitch Albom, "Yo, Bud Selig, Blown Call Is a Perfect Call to Action," *Detroit Free Press*, June 3, 2010.

[187] Interview with Milt Pappas.

[188] Beck, "Galarraga Brings Lineup to Tearful Joyce."

Chapter 18

[189] Red Barber, "Moments in Sportscasting," *Family Weekly*, May 23, 1971, 4–5.

[190] Ibid.

[191] Jim Carlisle, "Mel Allen Remembered as among Best in His Business," *Dallas Morning News*, June 19, 1996, 5B.

[192] Barber, "Moments in Sportscasting."

[193] Red Barber, *1947: When All Hell Broke Loose in Baseball* (Boston, Mass.: Da Capo Press, 1982).

[194] D. Lammers interview with Robert Ford, October 6, 2014.

[195] Daniel Riley, "Vin Scully Remembers His Greatest Calls," *GQ*, October 2011.

[196] Don Page, "Vin Scully Gets Nod on All-Star Game," *Los Angeles Times*, July 9, 1960.

[197] Associated Press, "Can't Hide No-Hitter from Fans—Erskine," *Miami News*, June 5, 1960, 18.

[198] "St. Louis Cardinals vs. New York Mets," WFAN (New York), June 1, 2012.

[199] Ibid.

[200] D. Lammers interview with Bob Uecker, June 24, 2015.

[201] Diane Pucin, "Did Angels Announcers Make Right Call on Jered Weaver No-Hitter?" *Los Angeles Times*, May 3, 2012.

[202] Tom Jones, "Tom Jones' 2 Cents: Don't Jinx the No-Hitter," *Tampa Bay Times*, July 27, 2010, http://www.tampabay.com/blogs/twocents/content/dont-jinx-no-hitter.

[203] Interview with Robert Ford.

[204] D. Lammers interview with Steve Busby, May 20, 2015.

[205] "BB Moments: Righetti's No-Hitter," MLB.com, July 4, 1983, http://m.mlb.com/video/v3977857/bb-moments-7483-righettis-yankee-doodle-nono/?c_id=mlb.

[206] D. Lammers interview with Jim Bunning, May 1, 2015.

[207] Ibid.

[208] Ibid.

[209] Ibid.

DID YOU KNOW? SAVED BY THE GLOVE

[210] D. Lammers interview with Bill Schroeder, June 24, 2015.

[211] D. Lammers interview with Bob Uecker, June 24, 2015.

Chapter 19

[212] Neille Ilel and Donnell Alexander interview with Dock Ellis, "An LSD No-No," *Weekend America*, March 29, 2008.

[213] Kevin Mcalester, "Balls Out: How to Throw a No-Hitter on Acid, and Other Lessons from the Career of Baseball Legend Dock Ellis," *Dallas Observer*, June 16, 2005.

[214] Ibid.

[215] Interview with Dock Ellis.

[216] Mcalester, "Balls Out."

[217] Interview with Dock Ellis.

[218] Chuck Brodsky, composer and performer, "Dock Ellis' No-No," *The Baseball Ballads* (Decatur, Ga.: K. Bush, 2002).

[219] Interview with Dock Ellis.

[220] Vito Stellino, "Ellis Fires No-Hitter," *Times-News*, June 13, 1970, 7.

[221] David Wells with Chris Kreske, *Perfect I'm Not: Boomer on Beer, Brawls, Backaches, and Baseball* (New York: It Books, 2004).

[222] Robin Williams, "Weapons of Self Destruction," Home Box Office (Washington, D.C.), December 6, 2009.

Chapter 20

[223] Joe Gergen, "Perry Hurls No-Hitter at Cards," *Delta Democrat-Times*, September 18, 1968, 7.

[224] Herschel Nissenson, "Gaylord Perry Hurls No-Hitter at Cards," *Cumberland Evening Times*, September 18, 1968, 37.

[225] Gergen, "Perry Hurls No-Hitter at Cards."

[226] Associated Press, "Another No-Hitter: Washburn," *Des Moines Register*, September 19, 1968, 21–22.

[227] Ibid.

[228] Mike Recht, "Maloney Takes No-No Calmly," *Port Angeles Evening News*, May 1, 1969, 23.

[229] Ibid.

[230] Robert T. Moore, "Wilson Sets Down the Reds on No-Hit Shutout," *Beatrice Daily Sun*, May 2, 1969, 3.

[231] Ibid.

Chapter 21

[232] "Base-Ball: Chicago vs. Boston," *Chicago Daily Tribune*, August 20, 1880, 8.

[233] "Brilliant Close to the Championship Season by the Chicagos at Home," *Chicago Daily Tribune*, September 21, 1882, 8.

[234] "National League: Anson's Loss and Gain," *Inter Ocean*, August 7, 1890, 6.

[235] "Not One Hit Off Young," *Cincinnati Enquirer*, September 19, 1897, 2.

[236] "Pitcher Young Breaks Record," *San Francisco Chronicle*, May 6, 1904, 10.

[237] "No Hits for Yankees off Veteran Young," *New York Times*, June 1, 1908, 5.

[238] Ibid.

[239] United Press, "Some Feller! Sandlot Kid Has More Speed Than Johnson," *Xenia Daily Gazette*, July 10, 1936, 5.

[240] Ibid.

[241] Jack Hand, "Bob Feller Unfolds No-Hitter," *Evening Citizen*, May 1, 1946, 14.

[242] Ibid.

[243] United Press, "Bob Feller Pitches His 3rd No-Hitter: But Stengel Shuns Him as All-Star," *Pittsburgh Press*, July 2, 1951, 18.

[244] Ibid.

Chapter 22

[245] B. Olney interview with Clayton Kershaw, *SportsCenter*, ESPN, September 2, 2014.

[246] Associated Press, "Ryan Passes Koufax with 5th No-Hitter," *Ludington Daily News*, September 28, 1981, 11.

[247] M. Glickman interview with Sandy Koufax, Sports Record Talking Baseball Card, Sports Champions, Inc., 1964.

[248] Sandy Koufax, "Sanford Koufax—Induction Speech," National Baseball Hall of Fame and Museum, August 7, 1972, http://baseballhall.org/node/11133.

[249] Ibid.

[250] "Catcher Norm Sherry's Advice Started Koufax on Way to Top," *Naugatuck Daily News*, September 10, 1964, 4.

[251] Charles Maher, "Dodgers Finally 'Harness' Koufax," *San Bernardino County Sun*, July 2, 1962, 12.

[252] Charles Maher, "Koufax Says Saturday No-Hitter Top Thrill," *Park City Daily News*, May 12, 1963, 9.

[253] Lee Mueller, "Joe Borden, Author of First No-Hitter, Never Knew He Made Baseball History," *Gadsden Times*, June 27, 1969, 14.

[254] D. Lammers interview with Jeff Torborg, October 6, 2014.

[255] Ibid.

[256] Vin Scully, *Happy Anniversary to Koufax's Perfect Game* (video), September 9, 2014, MLBlogs Network, http://dodgers.mlbogs.com/2014/09/09/video-happy-anniversary-to-koufaxs-perfect-game.

[257] George C. Langford, "Koufax Perfect Game Makes Four No-Hitters for Lefty," *Naugatuck Daily News*, September 10, 1965, 4.

Chapter 23

[258] Fred Down, "Will Nolan Ryan Get Another One?" *Times Standard*, July 16, 1973, 10.

[259] D. Lammers interview with Jeff Torborg, October 6, 2014.

[260] Nolan Ryan, "Lynn Nolan Ryan—Induction Speech," National Baseball Hall of Fame and Museum, July 25, 1999, http://baseballhall.org/node/11303.

[261] Interview with Jeff Torborg.

[262] Larry Paladino, "Ryan Wanted Shutout, Got No-Hitter," *Reading Eagle*, July 16, 1973, 18.

[263] Milton Richman, "Ryan's Mother Happy, Wants Perfect Game," *Daily Herald*, July 16, 1973, 8

[264] Interview with Jeff Torborg.

265 United Press International, "Big Balaz Catch Saves No-Hitter," *El Paso Herald-Post*, September 30, 1974, 24.

266 Mike Rubin, "Ryan Hurls Fourth No-Hitter," *Courier News*, June 2, 1974, 15.

267 Associated Press "Ryan Passes Koufax with 5th No-Hitter," *Ludington Daily News*, September 28, 1981, 11.

268 Ibid.

269 Dick Brinster, "Nolan Ryan again Pitches No-Hitter," *Daily Sitka Sentinel*, June 12, 1990, 8.

270 Gerry Fraley, "Rangers' Nolan Ryan Throws His Seventh Career No-Hitter," *Dallas Morning News*. May 2, 1991.

Chapter 24

271 United Press International, "A's Dave Stewart No-Hits Blue Jays," *Tyrone Daily Herald*, June 30, 1990, 5.

272 Associated Press, "A's Stewart No-Hits Blue Jays: 4th in Majors This Season; 3rd in June," *Standard-Speaker*, September 30, 1990, 13.

273 United Press International, "A's Dave Stewart No-Hits Blue Jays."

274 "Fernando's Memorable No-Hitter," MLB.com, accessed August 7, 2014, http://m.mlb.com/video/v24097343/fernando-valenzuelas-1990-nohitter.

275 Ibid.

276 Ibid.

277 "Phenomenal Pitching Feats: Hughes Shuts Out Boston and Breitenstein Shuts Out Pittsburg without a Hit," *Chicago Daily Tribune*, April 23, 1898, 7.

278 Ibid.

279 "Two Great Pitching Feats," *Harrisburg Telegraph*, April 23, 1898, 2.

Chapter 25

280 Allan Ryan, "Oh So Close—Again! Stieb's Perfect Game Is Spoiled with Two Yankees Out in Ninth," *Toronto Star*, August 5, 1989, C1.

281 Ibid.

282 Steve Nidetz, "Jays' Stieb Keeps It All in Perspective," *Chicago Tribune*, August 26, 1985, 1C.

283 Ibid.

[284] Associated Press, "Jays' Stieb Inflicted by Deja-Vu," *News-Journal*, October 2, 1988, 4D.

[285] Ibid.

[286] Postgame interview with Dave Stieb, CTV, September 2, 1990, https://www.youtube.com/watch?v=EO_pEfD99lQ.

Chapter 26

[287] United Press International, "Gomez Booed for Controversial Move: Deprives Kirby of No-Hit Bid," *Progress Bulletin*, July 22, 1971, E3.

[288] Associated Press, "Gomez Puts Win before No-Hitter: Kirby Lifted Three Outs from Fame," *Sarasota Herald-Tribune*, July 23, 1971, 2C.

[289] Ibid.

[290] United Press International, "Gomez Booed for Controversial Move."

[291] Tom Emory, "Padres' Steve Arlin Has Near No-Hitter until Manager 'Messes It Up' in Ninth," *Daily Reporter*, July 19, 1972, B3.

[292] Mel Antonen, "Despite Close Calls, Padres Only Members of the No No-Hitters Club," *Sports Illustrated*, July 13, 2012, http://www.si.com/more-sports/2012/06/13/padres-no-hitters.

[293] Mike Bryson, "Expos' Bill Stoneman Hurls First No-Hitter," *Corbin Times-Tribune*, April 18, 1969, 2.

[294] Associated Press, "Gomez Right Says Astros' Don Wilson," *Victoria Advocate*, September 6, 1974, 5B.

[295] Ibid.

[296] Ibid.

Chapter 27

[297] Associated Press, "Martinez Hurls Perfect Game," *Pharos-Tribune*, July 29, 1991, B1.

[298] Lynn Elber, "'Tonight' Sidekick Ed McMahon Dies in LA at 86," *San Diego Union-Tribune*, June 23, 2009.

[299] D. Lammers interview with Don Larsen, September 30, 2014.

[300] Ibid.

[301] Steve Rosenbloom, "All Stress, No Glory," *Chicago Tribune*, May 12, 2012.

[302] D. Lammers interview with Clay Buchholz, May 20, 2015.

[303] Ibid.

[304] Thomas Kaplan, "Red Sox' No-Hitter Puts Varitek in Record Books," *New York Times*, May 21, 2008.

[305] Greg Garno, "Ruiz ties MLB mark for catching no-hitters," MLB.com, September 4, 1993. http://m.mlb.com/news/article/138728956/carlos-ruiz-has-caught-four-no-hitters

[306] David Jones, ed., *Deadball Stars of the American League* (Washington, D.C.: Potomac Books, 2006).

[307] D. Lammers interview with Jeff Torborg, October 6, 2014.

[308] Associated Press, "Erskine Spins No-Hit, No-Run Game," *Kingsport Times-News*, May 13, 1956, 21.

[309] Don Larsen with Mike Shaw, *The Perfect Yankee* (Champaign, Ill.: Sports Publishing, 1996).

[310] Lawrence Baldassaro, *Beyond DiMaggio: Italian Americans in Baseball* (Lincoln: University of Nebraska Press, 2011).

Chapter 28

[311] D. Lammers interview with Andy Hawkins, May 20, 2015.

[312] D. Lammers interview with Fay Vincent, October 6, 2014.

[313] Seymour Siwoff, *The Elias Book of Baseball Records* (New York: Elias Sports Bureau, 2014).

[314] Jim Donaghy, "Houston Loses to New York as Cone Loses No-Hitter," *New Braunfels Herald-Zeitung*, April 29, 1992, 8.

[315] D. Lammers interview with Andy Hawkins, May 20, 2015.

[316] Murray Chass, "On Baseball: What Is a No-Hitter? Matt Young Knows," *New York Times*, April 17, 1992.

[317] Interview with Fay Vincent.

[318] Siwoff, *The Elias Book of Baseball Records*.

[319] Associated Press, "Haddix No-Hitter Is Axed," *Telegraph*, September 4, 1991, 47.

[320] Siwoff, *The Elias Book of Baseball Records*

[321] Associated Press, "Haddix No-Hitter Is Axed."

[322] Chass, "On Baseball."

Chapter 29

[323] Charles Maher, "Dodgers Finally 'Harness' Koufax," *San Bernardino County Sun*, July 2, 1962, 12.

[324] James Bacon, "Guys, Gals and Parties—Featuring Bo Belinsky," *Standard-Speaker*, June 14, 1962, 24.

[325] Sam Feldman, "High & Inside by Jim McKone," *San Bernardino County Sun*, July 12, 1962, 25.

[326] Milton Richman, "Belinky Frowns on Trade to A's," *Daily News-Texan*, September 5, 1962, 6.

[327] Vernon Scott, "The Hollywood Scene," *Eureka Humboldt Standard*, February 8, 1963, 4.

[328] Associated Press, "Belinsky Suspended for Striking Writer," *Daily Telegram*, August 15, 1964, 8.

[329] Murray Olderman, "Where Has All the Glamor Gone? The Last Fling for Bo Belinsky," *Mt. Vernon Register-News*, June 19, 1973, 14.

[330] Richard Goldstein, "Bo Belinsky, 64, the Playboy Pitcher, Dies," *New York Times*, November 27, 2001.

[331] Ibid.

DID YOU KNOW? TWINS' FARM CLUB HURLS 18-DAY, TWO-STATE NO-NO

[332] Associated Press. "Kralick: 'Walking Alusik Better Than Hit,'" *Winona Daily News*, August 27, 1962, 12.

[333] Danny Wild and Jake Seiner, "'Wings' Darnell, May Combine on No-Hitter," MiLB.com, August 11, 2014, http://www.milb.com/news/article.jsp?ymd=20140811&content_id=89120466&fext=.jsp&vkey=news_milb.

Chapter 30

[334] Dewayne Staats, "Abbott's No-Hitter," MLB.com, September 4, 1993, http://m.mlb.com/video/v2685734/9493-jim-abbotts-nohitter.

[335] Associated Press, "Abbott Hurls No-Hitter as New York Downs Cleveland," *Times-News*, September 5, 1993, 1C.

[336] Jim Abbott and Tim Brown, *Imperfect: An Improbable Life* (New York: Ballantine Books, 2012).

[337] Dwight Gooden and Ellis Henican, *Doc: A Memoir* (Boston, Mass.: Houghton Mifflin Harcourt, 2013).

338 Associated Press, "Doc's Not Done: Gooden No-Hits Mariners 2-0," *Daily Globe*, May 15, 1996, 8.

Chapter 31

339 Edwin Jackson talks to broadcasters about his no-hitter and receives a "gift" from his teammates, "Arizona Diamondbacks at Tampa Bay Rays," Fox Sports Arizona, June 25, 2010.

340 Ibid.

341 Bernie Wilson, "Lincecum Still the Freak after 148-Pitch No-Hitter," Associated Press, July 14, 2014.

342 Gary Kale, "Reds' Maloney Loses 10-Inning No-Hitter," *Daily Times*, June 15, 1965, 10.

343 L. B. Pettit interview with Jim Maloney, "Cincinnati Reds at Chicago Cubs," WGN Television, Chicago, Ill., June 14, 1965.

344 Kristie Ackert, "Year after Johan Santana No-Hitter, Mets Manager Terry Collins Managing Emotions," *New York Daily News*, June 1, 2013.

Chapter 32

345 Clark Spencer, "Henderson Alvarez Closes Miami Marlins Season with No-Hitter; Marlins 1, Tigers 0," *Miami Herald*, September 30, 2013.

346 "Detroit Tigers vs. Miami Marlins," Fox Sports Florida, MLB.com, September 29, 2013, http://mlb.mlb.com/news/article/mlb/marlins-right-hander-henderson-alvarez-tosses-no-hitter-against-detroit-tigers?ymd=20130929&content_id=62119746.

347 Associated Press, "Fowler for Macks Pitches No-Hitter," *Kane Republican*, September 10, 1945, 3.

348 Harry Stapler, "Virgil Trucks Hurls No-Hitter as Tigers Nip Nats 1-0," *Oneonta Star*, May 16, 1952, 12.

349 Joe Starkey, "Cordova, Rincon No-Hitter Carved a Place in History," *Pittsburgh Tribune-Review*, July 8, 2007, http://triblive.com/x/pittsburghtrib/sports/pirates/s_516245.html#axzz39QtpUaK4.

350 Ibid.

INDEX

S